Lawyers Then and Now

Lawyers Then and Now

An Australian Legal Miscellany

Keith Mason

THE FEDERATION PRESS
2012

Published in Sydney by
The Federation Press
PO Box 45, Annandale, NSW, 2038.
71 John St, Leichhardt, NSW, 2040.
Ph (02) 9552 2200. Fax (02) 9552 1681.
E-mail: info@federationpress.com.au
Website: http://www.federationpress.com.au

National Library of Australia
Cataloguing-in-Publication entry

Mason, Keith
Lawyers then and now : an Australian legal miscellany/Keith Mason.

Includes index and bibliography.
ISBN 978 186287 890 7 (hbk)

Law - History.
Lawyers - Australia - History.
Lawyers - Australia - Anecdotes.
Judges - Australia - Anecdotes.
Attorney and client - Australia - Anecdotes.

340.0994

Typeset by The Federation Press, Leichhardt, NSW.
Printed by Ligare Pty Ltd, Riverwood, NSW.

Contents

Preface

Our system of government under law may be divinely instituted. But its functioning depends on the human actors who participate as litigants, lawyers, judges and academics. Fascination with them has driven my selection of themes and incidents in this work. Recognising that most people perform well most of the time, I have inevitably been drawn to the exceptional, disfunctional, unplanned, humorous and at times bizarre or ugly aspects of the men and women in the law.

My primary aim has been to collect, arrange and preserve illustrative stories about Australian law and lawyers from written and oral legal history, case law and the statute book. I am sure to have overlooked many good stories. And many of them have been told before, not that this is a bar in itself.

A second broad goal, indicated by the *Then and Now* in the title, is observing the constancies and changes in behaviour. As recounted in the final chapter, some patterns illustrate the constancy of our frailty. Others show that every era and every individual have blind spots (at least in the eyes of others).

Why turn to fiction when history, law reports, legal textbooks and the chatter of common rooms provide such rich veins? The idea of this work (and some of its content) emerged over many years in conversations with my friend Leslie Katz to whom the book is dedicated. Sir Robert Megarry's *Miscellany at Law* series suggested themes while setting standards of scholarship and literary verve I could not expect to emulate.

I am deeply indebted to John Bennett, Alex Castles and Bruce Kercher for making Australian legal history popular and accessible. Many friends have provided stories or assistance, particularly Mark Aronson, Tony Blackshield, Gerard Brennan, Tom Brennan, John Bryson, Michael Colbran, Maurice Cullity, Colin Fong, Alexandra George, Ken Handley, Deborah Healey, David Ipp, Bruce Kaye, Hugh Mackay, Marianna Matevosian, Adrian McMinn, Margaret McMurdo, Jim Merralls, Geoffrey Muecke, Garth Nettheim, Malcolm Park, Aladin Rahemtula, Mehera San Roque, Philip Selth, George Williams, Derek Wong and Peter Young. Finally, I thank the people at The Federation Press who have so skilfully organised the publication especially Kathryn Fitzhenry, Rebecca Fung and Christopher Holt.

Keith Mason
Sydney, October 2012

For
Leslie Katz

Part 1

Beginnings

1 Beginnings

Indigenous law

Humans first came to Australia about 40,000 years ago.

The observations of anthropologists and early settlers and the oral histories of Aboriginal descendants attest to Aboriginal customary law.[1] As with European law, sanctioned and unsanctioned behaviour patterns enjoyed moral and religious underpinnings. For what it is worth, authoritative caselaw also agrees that Aboriginal lore was and is indeed law.[2] The harder question relates to its coexistence with the predominant system of statutory and common law deemed to stem from white settlement.

The Aboriginal customary rules, which were not necessarily uniform, spanned aspects of land law, environmental law, sacred law, kinship, marriage, initiation and other parts of family law. And there were sanctions, including spearing designed to cause death in some cases, injury in others, indications of a graduated scheme of public wrongs.

To modern eyes there was a good deal of self-help, but any student of English common law or European civil law knows that this is a badge of any legal system especially in its primitive phase. As to processes, there were roles for elders whose word was law in various matters and who, like the judges at common law, were the primary medium for explicating and enforcing the tradition.[3] Indigenous legal systems recognised processes akin to trials.[4] These were rudimentary explorations for truth that put a premium on consensus-seeking dialogue, the bedrock of formal mediation processes that white man's law would embrace with enthusiasm in the late 20th century.

---

1 See Kenneth Maddock, "Aboriginal customary law" in Peter Hanks and Bryan Keon-Cohen (eds), *Aborigines and the Law: Essays in Memory of Elizabeth Eggleston*, George Allen & Unwin Australia Pty Ltd, 1984.

2 *Milirrpum v Nabalco Pty Ltd* (1971) 17 FLR 141 esp at 265-8; *Mabo v Queensland (No 2)* (1992) 175 CLR 1 at 39, 186.

3 At the ceremony to mark his retirement in 2011, Spigelman CJ remarked that: "Just as the elders of the Gadigal Clan of the Eora people have been the custodians of the land on which we meet, the 16 Chief Justices of New South Wales, including myself, have been the custodians of the institutional traditions of the rule of law, since this Court was established almost exactly 187 years ago".

4 See eg Castles and Harris, *Lawmakers and Wayward Whigs*, p 24.

Yet by a western conceit, Indigenous laws and customs were entirely disregarded (by the white settlers) until long after occupation of the eastern seaboard which commenced with the arrival of the First Fleet in 1788. The Aboriginal peoples inhabiting Australia were variously ignored, attacked and exploited by the settlers and their descendants. Sometimes they retaliated. Sometimes they acted in self-defence or the assertion of a claim of right (had their evidence been acceptable, which it was not until many decades after white settlement). Sometimes they, like the white people, did things that contravened both their own laws and the English law that was haltingly applied to them in the frontier colony. Sometimes they did no more than oppose the encroachment of settlers upon the lands which would not be recognised as theirs until 1992, long after they had been killed or moved away as "trespassers". In Tasmania, there were well-documented incidents of Aborigines being hunted down and killed by employees of the Van Diemen's Land Company because they had resisted the abduction of their wives or for spearing company sheep believing them to be game.[5]

In the 1992 *Mabo Case* the High Court rejected the application of the *terra nullius* doctrine in Australia.[6] It was declared that native title was capable of surviving the Crown's acquisition of sovereignty and radical title to land in Australia. Sadly, *Mabo* was a decision whose symbolic impact was not matched by any significant redress of past wrongs. There were two broad reasons. At a practical level, it has proved highly difficult and expensive to identify the content of native laws and customs extant at the time of white settlement. And at a legal level, the march of white settlement meant that Crown grants of freehold and other acts of occupation simply overreached native title so that it was incapable of revival. In Brennan J's memorable words:[7]

> The common law can, by reference to the traditional laws and customs of an indigenous people, identify and protect the native rights and interests to which they give rise. However, when the tide of history has washed away any real acknowledgment of traditional law and any real observance of traditional customs, the foundation of native title has disappeared. A native title which has ceased with the abandoning of laws and customs based on tradition cannot be revived for contemporary recognition.

Mabo is generally seen as a case about land rights, although the judgments recognised the theoretical possibility that other aspects of customary law, including rights to hunt and fish,[8] could have survived white settlement. But the criminal law was not one of them, according to Mason CJ in *Walker v*

5 See Castles, *Lawless Harvests or God Save the Judges*, p 141.

6 *Mabo v Queensland (No 2)* (1992) 175 CLR 1.

7 *Ibid* at 60.

8 See *Yanner v Eaton* (1999) 201 CLR 351.

New South Wales.[9] He held that the principle of equality before the law and the universal language of criminal law statutes left no room for incompatible systems of native law to endure. However, the possibility of a defence based on honest claim of right has been noted[10] and there has been limited recognition of a role for customary punishments to be taken into account when sentencing.[11]

The trial of the *Batavia* mutineers

It is often asserted that the first application of non-Indigenous law occurred in the days following the landing of the First Fleet at Sydney Cove on 26 January 1788. But one well-documented instance of white man's law took place many years earlier. The first trial according to European law occurred over 140 years before Captain James Cook "discovered" the eastern seaboard and, on behalf of King George III, purported to annex two-thirds of the continental land mass, including Van Diemen's Land, naming the entire eastern mainland New South Wales.[12]

By the early 17th century Portuguese and Dutch sailors became aware of the great southern continent which they called *Terra Australis Incognita*. The routes by which they sailed from the Cape of Good Hope to the Javan town of Batavia (modern Jakarta) brought them close to, and at times onto, the shores of modern Western Australia. In October 1628 the Dutch East India Company ship *Batavia* sailed from The Netherlands on her maiden voyage to the town of that name. The *Commandeur* of the venture was Francesco Pelsaert, a senior merchant in the employ of the company. The skipper on board was Ariaien Jacobsz. The two men were old enemies and things got even nastier when Pelsaert publicly shamed Jacobsz over an incident involving a woman passenger whom Jacobsz and others were bedding at the time.

Although Pelsaert would not discover this until later, Jacobsz and the undermerchant Jeronimus Cornelisz were planning to mutiny. But before their plan could be hatched the ship ran aground on a reef within the Houtman Abrolhos, a chain of 122 islands and coral reefs in the Indian Ocean some 40 miles from the coast of mainland Australia near modern Geraldton. About 180 passengers and crew were offloaded onto an island soon to be named Batavia's Graveyard. Pelsaert, Jacobsz and some 30 others, mostly sailors, landed on a smaller island with the bulk of the supplies.

Pelsaert, Jacobsz and a hand-picked team went in search of water but, finding none, they set sail to Batavia for food and help. They were too fearful of being overpowered by the already unruly and desperate survivors on shore

9 (1995) 182 CLR 45.

10 See *Walden v Hensler* (1987) 163 CLR 561; *Mueller v Vigilante* [2007] WASC 259.

11 See eg *R v Minor* (1992) 2 NTLR 183.

12 Victoria and Queensland would be hived off in 1851 and 1859 respectively.

to set foot again on Batavia's Graveyard. Instead, they left a note about their intentions. Those left behind felt so betrayed by this desertion that they named the smaller island Traitors' Island.

A handful of passengers perished from thirst before rain fell. Perhaps they were the fortunate ones, because over 120 other surviving men, women and children were, over the next three months, slaughtered (by clubbing, drowning or stabbing) by a group sworn or pressed into loyalty by Cornelisz. He was an eloquent psychopath with religious attitudes that would have been heretical in any age. His initial motive may have been to reduce to about 45 the number of survivors vying for limited resources. But other survivors were killed to prevent betrayal of the mutineers when and if Pelsaert returned. The murders became utterly indiscriminate as time progressed, appearing to serve no function beyond the relief of boredom or the assertion of naked power in a society where the bonds of religion, morality and law fell apart.

About three and a half months after sailing off from Traitors' Island, Pelsaert returned on the yacht *Sardam* with detailed instructions and armed support. A race to intercept his vessel was won narrowly by the loyalist group headed by a man named Wiebbe Hayes that had survived repeated attempts at extermination by the mutineers. The suspects were then rounded up and the full horrors of what they had done came quickly to light.[13]

Pelsaert's journal offers a detailed account of the trials and punishments of the leading mutineers.[14] It is the first record of legal proceedings in Australian history. By any standard, it is as good as any memorial of a trial in Australia before the advent of official shorthand transcription or electronic recording in the detail it offers of the evidence, processes, formal findings and sentences. Pelsaert was obviously intent on writing history as he wanted it to be viewed, but historians have seen little reason to doubt the accuracy of his detailed account.

Dutch law permitted the extraction of evidence through torture, subject to requirements that there should first be a reasonable presumption of guilt and that any confession thus obtained had to be repeated "free" not more than 24 hours after the torture had stopped. The retraction of confessions made under such duress was not the end of the matter and generally led to the application of even harsher tortures. "Since the end result was almost inevitably the same, the Dutch insistence on freewill confession was thus something of a fig leaf".[15] (Australian common law has its own share of legal fictions.) Pelsaert's record faithfully details torture by water not unlike the waterboarding that the Bush

13 Jacobsz was later imprisoned in Batavia where he probably died awaiting trial.

14 This account and the quotations from a translation of the journal that are set out below are taken mainly from Henrietta Drake-Brockman, *Voyage to Disaster The Life of Francisco Pelsaert*. See also Mike Dash, *Batavia's Graveyard* and Simon Leys, *Wreck of the Batavia*, Atlantic Books, 2007.

15 Dash, *op cit*, p 177.

administration in the United States used on suspected terrorists in Guantanamo Bay. The accused was tied up, sometimes spreadeagled in a doorway or between posts, with a cloth wound around his neck and face to form a funnel. Water was then poured softly upon his head until the cloth was full up to the mouth and nostrils. The victim had to swallow to keep from drowning and this caused his body to bloat and the eyes almost to pop out of his head.[16]

Commandeur Pelsaert's graphic record of the trial and execution of the ringleader, Jeronimus Cornelisz opens as follows:[17]

> First there will follow the examinations of Jeronimus Cornelisz, from the day when he was brought to us as a prisoner until today; have been busy with him daily; as well as his freewill confession concerning the evil misdeeds done and intended by him. ___Whereupon his sentence has been passed on him, as well as on his Accomplices___follows___
>
> Today 17 Sept 1629, after noon has been resolved by the Commandeur *Franco Pelsart* and the Ship's council to bring forward the captured Jeronimus Cornelisz of Haarlem, Apothecary, and later under Merchant on the ship *Batavia*, in order to examine the gruesome deeds which had done, and still had in mind to do, and if necessary to put to torture; on the Yacht Sardam___*date as above.*
>
> JERONIMUS CORNELISZ brought in, has been asked by the Commandeur why through the devil he has denuded himself of all humanity, and why he was more evil than if he had been changed into a tiger animal, so that he had to let flow so much innocent blood; and also has had the intention also to do that with us. Whereon he says, 'Everything that has been done is not my fault, but David Sevanck [*and other named persons*] have thought of it and forced me to do it, otherwise I had to die.' ... [*Details of some of the murders then are given, with Cornelisz maintaining that he was no more than an unwilling witness.*]

Later in the record for that day Pelsaert states that:

> Jeronimus Cornelisz, being bound, and having started to torture him a little, requests a postponement, for he wished to tell that which one had asked him, and what he knew.

Some further information is obtained under this "gentle" inducement and recorded. But the next day (when the trial had moved to Batavia's Graveyard) things got down to business. The record opens with the matter of fact statement that:

> Jeronimus Cornelisz, bound, and made ready for torture, requested pause; that he would say truthfully what he knew.

Confessions of at least attempts to seduce a woman on the ship, and failing her, her maid, are then recorded along with a version of the events leading up to the shipwreck, still largely exculpatory of Cornelisz. The record continues:

16 Drake-Brockman, *op cit*, p 101; Dash, *op cit*, pp 213-14.

17 Drake-Brockman, *op cit*, p 158.

> The Commandeur asking him [Jeronimus] further, because he wished to know when the decision to seize the ship had been made, denied knowing anything about it. Therefore again made ready to torture. And after a little water had been poured out, says he will say all that he knows.

More evidence thus extracted is recorded, interspersed with the testimony of other witnesses who in Cornelisz's presence recount their testimony, at first "free and unbound" and then "after the beginning of the torture" (on themselves). The journal continues:

> Jeronimus Cornelisz, again brought into the tent, and being bound for torture, as one could not get from him the straight truth, and asked ... confesses ...

This most meticulous of reports states that over the ensuing days Cornelisz confessed in detail to a series of misdeeds, including mutiny, mass murder and rape. The record at this point is careful to note that the later confessions were "free and unbound, without torture".

The record then states the findings of the seven-man council, including Pelsaert, who conducted the trial, adding their signatures at this point. Sentence was then pronounced. There was to be a delay of two days to enable Cornelisz to be baptised.[18] He was then to be taken to one of the islands called Seals' Island there to have both of his hands cut off and to be hanged. Ever concerned with monetary matters, the council stipulated that the prisoner was to suffer confiscation of "all his goods, Moneys, Gold, Silver, monthly wages and all that he may have to claim here in India against the General East India Company, our Lord Masters".

Cornelisz begged to be brought to Batavia to see his wife before what he realised would be inevitable execution. But this application for a stay of execution was refused. After a failed attempt at poisoning himself on the eve of his execution, Cornelisz (in Pelsaert's record) "died stubborn", invoking God's justice "because he had not been able to get it here on Earth".[19] Other ringleaders were dealt with by similar processes and with similar outcomes, except that they were to keep one of their hands before execution. Lesser offenders in their teens got off with triple keel-hauling, flogging and loss of all wages.

One of the men sentenced to die on Seals' Island was a youth whose pleas at the scaffold led Pelsaert to respite execution in favour of putting him "on an island or the continent according to occasion occurring". This young man was in fact put ashore on the "main SOUTHLAND" in the company of a second "death-deserving delinquent".[20] They were handed a written instruction to

18 Cornelisz was an Anabaptist who did not believe in baptism. According to Simon Leys (*op cit*, p 43), his request for baptism was a stalling tactic and he eventually declined baptism.

19 Drake-Brockman, *op cit*, pp 212-13.

20 *Ibid*, pp 213, 229-30. The names of these earliest recorded entrants to Australia were Wouter Loos and Jan Pelgrom de By van Bemel.

"make themselves known to the folk of this land by tokens of friendship". They were provided with a stash of trinkets "of which shall give to the Blacks only a few until they have grown familiar with them". They were also counselled to keep eyes open for the continuing trade interests of the Company and for any passing ship that might be available to rescue them. The Instruction concluded with a commendation to God's grace and protection. Hopefully their lives looked up from that point onwards. They were never seen again by the Dutch.

Had the likes of the Sydney *Daily Telegraph* been then in print, there would have been howls of protest at the leniency of the lesser sentences. Sydney radio "shock-jocks" might even have weighed in about the evils of such unscheduled arrivals on "our" shores of these boat people.

Australia is claimed by the Europeans

In 1493 Pope Alexander VI divided the entire "discovered" and undiscovered world between Portuguese and Spanish spheres of influence. The Treaty of Tordesillas between the two nations, mediated by the Pope the following year, made a smallish adjustment that delivered Brazil to Portugal. The notional line that ran around the globe intersected Australia by the 129th meridian and came by degrees to serve as the boundary of Western Australia.

When, in 1770, Captain Cook claimed "New South Wales" for the British Crown, the land area comprised all of the modern New South Wales, Queensland, South Australia, Tasmania, Victoria and the Northern Territory. The western extremity was initially latitude 135 degrees west but this was extended to the 129th meridian in 1828, thereby ensuring that the demarcation was as antipodean extension of the pope's line. "Possession" of Western Australia was taken by Captain Stirling in 1829, as far east as the 129th meridian.[21] One suggested reason for delaying until the 1820s to annex the western part of the continent was respect for the British East India Company which was seen as the inheritor of the shadowy Portuguese entitlement in the Indian Ocean. By this reasoning, the hand of a medieval pope can be seen as having determined the boundary of modern Western Australia.

In 1642 the Dutch explorer Abel Tasman, sailing under the patronage of the colonial Governor Anthony Van Diemen, claimed the large island to the south of the mainland for the stadtholder of The Netherlands. That island would bear his patron's name until 1856 when it was decided that Tasman himself should be honoured this way. The Dutch claim was doubly inchoate: legally, because international law required occupation or "settlement" to accompany such an assertion (at least in relation to *terra nullius* as Terra Australis Incognita was

21 See *Rogers v Squire* (1978) 46 FLR 372. For a fuller account, see *Western Australia v Commonwealth* (1995) 183 CLR 373 at 422-9.

then regarded);[22] and practically, because there was no way that the British would acquiesce in such conduct by their Dutch rivals. Whatever their status under international law, these assertions of Dutch sovereignty were never recognised by the British who, interestingly enough, called the great southland New Holland until well into the 19th century.

English law comes to Australia: The earliest trials in New South Wales

The process whereby English law was received into Australia has recently received exhaustive study.[23] According to a 1722 decision of the Privy Council[24] and the writings of William Blackstone,[25] English law (common law and statute law, so far as applicable) was carried abroad as a "birthright" or inheritance by British subjects who settled in overseas dominions. The birthright notion was selectively ignored by early Governors who purported to issue licences and regulations inconsistent with the liberties of free Englishmen. But it was adopted by early decisions of the Supreme Court of New South Wales and has been confirmed by the High Court.[26] Reception was endorsed by colonial legislation which also supplied a cut-off date.

New South Wales was originally administered by the Governor assisted by military and naval officers acting under letters patent requiring the application of English criminal law.[27] Civil jurisdiction was imposed as a prerogative act. The constitutional bases of gubernatorial and judicial power remained controversial until 1824 when Supreme Courts were established by letters patent in Van Diemen's Land and New South Wales by charters issued under Imperial legislation.[28] Van Diemen's Land was carved out of New South Wales in 1825 (its name being changed to Tasmania in 1856), Victoria in 1851 and Queensland in 1859. Legislation to constitute a colony in Western Australia was first enacted in 1829. South Australia was proclaimed a separate settlement in 1836 pursuant to a British Act that stipulated, among other things, that there were to be no convicts.[29]

22 BH McPherson CBE, *The Reception of English Law Abroad*, Supreme Court of Queensland Library, 2007, pp 42-3, 310.

23 *Ibid.*

24 *Anonymous* (1722) 2 P Wms 75; 24 ER 646.

25 William Blackstone, *Commentaries on the Laws of England*, Facsimile of the First Edition of 1765-1769, vol 1, p 105.

26 See eg *R v Farrell* (1831) 1 Legge 5 at 10. See also *Skelton v Collins* (1966) 115 CLR 95 at 135; *Dugan v Mirror Newspapers Ltd* (1978) 142 CLR 583 at 589-90.

27 Castles, *An Australian Legal History*, chs 3 and 4.

28 It was the *New South Wales Act 1823*, 4 Geo 4 c 96 (Imp), which also applied to Van Diemen's Land.

29 The *South Australia Act 1834*, 4 & 5 Will 4 c 95 (Imp).

The first English trial on Australian soil occurred just over two weeks after white settlement. On 6 February 1788 the women of the First Fleet landed at Sydney Cove. That evening there was an uproarious celebration that continued over the next couple of days. One of the revellers, a convict named Barsby, was charged with personally abusing a drum major, striking a drummer with a cooper's adze and repeatedly abusing the sentinel and other soldiers on the guard while in custody. He was convicted and sentenced to 150 lashes with a cat of nine tails.[30] (This illustrates two aspects of convict law in Australia: the use of legal processes as a prelude to punishment of the convicts and the savagery of the ensuing sentences.)

Over the next few days the Court of Criminal Jurisdiction determined several cases involving the theft of scarce food rations. The condign punishments obviously failed to deter the desperately hungry convicts. On 27 February 1788 a convict named Barrett was convicted and sentenced to death for stealing food rations.[31] Two days later, another convict (Freeman) was also sentenced to death for a similar crime.[32] It is not clear who was deputed to carry out Freeman's execution but, as he stood at the foot of the gallows, he was informed of the Governor's conditional pardon, the condition being that he become the common executioner. After a little time pondering whether to accept the proposal, he reluctantly agreed and his first official duty was to hang Barrett.

Sometimes the rigours of the English law were neglected or overlooked. The first civil case, widely hailed as showing the rule of law in the convict colony, was a claim by two convicts against the master of the ship that had transported them to New South Wales in 1788. The successful action in detinue for the loss of the convicts' luggage resulted in an award of £15.[33] The Deputy Judge Advocate[34] overlooked or turned a blind eye to the English law of attaint that, if applicable as the High Court of Australia was to rule 190 years later in *Dugan's Case*,[35] would have precluded the plaintiffs (as convicted felons) from both suing and giving sworn evidence during the full period of their transportation. The plaintiff Cable (or Kable) went on to become a constable, then a leading merchant in the colony, though he later fell into deep financial difficulties.

The convicts, soldiers and free settlers who formed the early colony did not enjoy all of the rights of their English counterparts. As time went by this

30 *R v Barsby* [1788] NSWKR 1. This is the citation of *The Kercher Reports, the published decisions of the New South Wales Superior Courts 1788 to 1827* edited by Bruce Kercher and Brent Salter. The case notes by the learned authors are the source of the information provided below.

31 *R v Barrett* [1788] NSWKR 4.

32 *R v Sherman and Freeman* [1788] NSWKR 5.

33 *Cable v Sinclair* [1788] NSWKR 7.

34 David Collins, a marine officer with no legal training.

35 *Dugan v Mirror Newspapers Ltd* (1978) 142 CLR 583.

became more and more contentious, with calls for trial by jury of "peers", ie non-officers, becoming more and more strident.[36] But other trappings of English common law were applied from the outset, as with the case of Ann Davis who in 1789 was convicted and sentenced to death for stealing from a dwelling house. She claimed to be pregnant and thus incapable of (prompt) execution. A jury of twelve matrons was summoned and it was only when they declared Davis not to be pregnant that she was hanged.[37]

Blackstone's birthright principle was not, however, self-enacting. Whether because of ignorance or intent, or because most of life was lived beyond the reach of the law, "what passed for law in the colony often differed strongly from English law and often contradicted it".[38] For example, it was not until 1820 that a European was convicted and executed for the murder of an Aboriginal native; and even here the concern of the authorities was that the accused had breached the protocols of diplomacy as much as broken the law.[39]

36 Trial by jury for serious offences was not finally established until 1839.

37 *R v Davis* [1789] NSWKR 5. See also Barker QC, *Sorely Tried*, p 211 for another occasion when there was such a jury. Another unusual form of jury inherited from the English common law was the jury *de medietate linguae* which an alien could require if he or she did not speak or understand English. Such juries were composed of six ordinary jurors and six of the accused's own countrymen. For an example of its use in 1875 in what is now the Northern Territory, see Mildren, *Big Boss Fella All Same Judge. A history of the Supreme Court of the Northern Territory*, p 9. When, in modern times, an Aboriginal man sought a "jury of peers" consisting of Aboriginal elders his application was rejected: *R v Buzzacott* (2004) 149 A Crim R 320.

38 Bruce Kercher, "A Convict Conservative: George Crossly and the English Legal Tradition" (1998) 16(1) *Law in Context* 17 at 24. See generally Lisa Ford, *Settler Sovereignty: jurisdiction and indigenous peoples in America and Australia*, Harvard University Press, 2010. Many examples of the dissonance between law and practice, and their impact on the distinctiveness of Australian law and legal history, are referred to in this work. They include the situation of Aborigines, women and convicts.

39 See the notes to *R v Kirby and Thompson* [1820] NSWKR 11.

Part 2

People of the Law

2 *Just Folks*

Names and dynasties

For many Australian judges, their names alone have generated hope or fear in those before them, whether as litigants or counsel.

One feels instinctively that all will be well in a court presided over by Judge Just or Justice Wright (there have been two of them as well as a Judge Wright). An enjoyable day will start before Bongiorno J. Things should be sweet before Bonney J, Cantor J or Sugerman P. Don't expect too many bumps or much judicial activism from Stable SPJ. But consider being called before a judge named Bent, Barker, Boo[th]by, Bray, Bulley, Bunny, Cross, Cussen, Gamble, Madden, Pain, Quirk, Rath, Row, Shaw, Sly, Viol, Wearing, Wolfe or Wylde? And would one expect ready empathy from a Barron Field, Frost, Hidden, Leech, Nettle or Stone?

For the well-prepared advocate, things will be looking up if listed before judges named Bright, Cope, Crisp, Einstein, Good, Keane, Power, Powers,[1] Sharpe, Smart, Solomon, Virtue or Wise. Don't dawdle in front of the likes of Flick, Fox, Gallop, Preston, Quick or Sharpe although an easy pace may suffice for Miles and Walker JJ.

One might anticipate cutting or grating remarks from judges called Barber, Barbour, Cheeke, Docker, Finn, Glass, Hackett, Harper, Skinner or Slicer and a pounding from the likes of Box, Blow, Knox, Mason, Pepper, Smith, Stone or Wood. Criminal cases should go well for the accused before Freeman DCJ or Robin DCJ but not before Hanger J (or DCJ) or Birchall DCJ. Hopefully you would not be appearing for a creditor before Hock DCJ, any of the four Owens or Spender J. Far better Rich J. Environmentalists may anticipate favour from judges named Field, Forrest, Grove or Hill.

Those representing women whose right to ordination as Anglican priests was at issue in *Scandrett v Dowling*[2] may have seen divine intervention when the majority of the Court of Appeal who found in their favour had the names of Priestley and Hope. The involvement of Judge Bishop would have been

1 Although Owen Dixon is reputed to have said that he did not fully understand the meaning of *ultra vires* until he read a constitutional judgment of Powers J.

2 (1992) 27 NSWLR 483.

premature both legally and ecclesiastically. Angel J only sat briefly as an Acting Judge in New South Wales.

Those disappointed with coming before judges called Blanch, Bland, Black, Dunn, Gray or White would cheer up if they encountered more colourful jurists named Brown, Browne, Brownie, Green or Rose. Judge Rainbow would appeal to those hoping for variety.

Some judges have acquired colourful nicknames. The Commonwealth's first Chief Justice was "Oily Sam" (Griffith) – a tag picked up at school for his ability to argue on any side of any argument. A chilly demeanour earned for Irvine CJ the name "Iceberg" (with his appearance of prim austerity and his monosyllabic, incisive method of speech) and for Jordan CJ the name "Frigidaire Freddy".[3] The diminutive Catholic judge, Paul Flannery, was called "The Pope's Jockey". Both Owen Dixon and Michael Kirby were at times referred to as "the Great Dissenter".

Some nicknames point to more serious defects of character and, like all Bar-room gossip, need to be taken with caution. Nevertheless, I record that Judge Harvey Prior was known as "Fletcher Jones" because of his reputation for "fitting up" accused persons; Justice Freddy Myers was known as "Funnelweb Freddy" because of his penchant for laying traps for the unwary;[4] and Justice Alkin Wallace was called the "Cobra" because he used to nod enthusiastically as submissions were put to him that he would later reject out of hand. Only the knowing realised that the nod could be the kiss of death. By contrast, Chief Justice Gleeson's moniker, "The Smiler", stemmed from his invariably upbeat personality. The nickname at the Bar for the current Chief Justice of New South Wales (Tom Bathurst) was "the Shuffling Assassin": litigants be warned! Judge Joseph Moore was often in trouble with the New South Wales Court of Criminal Appeal for imposing overly lenient sentences: it was a case of Moore giving less, more or less.

---

3 Jordan confirmed his reputation when the associate to Milner Stephen J rushed into his chambers while he was reading Greek poetry to announce that the judge had died suddenly and that "the jury was still out". Pausing to consult a practice book, Jordan answered the young man "That is all right. You can take the verdict" before returning to his poetry. Dr Bennett's entry about Jordan in the *Australian Dictionary of Biography* quotes an unidentified source as stating that he "adopted a manner in his robes that was not merely cold, but chilling. He had a high-pitched voice of frosty intonation, and his thin-rimmed spectacles added to the severity of his demeanour". For instances of Jordan's dry humour, see *Spilsted v Spilsted* (1944) 44 SR (NSW) 242 at 245.

4 One well known story is that he persuaded a reluctant barrister to amend a pleading that he promptly ruled to be demurrable. Another relates to a probate suit where he barred counsel for an executor from splitting his case when he customarily sought to lead evidence on the issue of testamentary capacity in reply. The judge ruled that counsel had led such in chief evidence when, in the course of providing the evidence going to execution of the will, the polite conversation had included "Good morning Mr X. How are you?" "I am fine thanks."

The Australian judiciary has had so many dynasties that the English appear upwardly mobile by contrast. At the apex stand the Douglas clan with six senior judicial officers.[5] Next come the four Stephens,[6] three Macrossan CJs, three Street CJs, three Owens, Windeyers, Winnekes and Evatts, and the (presently) smaller judicial dynasties of two bearing the names of a'Beckett, Andrews, Barton, Brennan, Brereton, Burt (two Chief Justices), Cohen, Curlewis, Davies, Dowling, Dovey, Ferguson, Garling, Gavan Duffy, Flannery, Forbes, French, Fullagar, Hanger, Hart, Heenan, Herron, Jackson, Jeffcott, Joske, Kirby, Levine, Long Innes, Macfarlane, Mansfield, Maxwell, McLelland (two CJs in Eq), McLoughlin,[7] McMurdo, Molesworth, Nicholas, Noel, O'Bryan, Slattery, Smith, Smithers, Starke, Studdert, Williams, Winneke and Woinarski? If I have left any off, I apologise.

Judges who are married to each other are now fairly commonplace, especially in Queensland, the home of many legal propinquities.

Brian Frank Martin was Chief Justice of the Northern Territory between 1993 and 2003. His successor was a man of almost the same name (Brian Ross Martin). Rumours circulated that the Territory government was too strapped for cash to afford new stationery or to paint a fresh name on the door.

I know of two families that have produced three successive generations of senior counsel: the Shands (Alexander Barclay Shand KC, John Wentworth (Jack) Shand KC (later QC), and Alec Shand QC) and the Streets. The first Street CJ (Phillip Whistler Street) never took silk, but his son (Kenneth Whistler Street), grandson (Laurence Whistler Street) and great-grandson (Alexander Whistler Street) were all appointed senior counsel.

The Wentworths are a legal dynasty of a different order. Their progenitor D'Arcy Wentworth was twice acquitted of a capital crime and left England quickly for New South Wales in 1789 to avoid a third brush with death or

5 Robert Johnstone Douglas was the Northern Judge in Queensland between 1923 and 1935; his elder brother Edward Archibald Douglas was a Supreme Court judge between 1929 and 1947 (he was passed over for the position of Senior Puisne Judge in controversial circumstances: see p 79); his son James Archibald Douglas was appointed to the Supreme Court in 1965; James' son Robert Ramsay Douglas was a judge of the same Court from 1999 until his untimely death in 2002; Robert's brother James Sholto Douglas was appointed to that Court in 2003. Naming the sixth, another son of James, Francis Maxwell Douglas QC, who for a short time was a Judge of the Court of Appeal of Fiji, requires only a slight poetic licence. Fiji's admission as an Australian State was contemplated at federation and, as with New Zealand, is provided for in s 121 of the Constitution (see *Western Australia v Commonwealth* (1975) 134 CLR 201 at 273-4).

6 John Stephen was the first puisne judge of the Supreme Court of New South Wales; his son Alfred was Chief Justice between 1844 and 1873; his son Matthew Henry was a judge between 1887 and 1904 and Matthew Henry's younger brother, Edward Milner Stephen, held the like office between 1929 and 1939.

7 Bernard and Cornelius McLoughlin were brothers who served concurrently on the District Court of Queensland in the 1970s. Another pair of brothers to serve together on the Supreme Court in that State were EA and RJ Douglas.

transportation. He had no legal training but rose to become Chief Magistrate in the colony much to the disgust of the Exclusives. His illegitimate, native born son[8] William Charles, dubbed by his biographer Australia's greatest native born son, was an explorer, barrister, publisher, politician and statesman. He became President of the Legislative Council in 1861 and gave his name to the blue-ribbon federal electorate to which his great-grandson Billy Wentworth and Billy's niece Kate Wentworth would at times unsuccessfully seek election. Billy was a barrister and successful Liberal Party politician, holding the federal seat of Mackellar between 1949 and 1977. Kate Wentworth's campaign under the banner of "Wentworth for Wentworth" was unsuccessful. For many years she was engaged in litigation with past and present members of her family and others. A summons to have her declared a vexatious litigant was, however, dismissed.[9] Ms Wentworth later obtained legal qualifications, but her application to be admitted to the Bar was rejected by the Court of Appeal on the ground that she was not "suitable ... for admission".[10] A Bill was introduced in the Legislative Assembly for Ms Wentworth's admission, but it lapsed.

The Pedens are a fine dynasty of legal academics. Sir John Peden KC was Professor of Law and Dean at the Law School of Sydney University[11] where his great-granddaughter Elisabeth Peden is currently a professor. Elisabeth's father Professor John Peden taught at the same Law School before becoming Dean at Macquarie University Law School.

Family connections: Appearing before relations

The children of many distinguished lawyers have followed the legal footsteps of their fathers and mothers.[12] As indicated in the previous section, some of them followed onto the Bench. But, for a handful of lawyers related to judges in earlier days, their following was too close because the ponds in which the father and son both swam were too small. It was not always possible for matters to be listed before a non-relation. Sometimes it was possible, but not easy. Sometimes the more relaxed ethical standards of earlier times did not require the judge to step aside if a close relative was appearing before him.

8 A "currency lad". Governor Macquarie's locally issued paper money or currency was regarded as inferior to sterling.

9 *Attorney-General v Wentworth* (1988) 14 NSWLR 481.

10 *Wentworth v New South Wales Bar Association* (unrep, NSW Court of Appeal, 14 February 1994), relying on *Legal Profession Act 1987* (NSW), s 4(2). Special leave was refused: (1994) 68 ALJR 494.

11 He was also, for a time, the President of the Legislative Council of New South Wales who lent his name to the leading constitutional law case of *Trethowan v Peden* (1930) 31 SR (NSW) 183.

12 The recent President of the Victoria Bar, Mark Moshinsky SC, is the son of Victoria's third female Queen's Counsel, Ada Moshinsky QC.

The stormy judicial career of Algernon Montagu ended in the wake of a case relating to the validity of a local Dog Act decided by Pedder CJ and himself in 1847.[13] Counsel for the party whose success so enraged the Lieutenant-Governor as to propose the dismissal of both judges was Montagu J's own brother, Alfred Otter Montagu.

Septimus Burt practised in Western Australia as a barrister in the 1870s and 1880s when his father, Sir Archibald Burt, was the chief and only justice on the Supreme Court. This led to several allegations of bias, culminating in a case in 1873 when a disputed election result came before the Chief Justice with the son representing the successful petitioner.[14] Burt CJ and his son each despised the Crown Solicitor, George Walpole Leake, and waged a running battle on several fronts. Leake once threw an inkstand at Burt jnr in a fit of rage during an arbitration, apologising later saying that he had been annoyed with him for 10 years. In 1873 Leake wrote to a friend declaring that it was "but natural that a father should exhibit complacency to a son. But this complacency became as I thought excessive ... [Many] (of the lower orders [of the legal profession]it is true) did not hesitate to avow that they selected Mr Septimus Burt as their legal adviser in order that they might ensure the sympathies of His Honour". The Chief Justice's reciprocal low opinion of the Crown Solicitor kept Leake from attaining any permanent appointment on the Bench. Burt once described Leake as working "as the monkey in the fable is said to have done when using the cat's paw for raking his roasted chestnuts. He is a lamentable and incorrigible sinner and a baneful example to the young and inexperienced practitioners of my court".[15]

Sir Julian Salomons was representing a client before a judge whose son was on the other side. The judge appeared, to Salomons, to be turning a deaf ear to his persuasive arguments. Salomons declared: "I think I see what the trouble is". He looked first at the court window through which the sun's rays were streaming, and then very fixedly at his learned friend. "The son must have got in your Honour's eyes, and you can't see the law."[16]

During his later years as Chief Justice of Queensland, Sir Charles Lilley often tried matters in which his son Edwyn was counsel. The barrister's victories became so frequent that they were once ascribed flippantly to "the light of the son". Unsurprisingly, these successes boosted the son's practice even further,[17] thereby generating both envy and legitimate concern.

---

13 See pp 114-15.

14 Bolton and Byrne, *May it Please Your Honour*, p 57.

15 Bennett, *Sir Archibald Burt*, p 93.

16 Jacobs, *A Lawyer Tells*, p 152.

17 While he was at the junior Bar, the author was told by a solicitor that he had stopped briefing him when he learnt that he was *not* related to Sir Anthony Mason, then Chief Justice of Australia.

A storm erupted when the son's client won a high profile case in which the Queensland Investment and Land Mortgage Co Ltd of London (QILM) was suing its local directors for fraud. Lilley jnr represented the plaintiff. His father's rulings created a reasonable apprehension of bias with spades on, especially since the defendants included a bitter political rival of the father when he had been Premier of Queensland. The judge allowed the plaintiff a controversial amendment 37 days into the trial, then discharged the jury after its findings in favour of the defendants offended his conscience, and later awarded the plaintiff substantial damages. There were not enough judges on the Queensland Bench who were able to sit when the matter was taken on appeal. Accordingly, special legislation was passed to enable Sir William Windeyer of the Supreme Court of New South Wales to preside in the appeal (which was upheld).[18] In 1891 a parliamentary motion that no judge should sit alone or in chambers in any matter in which his son was counsel was deferred several times because the QILM case was sub judice. It was passed by a huge majority a few months later, although not translated into legislation.[19]

Lilley CJ announced his retirement from the Bench while the appeal was pending. Shortly afterwards he stood for election against Sir Thomas McIlwraith, one of the (now vindicated) defendants in the fraud case. McIlwraith and his running mate won handsomely.

For Septimus Burt and Edwyn Lilley, the son was attacked as a means of getting at the father. During the height of the controversies, legislation was introduced in both Western Australia and Queensland blocking a barrister from appearing before a closely related judge. In each instance the Bill was opposed by legal members of parliament and did not eventually pass into law. In modern times, these problems are avoided because there will always be a large enough pool of judges to constitute a trial or appeal court without embarrassment, even when the trial judge is closely related to one of the potential appeal judges.[20]

It is not quite so easy with the High Court because, as a final court of appeal with responsibility in constitutional matters, all judges should sit in important cases if available and some judges have had rising stars of the Bar in their families. Charles Gavan Duffy was appointed to the Supreme Court of Victoria while his father was Chief Justice of Australia. But the father was

18 See (1893) 4 QLJ 224. The legislation remained on the Queensland statute book until 1991 when the Queensland Court of Appeal was set up. In 2000 the New South Wales Court of Appeal was faced with constituting a court for an appeal from the decision of a judge who was by then a member of that Court in which one of the appellants had recently become a member of that Court (see *Heydon v NRMA Ltd* (2000) 51 NSWLR 1). Three judges from interstate sat as acting judges of appeal, one of them from Queensland, thereby discharging the debt of honour that had been incurred over a century before with the borrowing of Windeyer J.

19 Elvery, *In My Opinion*, p 64.

20 For example, McMurdo P and McMurdo J are wife and husband, as are their fellow judges on the Queensland Supreme Court, Ann and Peter Lyons.

nearing the end of his very long judicial career and it would have been highly unlikely that any appeal from the son would be heard by the father.[21]

With the advent of women into the legal profession, the prospect of a barrister appearing before a spouse or partner has increased markedly. So too has the possibility of sexual partners being pitted against each other in the courtroom.[22] The Queensland Court of Appeal set aside the conviction of a man who, despite being competently defended on a rape charge, was not told that the prosecutor and his defence counsel were in an "on again off again" sexual relationship. The platonic latency of that relationship during the trial itself (on circuit) did not excuse its non-disclosure, applying the test of reasonable suspicion or apprehension of bias in a fair minded, informed observer. Thomas JA concluded that:[23]

> [D]espite the suspended state of the relationship at the time of the trial, a frank disclosure should have been made to the client of the former relationship and of the continued friendship (or whatever the nature of the current relationship was). It is appreciated that in such a situation future predictions may be impossible. However the degree of association which followed so soon after the trial justifies the inference that there existed an interest in renewal.

But no one would have been deceived when Anthony Bellanto, Crown prosecutor, found himself opposed by his father, Tony Bellanto QC, representing an offender called up to be sentenced. According to the son's reminiscence, the father knew how to get his way when he referred to the son as "the very learned and fair crown prosecutor". He had never spoken to him in such glowing terms before.[24]

I am aware of only one instance where a father who was a practising barrister might possibly have been briefed to appear before his son. Wilfred Sheppard was called to the New South Wales Bar in 1915 and he was still practising in the late 1970s. His son Ian Fitzhardinge Sheppard was successively a judge of the New South Wales Industrial Commission (appointed 1970), the New South Wales Supreme Court (appointed 1973), the Federal Court of Australia (appointed 1979) and, after retirement (on reaching the statutory age) as an Acting Judge of the New South Wales Court of Appeal in a most distinguished judicial career. The late Christopher Gee QC had the pleasure, believed to be unique, of taking his bows as a new silk before his father Judge Kenneth Gee QC.

---

21 The Macrossan brothers, Hugh and Neal, each of whom would become Chief Justice of Queensland, appeared on opposite sides in the McCawley litigation. Robert Douglas J was a member of the majority in the Full Court that reversed the decision of his brother Edward Douglas J (see p 79).

22 The first husband and wife to appear on the *same* side of the record in the High Court were David Bennett (later the Commonwealth Solicitor-General) and Annabelle Bennett (now Bennett J) in *Datt v Law Society of New South Wales* (1981) 148 CLR 319.

23 *R v Szabo* [2000] QCA 194 at [64].

24 Anthony J Bellanto QC, "Reflections of a Criminal Barrister" *Bar News*, Winter 2011, at 80.

Until recently, many young lawyers acted as the associate to their father on the Bench. On some occasions, the judge's wife also served in this capacity. Concerns about nepotism and equal employment opportunities have seen such practices abandoned by the late 20th century.

Humorists and "hip"sters

Volumes have been written about humour and the law. The expression "gallows humour" reminds that the most sombre of legal occasions have been brightened by humorous diversion. Humour may defuse tension or deflect anger. Its intrusion may be deliberate or intentional. The jokes that are remembered about a person will, regardless of their truth, often be revelatory, both of the person remembered and of the jokester.

Writers may decry judicial humour that is excessive or inappropriate.[25] And a modern judicial officer who takes advantage of a captive audience to belittle or embarrass can expect disciplinary inquiry on top of Bar gossip. In keeping with one of the recurring themes in this book, one recognises that what may be funny in one generation may bemuse or appal the next. Instances of spontaneous humour in the cut and thrust of litigation are collected throughout this work. For the present, I focus on examples that may illuminate the character of the lawyer involved, or at least his or her reputation.

Sir Julian Salomons could use jokes to enforce a point. On being briefed to appear at East Maitland Circuit he said: "I am always glad to go there – I appreciate my home so much afterwards!" On another occasion he said to a solicitor who brought him a brief, "What bad fives you write!" and proceeded to alter the 30 guineas marked on the brief to 50.[26]

Sir Owen Dixon's humour could be abstruse.[27] It often betrayed a natural superiority of mind and a world-weariness bordering on cynicism. His biographer describes him as having "a wry, occasionally unkind sense of humour (though he would never be directly hurtful to an individual)".[28] In response to a woman at a dinner party who gushed about it being wonderful to dispense justice, Dixon retorted:[29]

---

25 For example, Francis Bacon observed that "judges ought to be more learned than witty" (*Of Judicature*) and Gilbert slated the "nisi prius nuisance ... the judicial humorist" (*The Mikado*).

26 AM Cohen, "Sir Julian Emanuel Salomons Kt KC. His Life Till 1886" (1945) 2 *Australian Jewish Historical Society Journal & Proceedings* 97 at 107.

27 Especially when it involved some play on Latin or Greek: see Graham Fricke, *Judges of the High Court*, p 120. Dixon CJ was at his most droll in describing the functionality of a "ball-pointed fountain pen" in *Martin v Scribal Pty Ltd* (1954) 92 CLR 17.

28 Ayres, *Owen Dixon*, p 10. For further instances of Dixon's clever cattiness, see pp 15, 53, 57.

29 Philip Ayres, "Owen Dixon's Causation Lecture: Radical Scepticism" (2003) 77 *Australian Law Journal* 628 at 693.

> I do not have anything to do with justice, Madam. I sit on a court of appeal, where none of the facts are known. One third of the facts are excluded by normal frailty and memory; one third by the negligence of the profession; and the remaining third by the archaic laws of evidence.

Dixon's prose could at times be stilted, but he could also be very amusing. In *Transport Publishing Co Pty Ltd v Literature Board of Review*[30] the Court overturned a censor's ban of a group of magazines as "objectionable". They were pictorial romances in which the characters spoke through captions. McTiernan J, in dissent, found them to be "distinctly evil" and "likely to enflame the venereal passions of the classes of young persons likely to devour this trash".[31] But, in a sublime piece of sustained deadpan, Dixon CJ who wrote the majority joint judgment calmly observed that:[32]

> When we did turn to the publications their actual character proved quite unexpected and produced almost a sense of contrast. The theme of them all nearly is love, courtship and marriage. Virtue never falters and right triumphs. Matrimony is the proper end and if you are not told that happiness ensues it is the constant assumption. They are, of course, intended for feminine readers. The pages contain nothing prurient, lewd or licentious. The tone is the complete contrary. The vehicle for this romance and sentiment is the only too familiar crude drawings with the inset print of dialogue, usually issuing from the lips of the figures. Needless to say, there are adventures, hazards, threats of violence, and escapes to excite the apprehensions of a fond reader. Whatever sensations are aroused by the narrative must be short-lived. For a story seldom occupies more than a dozen pages. There are, of course, bad men and they are sometimes wealthy. But invariably the heroine escapes from them by the aid of the strong, embracing arm of a good young man upon whom fortune is yet to smile. Why then has this literature been considered unduly to emphasise matters of sex and exhibit a tendency to deprave? It is because the lovers are depicted as loving passionately. They embrace and they embrace closely. Their kisses, though pure are full and perhaps prolonged. Their feelings for one another are intense and joy and happiness are represented as coming from a love that is as deep and passionate as it is devoted. Moreover, the eyes of the heroine are drawn with lids either drooping or unduly raised and her lips, though drawn in black and white, are obviously rosy as lipstick can make them. There is, too, an evident though crude attempt to infuse the subject with glamour, in the modern technical sense of that term. Another element frequently recurring is love at first sight; and love at first sight is at times aided by the tacit acceptance of the "pick-up" as an ordinary social practice. The convention that requires formal introduction

30 (1956) 99 CLR 111.

31 *Ibid* at 124, 125.

32 *Ibid* at 116-18.

> seems safely to be ignored by the heroines and there is no reason to suppose that it is observed in the circles in which they and the expected readers move ... The whole atmosphere resembles that of the American cinema. The reason why these otherwise virtuous narratives have been held unduly to emphasise matters of sex and to be likely to be injurious to morality is because again and again they depict or describe love scenes in which the parties kiss and embrace and display an ardent passion one for another.
>
> ... [The] publications of the kind here in question ... contain ... an affront to the intelligence of the reader but hardly a real threat to her morals. The stories are extremely silly, the letter press is stupid, the drawings are artless and crude and the situations are absurd. But we are not concerned with the damage done to the intellect or for that matter to the eyesight of the readers of these foolish periodicals. Our duty is to apply our judgment to the question whether regard being had to the nature of the literature, to the persons and age groups among whom it is to be distributed and to its tendency to deprave or corrupt them it is objectionable for that it unduly emphasises matters of sex or is likely to be injurious to morality or to encourage depravity. An examination of the literature is enough to satisfy us that the proper judgment upon the literature is that it is not "objectionable" within the definition on any of those grounds.

In *Green v Green*, the New South Wales Court of Appeal was addressing a claim by a de facto wife to a constructive trust stemming from the deceased man's promise to provide her with a home. In his reasons, Gleeson CJ observed:[33]

> The deceased appears to have maintained simultaneous domestic establishments with all three women and their respective children. In terms of division of his time he appears to have given preference to Margaret Green, but it seems that he spent two nights a week, regularly, with the respondent and, at least according to her evidence, gave what she regarded as a plausible explanation of his absences. Presumably, over a number of years, he managed to achieve the same result with the other women. This is consistent with his apparent success as a used car salesman.

It is understood that this last remark drew forth a letter of protest from a body representing the interests of car salesmen. Perhaps this incident triggered his Honour's later lecturing of judges to be careful about judicial humour.[34]

Judicial puns can be more than usually excruciating, perhaps because judges get false cues of encouragement from the polite tittering of counsel. In *Bear v Priestley*, a question arose whether trade usage could be proved by evidence in an action at law. Michie, from the Bar table observed, mischievously, that "Bear was strictly speaking not entitled to one farthing. Bear could not bring

33 (1989) 17 NSWLR 343 at 346.

34 See eg Murray Gleeson, "The Role of the Judge and Becoming a Judge" 16 August 1998, <www.hcourt.gov.au>.

it to bear". (A suppressed groan was heard and several counsel were reported to have shuddered.) a'Beckett CJ could not resist the rejoinder, "That is really quite unbearable".[35]

Samuels JA observed that "judges are criticised in one breath for living in ivory towers, and another for attempting to steal out of their seclusion, and indicating the very basic knowledge that they do in fact have of the real world".[36] Unsurprisingly, one form of judicial humour is the attempt to appear "hip", "cool" or "with it". Lockhart J put himself in such a frame when remarking:[37]

> Shoppers in supermarkets are probably not anxious to prolong the agony of wheeling trolleys between rows of food products and avoiding collisions with other trolleys, often to the unwelcome accompaniment of clamorous babies, and children impatient to escape from the shop or to buy everything in it except the household needs. I say nothing about attendant spouses who, if husbands, wait in varying degrees of impatience to perform their function as beasts of burden. Shoppers are inclined to select their goods quickly.

Often, allusions to modernity can be strained, or at least will appear so on a second reading. Heerey J began his reasons in a 1994 case saying: "This case concerns a proposed bridge to Hindmarsh Island. It is a troubled bridge over waters".[38] Other judges have referred to popular films, such as *The Castle* (with its reference to the "vibes" of the Constitution) or well-known television shows. In a case involving a botched raid by the Australian Secret Intelligence Service Mason J observed that:[39]

> There is an air of unreality about this stated case. It has the appearance of a law school moot based on an episode taken from the adventures of Maxwell Smart.

Boris Kayser was cross-examining a kidnap victim before a Melbourne magistrate, and attempting to show that a co-accused was the obvious ringleader.

> Kayser: He was subject to violent swings of mood, was he not?
> Witness looks puzzled.
> Kayser: If you don't understand my question you only have to say so.
> Dugan SM: He might think you are referring to Benny Goodman.

In *Permewan Wright Consolidated Pty Ltd v Trewhitt* Stephen J donned mock solemnity when declaring that:[40]

---

35 JM Bennett, *Sir William a'Beckett, First Chief Justice of Victoria 1852-1857*, Federation Press, 2001, p 78.

36 *Dykstra v Head* [1989] Aust Torts Reports 68,984 at 68,986.

37 Lockhart J in *Stewart Alexander & Co (Interstate) Pty Ltd v Blenders Pty Ltd* (1981) 53 FLR 307 at 316.

38 *Binalong Pty Ltd v Conservation Council of South Australia Inc* [1994] ATPR ¶41-312. The title of the Simon and Garfunkel song is "Bridge Over Troubled Water".

39 *A v Hayden* (1984) 156 CLR 532 at 550.

40 (1979) 145 CLR 1 at 29.

> Eggs are so notoriously perishable that in their deteriorated state they have much enriched the English language in a number of picturesque phrases ... They are not merely perishable but are enigmatic to the ordinary shopper ...

Cripps JA affected insouciance in the following exchange with counsel:[41]

> "Where was the new Rule introduced?"
> Poulos QC: "It is in the New South Wales Government Gazette".
> Cripps JA: "I knew I had read it somewhere".

In family law proceedings before Waddy J, it was necessary for a pair of battered old shoes to be tendered. Debate ensued over the description of the exhibit. Counsel suggested that the shoes would speak for themselves to which the judge replied: "That's why they've got tongues, I suppose".

A handful of lawyers revel in a reputation for unworldliness. Some even go out of their way to appear antiquarian, the very antithesis of "hip". The late ("Roddy") Meagher JA developed this to an art form. When at the Bar he responded to a survey about changing court dress by urging the reintroduction of silver buckles. He repeatedly courted both the attention and animus of feminists. Meagher professed no knowledge of the internet or the geography of mainstream Sydney. A regular conceit was to refer to the western Sydney address of a party or witness, adding "wherever that is". In *JPQS Pty Ltd v Cosarnan Construction Pty Ltd*[42] he referred dismissively to "a joint venture engaged in the development of certain land said to be situated in Bossley Park (wherever that is)". This goaded me (with the concurrence of Beazley JA) to state:

> I have had the benefit of reading in draft the reasons of Meagher JA.
>
> I also have the benefit of having access to a street directory. Accordingly, I do not share his Honour's customary doubts about the location of well-known Sydney suburbs lying to the west of Darling Point which sit cheek by jowl with his Honour's customary lack of doubts about most other matters. A useful resource for those who need to locate Bossley Park is http://www.travelmate.com.au. By clicking on "map maker" one can find easy ways of getting from, say Darling Point to that suburb.

But Meagher had the last laugh. He was responsible for preparing the headnote that accompanies most judgments issued by the Court of Appeal. Portion of it reads:

> HELD per Meagher JA, dismissing the appeal (Mason P and Beazley JA agreeing):
>
> The appellant's duty of care to the respondents arose from the latter's reliance on the accuracy of the appellant's certifications, for the purpose of presenting the relevant reports to their bank ...

41 *Admax Processing Pty Ltd v Pan* (unrep, NSW Court of Appeal, 14 December 1992).
42 [2003] NSWCA 66.

> HELD per Mason P (Beazley JA agreeing)
>
> A useful resource for those who need to locate Bossley Park is http://www.travelmate.com.au. By clicking on "map maker" one can find easy ways of getting from, say, Darling Point to that suburb.

In *Videski v Australian Iron & Steel Pty Ltd*[43] another President was on the receiving end of Roddy's humour. Kirby P and Cripps JA had circulated reasons pointing to opposite conclusions, as to whether the trial judge had erred in how he took account of the histrionic conduct of the applicant for compensation during his time in the witness box. Kirby P warned against stereotyping and the drawing of false conclusions from the witness' failure to show more stiff upper lip. Meagher JA agreed with Cripps JA, but felt compelled to add the following reasons of his own:

> [T]here is one aspect of Kirby P's judgment which is so extraordinary that it requires comment.
>
> The trial judge found that Mr Videski exaggerated when he gave his evidence. On this slender, and one would have thought unexceptionable observation, his Honour develops an elaborate, and distinctly xenophobic, rodomontade. His Honour says that Mr Videski only exaggerated because he was a Macedonian, all Macedonians are untrustworthy exaggerators, in this respect they do not resemble Anglo-Saxons, and judges ought be re-educated unless they appreciate these truths. One cannot permit such sentiments to be uttered without protest.
>
> Alexander the Great was a Macedonian, and Arrian's *Life* of him emphasised his honesty and taciturnity. There was no evidence before the Court that his epigoni have changed. We cannot assume that they have. On the face of it they are not the only people who have exaggerated when giving testimony. Occasionally people of undoubted Anglo-Saxon stock do so. I should have thought that an unfortunate propensity to deviate from the paths of honesty is something which occurs regardless of ethnicity. Judges are capable of dealing with it wherever it occurs, and from whatever source.
>
> It would be unfortunate if his Honour were permitted to utter, with the apparent approval of his brethren, sentiments so markedly at variance with the United Nations' Optional Protocol on Human Rights, not to mention Article 5 of the International Convention on the Elimination of All Forms of Racial Discrimination.

Kirby and Meagher were lifelong friends. And Meagher's rhetorical style was well-practised. Nevertheless, the President was driven to protest at the "self-evident absurd[ity]" of his brother judge's propositions. He allowed himself "compensatory comfort from the new-found interest of Meagher JA in the international instruments of human rights and their application to Australian law".

43 Unreported, NSW Court of Appeal, 17 February 1993.

At the end of the day judges and lawyers find it impossible not to be themselves, more or less, both on and off the Bench.

Clubs and Bar dinners

Membership of a gentlemen's club was never open to all judges or sought by all of them. In times past, some judges of good repute (and aren't all judges in this class?) found it impossible to gain entry into one or more of these clubs, for example because they were Jews. Others may simply have avoided trying because, like Groucho Marx, they did not care to belong to any club that would have them as a member. More recently, judges have ceased to be exclusively gentlemen.

The future High Court justice Henry Bournes Higgins was blackballed from the Melbourne Club when he sought membership in 1885 because of his unfashionable Irish sympathies.[44]

It was also rumoured in Brisbane that Macrossan SPJ imposed a harsh sentence on a dishonest solicitor whom he understood to have blocked his own admission to a gentlemen's club many years before. This rumour was boosted by the strange lecture about the *lex talionis* in the vigorous dissent of Brennan J when the Court of Criminal Appeal upheld the sentence:[45]

> Seeing that the learned trial judge was unable to exercise a merciful discretion, it then became his duty to impose such a sentence in this case as would relieve the suffering and hardships of several of the victims, then no sentence of imprisonment could be too severe; but the nature of punishment cannot be based on lex talionis (or law of retaliation), where under, as mentioned in the law of the Jews and Egyptians by Josephus and Diodorus Siculus, whoever without sufficient cause was found with mortal poison in his possession should himself be obliged to drink it; nor again on the law of the Locrians, which demanded an eye for an eye.

In times past, it was not unusual for all available judges of a court to troop off to lunch together at gentlemen's clubs like the Melbourne Club, the Weld Club (in Perth), the Australian Club (in Sydney). This was partly driven by a stricter separation between Bench and Bar than prevails today. And there was less paperwork to read during the luncheon adjournment. Inevitably, things have changed in recent years, with a much larger and busier judiciary and different attitudes to segregation of all sorts. Perhaps judicial collegiality has changed as well. Sir Garfield Barwick's biographer detected the disintegration of previously happy collegiality in the High Court of the Dixon CJ era in that "it was not

44 John Rickard, *H B Higgins, The Rebel as Judge*, George Allen and Unwin, 1984, p 65.

45 *R v McCowan* [1931] St R Qd 149 at 155. The source of this story is Brennan's grandson, Tom.

unusual to see six or seven cars waiting in Taylor Square to take each judge, *separately*, to the Australian Club".[46]

With the arrival of female judges in the 1960s additional barriers to clubbishness opened up. Some leading clubs maintained their men-only stance and some (but not all) of the male judges maintained their membership of such clubs. Some resigned in solidarity with their female colleagues. Inevitably, and across the courts, tensions would surface when there was debate about continuing traditional venues for celebratory dinners.

Judge Helen O'Sullivan was reportedly thrilled when, on appointment to the District Court of Queensland, she received an invitation to join Tattersall's Club in Brisbane. She wrote back accepting, expressing her delight that the Club had at last changed its policy of restricting membership to men. When the mistake was discovered the invitation was withdrawn.[47]

In their *Guide to Judicial Conduct*, the Council of Chief Justices of Australia makes the following statement about judicial membership of clubs:[48]

> It is obvious that a judge should not be a member of a club that engages in unlawful discrimination. It is generally accepted that a judge should not be a member of a club that engages in any form of invidious discrimination, even though no breach of the law may be involved.
>
> Views differ on whether it is desirable for a judge to be a member of a club or society that permits only male or female members. In some courts, the collegiate view is that social functions organised by judges should not be held at such clubs.

This delicately phrased advice must have taken many hours to thrash out.

Bar dinners are nowadays held annually. In times past they were reserved for notable (and rarer) events like the appointment or retirement of a distinguished judge. The failure to call a Bar dinner promptly could be viewed as a signal of professional hesitation about the appointment, as occurred when Julian Salomons' chief justiceship was first announced.[49]

In January 1865 judges of the Supreme Court of Victoria and other legal dignitaries attended a function at the Melbourne Club feting the officers of the Confederate ship *Shenandoah*. The United States consul had requested that the ship be seized for piracy on Union ships, alternatively that Britain's treaty obligation to observe strict neutrality should be observed to the letter. Although Australian public opinion was generally in favour of the Confederates, the attendance of the judges was severely criticised by the *Age* on the basis that,

46 Marr, *Barwick*, p 215 (emphasis added).

47 In 2006 the Club committee's motion to allow women was lost by 106 votes when the members rejected it by 1683 votes to 1577.

48 Second edition, 2007, p 32.

49 See p 84. Other stories about notable Bar dinners are given in Chapter 12 of Jacobs, *A Lawyer Tells*.

as "Government officials, ... it cannot be permitted that they should commit a breach of the neutrality enjoined by Her Majesty, without being called to account". The ship was allowed to refuel and, despite ineffectual governmental attempts at prevention, to recruit additional crew. It sailed off from Port Phillip and later went about destroying 37 Union ships, mostly whalers full of sperm oil of considerable value. In fact the Civil War had by then ended, although the *Shenandoah's* captain refused to believe reports to that effect from masters of neutral vessels. The incident led to proceedings by the United States against Britain known as the Alabama Claims. An arbitration in Geneva awarded over 15 million dollars damages against the British government for this and other breaches of the neutrality obligation. There was a strongly worded dissent by Sir Alexander Cockburn, the English Chief Justice who was a member of the arbitral panel.[50]

Relations between Lord Gifford, the appointed Colonial Secretary in Western Australia, and Wrenfordsley CJ were particularly strained, even allowing for the judge's capacity to fight with anyone.[51] Governor Robinson was inevitably drawn into the brawls and he often tried to hose down Gifford's excesses. Dr Bennett records that the breaking point in the exchange of incivilities occurred at a dinner in the Governor's honour at Perth's Weld Club in August 1882.[52] Wrenfordsley had been elected Club President on his arrival in the colony. Being the sole judge in town he "never frequented the Club" although he made an exception on this occasion. Gifford, at an adjoining table, snorted during Wrenfordsley's remarks. He was called to order but replied angrily "I am not addressing you, sir". Wrenfordsley replied: "You spoke too loud sir". The next day, Gifford complained to the Club committee. Persuaded that a Baron outranked a Chief Justice, they called on Wrenfordsley to explain his actions. Wrenfordsley angrily resigned and refused to reconsider. The press enjoyed the squabble. One newspaper published an advertisement:

> Wanted, A President
> He must be ... portly, courtly, and of grave demeanour; free from all taint of radicalism; thoroughly acquainted with the politics of the *West Australian*;[53] a cordial hater of the present Administration; secretive; a good whist player, and partial to porter ...
> Apply, SECRETARY, WELD CLUB

Sir Arthur Dean reports a story involving Hodges J, a judge of the Supreme Court of Victoria between 1890 and 1919, and Hayden Starke, later to become

50 Ernest Scott, "The Shenandoah Incident" (1926) 11 *Victorian Historical Magazine* 55. See also Edward E Morris, *A Memoir of George Higinbotham*, Macmillan & Co, 1895, ch X.

51 See further p 123.

52 JM Bennett, *Sir Henry Wrenfordsley, Second Chief Justice of Western Australia*, Federation Press, 2004, pp 47-8.

53 A rival newspaper.

a justice of the High Court. Starke himself had a reputation for rudeness, but this time it was Hodges who had insulted Starke in court. At lunch they met in the urinal of their club. Hodges apologised for his behaviour, only to be brushed aside by Starke who said that "an insult offered in open court cannot be wiped out by an apology in a urinal".[54] (In 1913, Starke and others arranged for the Victorian Bar to pass a resolution deploring Hodges' violent discourtesy towards litigants, witnesses and members of the legal profession. The resolution, which also recorded the opinion that Hodges' conduct was most detrimental to the administration of justice, was forwarded to the judge and thereafter there were no more formal complaints.)

In 1971 a young, obviously pregnant, Mary Gaudron, was "Mr Junior" with the role of roasting the guest of honour, Attorney-General McCaw QC, at the annual Bar Dinner in Sydney.[55] She attacked the Askin government's law reforms, introduced by McCaw, for having infringed civil liberties. Then she turned to McCaw's judicial appointments. Stating that she had checked in *Who's Who* the biography of all of the recent appointees she continued:

> That check ... revealed that [McCaw's] appointments all had a single common characteristic. It was not their religion, their politics or their schooling but it was something so apparent that one should be able to use it to predict future appointments.

As Gaudron paused for the punchline, Mr Justice Reynolds of the Court of Appeal, one of McCaw's appointees, rose and loudly announced, "Mr Chairman, I do not propose to listen to any more of this rubbish". He stormed out, followed by a volley of bread rolls from some quarters. Reynolds undoubtedly assumed that the punchline would advert directly to a pattern of all appointments being male. The punchline never came and, according to some (but not all) accounts, Gaudron became too upset at this stage to do more than second the toast. She later revealed that, with respect to each of the recent judicial appointments, *Who's Who* mentioned the judge's father but not his mother. Her intention was to draw the conclusion that eligibility for appointment under McCaw depended on being motherless. No doubt she was intending indirectly to make the point that enraged Reynolds.

Menzies J, a justice of the High Court from 1958, collapsed and died shortly before he was to take his seat at the 1974 New South Wales Bar dinner. Several nurses married to barristers tried unsuccessfully to revive him, kneeling over him in their evening dresses.

---

54 Dean, *Multitude of Counsellors*, p 180. Sir Owen Dixon described Hodges as a judge who "proved uncertain and irascible": see p 39 below.

55 The following account is taken largely from Burton, *From Moree to Mabo. The Mary Gaudron Story*, pp 92-3. See also David Bennett, "Mary Gaudron's 'Mr Junior' Speech and High Court Debut" in Geoff Lindsay and Carol Webster, *No Mere Mouthpiece Servants of All Yet of None*, LexisNexis, 2002, p 262.

Governor-General Kerr's dismissal of Prime Minister Whitlam on 11 November 1975 is one of those events etched in the minds of contemporaries like the assassination of President Kennedy. Kerr QC and Whitlam QC had been close friends who practised in similar areas of the Bar and shared chambers on the Tenth Floor Wentworth Chambers, Sydney, before entering public life. Whitlam, who had advised Her Majesty to appoint Kerr CJ Governor-General, was still mightily pleased with his choice when a floor dinner was arranged to celebrate the event. I was then a raw junior who was privileged to witness the bibulous self-congratulations from both of the great men. In what would become the deepest of ironies, Kerr expressed the wish that his vice-regal role would "not be confined to opening flower shows". After The Dismissal, Whitlam refused to have any further dealings with the man he believed had betrayed both him and Australian democracy. This presented a peculiar problem for organisers of floor dinners that was resolved by each man not accepting an invitation to attend until informed by the floor's clerk, Ken Hall, that the other was unavailable to do so. The men made an exception for the dinner to celebrate Ken Hall's 50-year career as floor clerk. Each behemoth of state sat at the opposite ends of a large table.

Writers for pleasure

Many notable lawyers have contributed to the arts and fields of learning outside the law. Others have sought diversionary fulfilment in writing about the law. A handful have achieved world-wide fame by their exploits.[56]

Some lawyers have been notable more for their artistic or literary contributions than their legal ones and here I would include the poets Andrew Barton ("Banjo") Patterson and Bernard O'Dowd. The famed historian of World War One, CEW Bean, had once been a Sydney barrister. It is unclear if these men were motivated like the character Dick in Joseph Furphy's Australian classic *Such is Life* of whom it was written that "educated for the law, his innate honesty had shrunk from the practice of his profession".[57]

Other contributors to the arts or literature are yet to match their reputation as lawyers with fame for their literary endeavours. The list is amazingly long and stretches back to our earliest lawyers. Obviously there are the memoirs

---

56 I would include Sir James Cockle CJ who was elected a Fellow of the Royal Society for his contributions to mathematics, the late David Hodgson JA (who was a world authority on the philosophy of the mind and whose publications include *The Mind Matters* (1991) and *Rationality + Consciousness = Free Will* (2011), each published by Oxford University Press) and George Palmer J (whose musical compositions, frequently played on the ABC, have been performed in Britain and the United States and who was commissioned to write the music for masses celebrated during the World Youth Day visit of Pope Benedict in 2008).

57 Joseph Furphy, *The Annotated Such is Life,* Oxford: Oxford University Press (1991), p 97.

and autobiographies of lawyers who entered politics, or who skirted its boundaries like Robert Garran, Garfield Barwick and Michael Kirby, as well as the reminiscences of many other leading lawyers. But there have also been significant publications of history,[58] poetry,[59] plays,[60] essays,[61] personal and family histories,[62] and works on gardening[63] as well as music.[64] Then there were the lawyers who wrote novels some of them deserving to be called "potboilers" except that they were not necessarily written for gain.[65]

An early Australian judge whose literary fame was entirely undeserved (in the eyes of Sheller JA) was Barron Field J. When proposing a toast to Dame Leonie Kramer, who had compiled *The Oxford Anthology of Australian Literature*,[66] Sheller waxed lyrical:[67]

> [T]he Supreme Court can hold its head high in your presence. Mr Justice Barron Field, spelt "on" not "en", a judge well known to the New South Wales lawyers present, but for the benefit of others, named second of the judges of the 1814 Supreme Court of New South Wales. He was indeed unique. A poetic judge. The Bar has slight regard for his literary achievements. Our historian has written that Barron Field's verse was not well received by the critics when it was published, and since then it has been more laughed at than read.
>
> Disraeli, who somehow met Barron Field in Gibraltar, described him as a noisy, obtrusive, jargonic judge, ever illustrating the obvious, explaining the evident and expatiating on the commonplace – things nowadays not done on the Bench. But the *Oxford History*

58 For example, by James Spigelman who has published biographies of *Beckett and Henry* (2004).

59 For example, by William a'Beckett and John Bray.

60 For example, by Ian Callinan.

61 For example, by Sir Frederick Jordan CJ and "Roddy" Meagher JA. In Jordan's case, his collection of essays and an anthology of parallel passages in the writings of diverse authors were published posthumously in 1950 in a limited edition entitled *Appreciations*, illustrated by Sir Lionel Lindsay.

62 For example, by Chris Bevan, Judge Kenneth Gee QC and Judge Christopher Geraghty.

63 By Pembroke J.

64 By Sir Robert Garran and James Thomas JA.

65 Glass JA published two novels under the name "Benjamin Sidney" featuring a Sydney-based barrister called Paul Sherman. The novels are called *Discord Within the Bar* and *Sherman for the Plaintiff*. Glass told one of his friends that he hoped to be remembered more for them than for his judgments, a double error from this fine jurist. A much less distinguished lawyer, but well known to law students, was the Sydney barrister Archibald Nugent Robertson whose brush with the Balmain New Ferry Co at Circular Quay generated litigation that went to the Privy Council. Robertson wrote a book in 1914, *Her Last Appearance*, and had it published by Mills and Boon. The story is built around the inability of a wife to give evidence in a matter concerning her husband because of the fiction of marital unity. Strangely, this work was overlooked by the High Court when the law of spousal competence, compellability and privilege was recently considered in *Australian Crime Commission v Stoddart* [2011] HCA 47.

66 Oxford University Press, 1985.

67 *Bar News*, Spring 1985.

> *of Australian Literature* sees him in a different light. Lovingly it recounts that he published a tiny volume, modestly called *First Fruits of Australian Poetry*. This is not the place to start a revival of Barron Field's poetry, if that were possible. That is for the Supreme Court to do. But I would like to read part – well the first line – of the poem for which, according to the Oxford History, he is best remembered. The poem is called *The Kangaroo*. The first line consists of two words "Kangaroo, Kangaroo".
>
> Call your poem *The Kangaroo* and then say nothing in the first line but repeat the title twice, is surely illustrating the obvious and explaining the evident, if not expatiating on the commonplace. But who are we, poor lawyers, to challenge the authority of the *Oxford History of Australian Literature* and wonder how it has preferred such a poem to the treasure to be found in the New South Wales Law Reports?"

Sir Alfred Stephen spent his early career in Van Diemen's Land where he served as Solicitor-General and Attorney-General. He then became a judge and later Chief Justice of New South Wales, with a judicial term spanning 34 years. Twice married and with 18 children, he composed this poem in 1859 while sitting at Bathurst Courthouse during "a very long reply in a Squatting action":[68]

> *Twice nine, or judicial Impartiality Exemplified*
> Of children this Knight had no less than eighteen –
> Twice nine little heads, with a marriage between.
> He had nine when a barrister, nine when a judge,
> And of "sex" – thus to Nature he owed not a grudge –
> Nine precisely were girls, the other half boys,
> An equal division 'twixt quiet and noise;
> While, if by marriage the number be reckoned,
> There were nine of the first and nine of the second.
> Nine in Tasmania, nine in New South Wales,
> Then, to show with what justice he still held the scales,
> Since nine it was clear he could not divide,
> (A third sex as yet never having been tried),
> Five sons and four daughters in Hobart were born,
> And four sons, five daughters might Sydney adorn.
> Twin daughters, twin sons, complete the strange story
> Of this patron of "Wigs", though constant old Tory.

As young men, the future judges William a'Beckett and Samuel Griffith published poetry under pseudonyms.[69] In June 1892, long before the start of

68 Ruth Bedford, *Think of Stephen, A Family Chronicle*, Angus and Robertson, 1954, p 188. Stephen's biographer has observed that "even for days when large families were common, it is difficult now to visualize a household in which there was an interval of 30 years between the birth of the first and last of all 18 children. No wonder that Alfred so often complained of exhaustion and impecuniosity!" (Bennett, *Sir Alfred Stephen. Third Chief Justice of New South Wales*, p 103).

69 See pp 102-3.

his own judicial career, Frank Gavan Duffy[70] published in the journal of the Melbourne Articled Clerks' Society a poem called *A Dream of Fair Judges* which was a parody of Tennyson's *A Dream of Fair Women*. He used the pseudonym "Vie Manquee" and his authorship was for obvious reasons not disclosed for a long time. The name had a significance not associated with legal matters and the authorship was first attributed by literary journals and critics to many persons other than the actual writer.

Duffy rose to become Australia's fourth Chief Justice. Undoubtedly there were some who knew of his youthful authorship of the poem. It was revealed generally in 1935, after Duffy had retired when the poem was republished with assisting notes by CJ Ahern in *Res Judicatae* in 1935 and the *Australian Law Journal* in 1945:[71]

I read, before my eyelids dropped their shade,
    The Code of Tenures writ in Law French fair
By him who through the Feudal mazes strayed
    Ere Coke and Blackstone were—

Great Littleton, the Lawyer whose sweet breath
    Precluded those black-letter tomes that fill
The Learned Courts of Great Elizabeth
    With doubts that echo still.

And for a while his "Treatise on the use"
    Held me entranced in intellectual pain
And wonder at the art that can confuse
    Things in themselves most plain.

Feoffment and fine, feigned issue, plea of right,
    And all the jargon of the Lawyer Priest,
Muddled my mind with surfeit of delight
    Like mixed wines at a feast.

And lo! I dreamt that I too had passed out
    From the fair fellowship of human kind,
And felt the full immunity from doubt
    Of the judicial mind.

All human weakness that can mar a man
    Slipped from me like a garment, and I stood
A judge beyond men's blessing or their ban,
    Like H—s or like H—d.[72]

And then methought I sat enthroned afar
    Among my peers in scarlet ermine-bound,
Remote from the base rubble of the bar
    That stood expectant around.

70 He was a justice of the High Court between 1913 and 1931 and Chief Justice of Australia between 1931 and 1935.

71 I have drawn extensively on those notes.

72 References to Hodges J and Hood J, the most recent appointments to the Victorian Bench.

And a clear undertone from close beside
    Thrilled through mine ears in that exalted sphere,
"Welcome, good brother; here thou mayst abide
    Free from desire and fear."

And by me stood a form I knew of old,[73]
    With dome-like brow, a sweet mouth firmly set,
Features clear cut as newly-minted gold,
    And eyes of calm regret.

"I drank delight of battle with my peers,
    My name was once the people's battle-cry,
Alas, what is the end of hopes and fears—
    Splendid obscurity!"

His firm tones fell like strokes on silver pure,
    Tones to my weary ear familiar long
In laboured judgments lucidly obscure,
    Perspicuously wrong.

"What wonder — at thy word on battlefield
    Myself, illustrious Chief, had boldly died."
I answered free, and turning I appealed
    To one that stood beside.[74]

But he, with sick and scornful looks averse,
    To its full height his stately stature draws—
"My prime," he said, "is blasted with a curse,
    And this man is the cause.

"I am cut off from hope in dull despair,
    A wretched puisne who should be a chief,
My father suffered so, and now I bear
    Hereditary grief.

"And much it chafes me that I cannot bend
    His will, nor stir the calm propriety
Of my slow, solemn colleague — Prythee, friend,
    How fares the great QC?[75]

---

73 This and the following three verses, and the first and second lines of the following verse, refer to Higinbotham CJ who bitterly resented the slur on his judgments by the then unknown writer.

74 According to CJ Ahern (19 *Australian Law Journal* 43): "The last two lines of this verse and the next three verses refer to Mr Justice Williams, Senior Puisne Judge, who was of very stately appearance. He resented Mr Higinbotham's appointment to the Bench ahead of him, and always chafed under the Chief's seniority when the latter became Chief Justice. Mr Justice Williams' father had been the Senior Puisne Judge of the Supreme Court of Victoria, and was very wrathful when Sir William Stawell, who had earlier been Attorney-General, was appointed as Chief Justice many years earlier. These lines had additional significance, when, about seven months after they were published, Chief Justice Higinbotham died, and Dr Madden (afterwards Sir John Madden) was appointed from the Bar to the position of Chief Justice, and Mr Justice Williams thereupon wrote a strong letter of protest to the daily press". See further p 77 below, where Williams' letter is set out in full.

75 A reference to JL Purves QC, longtime leader of the Victorian Bar.

"The man, my leader in the olden time,
He of the fluent tongue and braxen brow,
With him I rode on fortune's neck sublime—
Our paths are parted now."

"Alas! Alas!" a low voice full of care
Murmured beside me, "turn and look on me:[76]
My youth in drafting settlements did fare,
My prime in Equity.

"And to the dreadful Moloch of the Law
I gave my human heart and brain of fire,
Toiling with stern resolve and modest awe,
And hope that would not tire.

"I won success and wear it — what avails?
'Tis but a right to labour at the oar,
To sift with painful toil discordant tales,
And o'er dull pleadings pore.

"For me life has no leisure and no fun,
No rest from long debate of wrong and right;
Visions of work undone, and to be done
Do haunt me day and night."

To whom, in accents clear and free from care
Replied his benchfellow in Equity,[77]
"I am the happy judge whom men call fair,
Take comfort then from me.

"I work, I play, I let the mad world rail,
I never lose my temper or my time,
My judgment and digestion never fail
From merry chime to chime."

His cheerful words stirred all the silence drear,
Like soft winds waking on a torpid sea;
Sudden I heard a voice that said, "Come here
That I may look on thee."

I, turning, saw the idol of my youth—[78]
When life had idols in the years gone by—
The man of iron will and fearless truth,
And matchless loyalty.

He, flashing forth a haughty smile, had spoke,
But that I stayed him with preventing tongue,

76 A reference to Mr Justice Holroyd, a painstaking, careful and slow lawyer, according to Ahern.

77 Mr Justice Thomas a'Beckett.

78 CJ Ahern writes (19 *Australian Law Journal* at 44): "The last two lines of this verse and the next five verses refer to Mr Justice Hodges, who had not been long appointed to the Bench, and with whom the author had often appeared as a junior, and for whom he had, when at the Bar, a great admiration". Further as to Hodges J, see above p 31.

And through all forms with glad impatience broke,
    As if I still were young.

"Oh, master, since the judgment-seat you fill
    What chemic change confuses all your blood,
That in your eyes the deeds of men are ill,
    And no cause seemeth good?

"Have all things turned to sinfulness and shame?
    Is there no virtue now outside yourself?
Is honour dead, and goodness but a name,
    And no God left but pelf ?

"Why greet your former friends with savage sneer,
    Or with contemptuous pity's chilling frosts?
Why should all victor litigants appear
    Unworthy to have costs?

More had I spoken, but his wrathful eyes
    Blazed on me, till I trembled and awoke.
And lo! My Littleton before me lies,
    And the dull embers smoke.

And so I saw not him who left us last,[79]
    Of whom men murmur with admiring stare,
"Behold ideal justice, fair and fast" —
    But less fast were more fair.

Sir Owen Dixon provided a further commentary to this poem in a 1932 letter to Dr Waddell:

> Many thanks for the copy of the "Dream of Fair Judges" which you so kindly sent me.
>
> The Excellence of its Versification is only equalled by the aptness of its illusions to the men with whom it deals. The Chief was then Higginbotham who had been an aristocratic radical. The puisne "who should be a chief" is Sir Hartley Williams, whose father Edward Eyre Williams was appointed in 1852 and retired in 1874. He considered that he should have been made chief when Stawell was appointed in 1857. Hartley Williams thought that Higginbotham 's appointment was a political denial of his own claims to the Chief Justiceship but when, two or three years after the poem was composed, the office again fell vacant Madden was put over his head. The "low voice full of care" is that of Holroyd, perhaps the best of Victorian judges, a very clear headed man with a thorough knowledge of Equity. He was a son of a Comr. of Bankruptcy in England and a grandson of Holroyd J of the KB. The "accents clear and free from care" are a'Beckett's, a whimsical mind free of all vanity and full of common sense. His family were the founders of Quack and include the writer of the "Comic Blackstone". Hodges comes next. He came to the

79 The last verse refers to Mr Justice Hood, who had recently been appointed. The sting in the poem's final line was an additional reason for the author keeping his identity covered.

bench with a high reputation as an able common lawyer but proved uncertain and irascible. He was entirely without humour and it is said that when he read the poem he said to one of his friends "Did you see what Duffy wrote about me? My wife thinks it funny." Hood comes last. He was an older but frequent adversary of Duffy at the bar. He proved a very good common law judge something of the style of Pring.

With many thanks and kind regards,
Yours sincerely, Owen Dixon

The South Australian Chief Justice John Bray published books of poetry and essays. His *Hymn to Respectability* suggested that laws on hotel closing hours discriminated against the working classes:

Plump Bacchus must at dusk withhold
His foaming showers.
Strong liquors only can be sold
In working hours.
To shield the plebs thy care decrees
The shuttered pub.
Undaunted pass thy devotees.
They have their club.

Like Frank Gavan Duffy, Mary Gaudron would later go to the High Court. She was stung into a versified response, à la Edgar Allen Poe, when the head of the Attorney-General's Department was rash enough to requisition an annual report from the Chambers of the Solicitor-General:

On several midnights dreary, we have pondered weak and weary
Over many a quaint and curious volume of forgotten law,
And wondered if we sat in Chambers monitored ...
T'was new urgencies arriving at our very door,
Only this and nothing more.

Ah distinctly we remember it was drawing nigh September
Every parliamentary member quested for the floor
Eagerly we sought the morrow – vainly we tried to borrow
From the library anything we hadn't read before
To advise upon some matter growing urgent more and more
Forgotten now and for evermore.

Back into our volumes turning our wits a fevered burning,
Soon again we heard a tapping somewhat louder than before;
Surely this invasion must destroy our concentration
On the problems of the law,
So we postponed our advisings, the buggings to explore:
Only coppers – nothing more.

Then we pitched our voices to the ceiling – quoted sources quite revealing
But the words had little meaning and no relevancy bore,
For one cannot help agreeing that no living human being

Ever yet was blessed with seeing tapes transcribed without a flaw
And Bottom says there's more.[80]

There's been no diminution in the vigorous institution
Of the company prosecution – with success as heretofore,
And the Crown has kept appealing all sentences revealing
Any leniency in dealing with the disrespectful poor,
But there'll be no prosecution, much less due execution of our telegraphic law
Immunities Galore!

'Tho pedantic in our leaning we used no word with sexist meaning
With deference overweening to the Spirit of the law,
For there is no toleration of the least discrimination
But self-incrimination – now that's a different score.
We must aid each Royal Commission in its quest for an admission of corruption at the core –
Either now or evermore.

The demand for annual information is another indication
Of the woeful situation we dare not to ignore,
All assurances were token and all promises were broken
But our thoughts were not unspoken
For we advised yet more and more.
Herewith our summation for departmental lamination
Starting July 1 of 1984
The truth – nothing more.

Mary Gaudron was not asked to report the following year.

80 Bob Bottom OAM is a journalist honoured for his work "reporting upon and investigating organized crime" and the author of seven books on the subject. Investigative reporters are always stirring up leads that politicians, for good or ill, feel obliged to follow up. Hard questions about the admissibility and credibility of the information they dredge up are often placed on the desk of law officers or directors of public prosecutions.

3 Squabbling Jurists

Duellers and brawlers

Duelling was a popular and sometimes fatal diversion for "gentlemen" until the mid-19th century. Spigelman CJ described it as "the principal form of alternative dispute resolution" of the Rum Corps.[1] Those who participated, including the seconds, were liable as principals to murder if death resulted,[2] although convictions were rare and death sentences rarer.[3] Sir John Jeffcott was the founding judge of the South Australian Supreme Court. His involvement in a fatal duel that saw him prosecuted for murder is discussed elsewhere.[4] Australian society aped yet lagged behind England in this felonious practice. Duelling came to an abrupt end around the 1840s in England but lingered on later here.

There are several recorded instances of Australian lawyers getting involved in duels. The former Attorney-General Saxe Bannister's parting shot before sailing to England in 1826 was at the leading barrister Wardell in a duel from which both men emerged uninjured. William Charles Wentworth challenged Commissioner Bigge to a duel over the latter's suggestion that he, Wentworth, had written an anonymous poem defaming Lieutenant-Governor Molle. Indeed, Wentworth became so dangerously agitated that the Under-Secretary of State had to place him under police restraint.[5]

William Lyttleton was the police magistrate of Norfolk Plains in Van Diemen's Land in the 1820s. A wealthy settler, William Bryan, was angered at Lyttleton's conviction of one of his servants for cattle stealing. Bryan challenged Lyttleton to a duel, sending the challenge through a man named Lewis.

---

1 The Hon JJ Spigelman AC, "Bicentenary of the coup of 1808" (2008) 30 *Australian Bar Review* 129 at 138.

2 *R v Robert Atkins, Thomas Chambers and Henry Milton* (1828) Dowling's Select Cases 306.

3 Antony E Simpson, "Dandelions on the Field of Honor: Dueling, the Middle Classes, and the Law in Nineteenth-Century England" (1988) *Criminal Justice History* 99 discusses how the rules of honour were observed more than those of law. Convictions were very rare and, when they happened, capital punishment was reserved for the foreigner or the man who broke the conventions of honour in some heinous way.

4 See p 47.

5 Andrew Tink, *William Charles Wentworth. Australia's greatest native son*, Allen & Unwin, 2009, p 58.

Montagu J fined Lewis £150 and sent him to gaol for 18 months.[6] Hugh Cokeley practised for a time as a barrister in Hobart Town. He became Crown Solicitor in the 1830s. He was always in financial difficulties and narrowly escaped conviction for embezzlement in 1842. He sailed to New Zealand to take up private practice in Wellington. In 1844, after a legal dispute, he mortally wounded a fellow lawyer in a duel.

One of the earliest lawyers to practise in the Swan River Colony (later Perth) was William Nairn Clark. He got into a dispute with a merchant named Johnson whom he alleged to have defrauded a client. Clark approached him and his associates in a Fremantle street, stating: "you are a scoundrel and a blackguard, and if it were not for motives of prudence, I would give you a sound drubbing". Johnson challenged him to a duel which took place the following day. Both duellists fired a single shot. Johnson was struck near the hipbone and died the next day, declaring that he had no complaint at what had happened. Clark and the two seconds were charged with murder with Clark being kept in prison until his trial. At that trial he represented himself and was able to obtain acquittals for all the accused.

Charles Kingston QC was at various times Attorney-General and Premier of South Australia around the turn of the 20th century and he played a leading part in the Federation movement. When he was first elected Premier, he was on a good behaviour bond for organising a duel in Victoria Square, Adelaide. It was his response to being called "a coward, a bully and a disgrace to the legal profession" by Sir Richard Baker, a conservative member of the Legislative Council.

Although duelling was stamped out in the 19th century its code was still being advocated by Rich J in the 1940s when he described a libeller's invitation that the victim sue him as "an invitation to the adversary to substitute for methods of unregulated and desultory combat a duel to be fought in legal form with every weapon which the law allows, and as involving no promise that if it is accepted the challenger will fire in the air".[7]

Actual violence was threatened from the Bench in an episode involving Montagu J and Alfred Stephen, then the Attorney-General in Van Diemen's Land and later to become Chief Justice of New South Wales. Montagu commenced hearing a case whose prosecution by information lay under the law officer's control. Stephen ambled into court to be greeted with a judicial tirade probably unequalled in Australian legal history. It culminated:

> Sir, in your official capacity I shall always treat you with the courtesy and respect due to you. Were you elsewhere I should treat you after your conduct with even less courtesy than a dog or a cur as your

6 L Robson, *A History of Tasmania*, Oxford University Press, 1983, vol 1, pp 296-7, 468-9; McLaren, *Dewigged, Bothered and Bewildered*, p 161.

7 *Penton v Calwell* (1945) 70 CLR 219 at 248.

> conduct richly deserves. I say this, Sir, as an English gentleman, and only as such – perhaps in the capacity of a Judge I had better be silent.

Perhaps indeed!

In 1846 two prominent Sydney barristers were committed to prison for punching each other in court. In an otherwise pedestrian debt action before Stephen CJ, Richard Windeyer took umbrage at his opponent, John Darvall,[8] calling his client "a fellow". Windeyer protested that his client was at least an honest fellow – more than could be said for Darvall's client. As the judge tried to hose things down Windeyer repeated his assertion, adding that Darvall was a liar. As Stephen reported of the consequences:[9]

> Mr Darvall then struck Mr Windeyer forcibly with the brief which he held in his hand, on the neck or face. Mr Windeyer instantly started to the floor with his fists clenched and his arms squared at Mr Darvall; when – as he was striking, but before he struck, a blow – an officer in attendance placed himself between the parties.

Aghast at such behaviour, Stephen committed the two counsel to the custody of the Sheriff and adjourned for two hours while he consulted his colleagues. When he returned, the two combatants did not dispute his account of what had happened in the face of the court, but they tendered apologies. Unmoved, Stephen sentenced Darvall to 14 days' imprisonment, Windeyer to 20; and each was placed on a good behaviour bond for two years. The two lawyers spent Christmas behind bars.

Ratcliffe Pring was a "man of vigour and fiery temper". He was also a womaniser and a lover of horseflesh, waxing lyrical on his appreciation of both when he said:[10]

> To-day when I saw my beauty win, when I stroked his soft neck and felt his cold nose in my hand, I thought God only made one animal and that was the horse; then when I returned to the grandstand, the horse was displaced by the woman, and I felt that I'd hang before being compelled to choose between them.

Pring distinguished himself in 1872 when, as Attorney-General for Queensland, he threatened and assaulted another member of the House while drunk. The Speaker ordered his arrest, but, when the Sergeant-at-Arms approached him, Pring bolted, exclaiming: "You will have to catch me first". Pring was found guilty of contempt of Parliament, but in order to give him a chance to apologise, the Speaker's warrant for arrest was not signed. Pring resigned from Parliament the following day. The Speaker then went ahead and signed the warrant and Pring found himself arrested 11 days later when he arrived at Dalby to attend

---

8 Darvall later took silk and served as Attorney-General for New South Wales before resigning from politics and returning to England.

9 See Bennett, *Sir Alfred Stephen*, pp 157-8.

10 Elvery, *In My Opinion*, p 17.

the court sittings there. Since, however, Parliament had by then been prorogued, Pring came back to Brisbane in triumph. He later returned to Parliament, took silk and was appointed a judge of the Supreme Court of Queensland in 1880.

A Victorian barrister named Gerald Supple took conflict to a higher level. Deeply versed in the antiquities of his native Ireland, he was in a running battle with another barrister, the former Attorney-General, George Paton Smith, over a series of articles published in a newspaper edited by Smith. Supple's complaint centred around Smith having used the term "Celtic" to refer to Irish people. Supple's extreme short-sightedness had caused him to abandon practice at the Bar and, for a time, it looked as though it might save him from conviction for murder. Supple approached Smith in Latrobe Street, Melbourne. He walked up to him and peered into his face, as if making sure of his man. Then, being satisfied of his identity, he produced a revolver. Smith ran off as Supple fired several shots. Due to his blindness, the shots missed their intended target, but a bystander who intervened to help was struck and died from his wounds a few days later. The jury had no doubt about Supple's intent to kill, but recorded a finding that the fatal shot was accidental. The trial judge ruled that murder had been committed and this conclusion was upheld in the Full Court. The Chief Justice held that "a person who fires at A and shoots B, is guilty of murder, because the law connects the murderous intention of the accused with the event that follows".[11]

Dr Evatt KC led Garfield Barwick in a matter. During preparation, Barwick urged his leader to study a particular case and work up an argument based on it, but Evatt ignored his junior's suggestion. When the presiding judge asked why Evatt was not relying on the earlier decision, Evatt is said to have replied that his junior had not drawn his attention to it at which point Barwick said "Go to buggery" and left the court.[12]

Brawling between barristers need not get physical to be wounding. Stuart Littlemore QC and Tom Hughes QC were squared off against each other in a private prosecution for contempt before the New South Wales Court of Appeal.[13] I was the presiding judge. Tom Hughes junior was Tom Hughes senior's junior. The father permitted the son to cross-examine one of the witnesses but, as leaders do, kept prompting the son to ask additional questions. The volume was such that Littlemore eventually exploded in protest: "Your Honours. This is the noisiest ventriloquist act I have ever heard!"

After a particularly vigorous exchange between two Queen's Counsel Nathan J remarked that he felt like "a cook in a brothel; competent in my own right, but quite irrelevant to the real business of the management".[14]

---

11 *R v Supple* (1870) 1 VLR (L) 151 at 153. This is one of many fictions in the law. For a fuller account of this trial, see PA Jacobs, *Famous Australian Trials*, 2nd ed 1943, ch IV. See also Forde, *The Story of the Bar of Victoria*, pp 262-5.

12 Marr, *Barwick*, p 19.

13 *Harkianakis v Skalkos* (1997) 42 NSWLR 22.

14 *Order in the Court*, p 87.

Lawyer litigants

Leading lawyers, including judges or former judges, have at times been involved in litigation that is memorable or significant. Some have made fools of themselves in the process.

The fractious Jeffrey Hart Bent[15] made himself the laughing stock of many Sydneysiders when, in September 1815, he refused to pay toll-bar fees which he considered illegal. He so conducted himself at the toll gates that he was fined £2 by D'Arcy Wentworth JP. He had ignored the summons to appear before the Court of Petty Sessions claiming that, "as judge of the Supreme Court, he was by no means amenable to any criminal jurisdiction in this Territory".[16] This assertion was clearly untenable.

Many early colonial judges were reckless or overstretched in their financial affairs.[17] Some had sought colonial appointments to escape creditors only to run up fresh debts they could not meet after arrival in Australia. This presented particular problems when creditors sought justice against the judge or third parties in the judge's own court. Impoverished court officials were also prey to temptations, and several yielded to them. It was not until the mid-19th century that the authorities began to take a stronger line on the risk of abuse or miscarriage stemming from judicial indebtedness. When Pedder CJ and Montagu J ruled in 1847 that their (two man) Supreme Court of Van Diemen's Land had no jurisdiction to entertain an action brought against Montagu by one of his creditors, this became the basis for Montagu's amoval from office by the Lieutenant-Governor whose actions were upheld by the Privy Council.[18] Horne J reigned from the Tasmanian Bench to avoid dismissal when he sought a loan from a litigant in a pending case.[19] A Queensland District Court judge was also removed from office in 1878, primarily for using his office to impede his creditors.[20]

Dowling CJ's brush with the law was uncomfortable, but did him no discredit. He liked to walk to work and once set off early to cover an 18 kilometre journey from a friend's house at Parramatta to the city. The police

15 See further pp 110-12.

16 Dr CH Currey, "Bent, Jeffrey Hart (1781-1852)" in *Australian Dictionary of Biography*. Dr Currey adds: "As the alleged offence was not committed by him in his judicial capacity in a court of justice, there would seem to have been no firm basis for this claim to immunity".

17 Of the early Deputy Judge Advocates in New South Wales, Collins, Atkins, Bent and Dore died insolvent: Kercher, *Debt, Seduction and Other Disasters*, p 37. Bankruptcy does not, of course, necessarily betoken any moral failing. Garfield Barwick was made bankrupt in 1930 at the age of 27 after he had effectively stood guarantor for his younger brother who started out in business on the eve of the Great Depression.

18 See *Montagu v Lieutenant-Governor and Executive Council of Van Diemen's Land* (1849) 6 Moo PC 489, 13 ER 773. On amoval generally, see p 108 below.

19 See pp 117-18.

20 Hirst DCJ. See pp 125-6.

were doing a sweep for bushrangers and they picked up the dishevelled Chief Justice and threw him into the watchhouse. It was only after he convinced them that he was the colony's senior judge that he was able to take his seat in the court and not the dock.

Many 19th and some 20th century judges have rushed to law, seeking damages for libel. Others even commenced criminal defamation proceedings to punish and (temporarily) silence their critics.[21] Some were vindicated, others left with a humiliating flea in the ear.

Judge Advocate Atkins was frequently in trouble over money, alcohol or legal incompetence (or all three at once). He held the office before the arrival of Dore JA in 1798 and resumed it in 1800 after Dore's death. During an interregnum in 1799 Atkins went before Dore JA, suing the surgeon John Harris for defamation based on Harris having called him a swindler. Harris pleaded truth, contending that Atkins was not only a swindler but of so depraved a character that to associate with him was to become infamous. He also contended that Atkins' reputation was already in tatters and that slander caused no compensable damage. Calling John Macarthur as his first witness, Harris set out to prove various frauds in private and public dealings as well as a long history of financial default on Atkins' part.

One witness, a convict who was allowed to testify despite the common law, swore that Atkins owed him £4 and that, when he asked him for it, Atkins threatened to flog him and put him in irons. Atkins in reply did not try to conceal his indebtedness but argued vigorously that there was a distinction between defaulting on debts and dishonesty. He contended that the action was really part of a conspiracy by John Macarthur, who was "hiding his diminished head like a toad in a hole feeding on his own poison [stalking] abroad like sin and death seeking whom he may devour". Dore's court found in favour of Atkins, but awarded only £50 damages, a fairly paltry sum for the libel alleged.[22] On one very technical view of the matter, the Rum Rebellion arose out of a judicial conflict of interest when Atkins JA refused to stand down in a case involving the prosecution of a man who was both his creditor and his enemy.[23]

Shortly after his arrival in South Australia, Boothby J launched a suit for specific performance of a house property. His new Chief Justice, Cooper CJ, found against him "on the basis of faulty proceedings, inadequate evidential support for his claim, and a failure to disclose a case for relief".[24]

---

21 Some early reported cases are discussed in *Mann v O'Neill* (1997) 191 CLR 204 at 230-5. See also BHMcP, "Defaming the Bench" (1996) 70 *Australian Law Journal* 948. While on the Bench, Sir Alfred Stephen launched and conducted a private prosecution for criminal libel: see p 105.

22 See *Atkins v Harris* [1799] NSWKR 4; Kercher, *Debt, Seduction and Other Disasters*, pp 30-1.

23 See *R v Macarthur* [1808] NSWKR 379.

24 McLaren, *Dewigged, Bothered and Bewildered*, p 194.

In 1886 a Police Magistrate in Perth sued a solicitor who, in an electioneering speech, called for a commission to inquire into Police Courts "with a view to weeding out corrupts, vindictive, mulishly wrongheaded, eccentric buffoons presiding there, who cruelly and inconsistently torture and punish as their whims incline". The magistrate boldly called evidence to show that many people took the words as being directed at himself. Damages of £100 were recovered with the verdict being upheld by the Full Court.[25]

More recently, a special magistrate in the Australian Capital Territory sued for defamation in letters of complaint written by a disappointed litigant. The letters questioned the magistrate's mental capacity. The High Court held (by majority) that the letters did not attract absolute privilege.[26] It might have been otherwise if the allegations had been made in support of a ground of appeal. Elsewhere I detail two instances where judges sued for libel based on their being falsely identified as the publisher of some embarrassing material.[27]

Sir John Jeffcott's South Australian appointment rescued his legal career from a marked trough. In 1830 he had become Chief Justice of Sierra Leone and the Gambia. In 1833, while on leave in England (where he was knighted), he fought a duel on Exeter racecourse, killing a young physician.[28] The "affair of honour" was a dispute about Jeffcott's truthfulness in his dealings with the man whom he hoped to become his father-in-law. Jeffcott fled to Africa, then to France. A warrant issued for his arrest on the charge of murder and the colonial authorities removed him from the office of Chief Justice. In 1833 his two seconds were tried for murder and acquitted. No one wished to press the charge against Jeffcott so it was arranged that, if he returned to England and stood his trial, no evidence would be tendered against him. Thus, he was tried and acquitted of the capital offence at the Exeter Assizes in March 1834. In May 1836 he was appointed the first judge of the colony of South Australia.[29] He drowned within months of taking up this later office.

Sir Robert Molesworth was a highly respected judge on the Supreme Court of Victoria between 1856 and 1886. He and his wife were married in 1840, when they lived in Ireland. He was 17 years her senior. The couple separated in 1856 and she went to England in 1862 where she gave birth to a son. Only with the passing of the *Divorce and Matrimonial Causes Act 1861* in Victoria did Molesworth became enabled there to seek the dissolution of his marriage. He petitioned on the basis of his wife's adultery with RD Ireland, a leading member

---

25 Russell, *A History of the Law in Western Australia*, pp 239-40.

26 *Mann v O'Neill* (1997) 191 CLR 204.

27 See pp 104-6.

28 See generally Hague, *Sir John Jeffcott, Portrait of a Colonial Judge*, ch 2. As to duelling and the law, see p 41.

29 According to Hannan, *The Life of Chief Justice Way*, pp 34-5, Henry Walter Parker was earlier appointed (at the ripe age of 26), but he resigned almost immediately over a pay dispute (see pp 86-7).

of the Melbourne Bar. The matter came on for hearing before the remainder of the Supreme Court, Stawell CJ, Barry J and Williams J, and a jury of 12. In a split decision, the Court upheld the technical objection that the petition was not served on the day on which it was presented to the Court.[30] The petitioner was granted leave to have the suit dismissed so that he could begin afresh.

Before he could do so, Mrs Molesworth herself petitioned for judicial separation on the ground of cruelty. Molesworth filed a counter-petition, also for judicial separation, on the grounds of various acts of adultery, including adultery with Ireland. By this time, Ireland had taken silk and was serving as Attorney-General for Victoria. Mrs Molesworth gave evidence of having been assaulted by her husband and she denied having committed adultery with Ireland or any other person. Ireland also denied having committed adultery. Molesworth led evidence of adultery, mainly based on the petitioner's admission to that effect. (She had earlier given evidence that such admission was false, and the product of bravado by way of retaliation for his treatment of her.) Questions submitted to the jury negatived her adultery with Ireland but were otherwise favourable to Molesworth, the respondent husband. The case came before the Full Court to determine what order was proper upon the findings of the jury and the evidence. Mrs Molesworth's petition was dismissed and Molesworth was granted a decree for judicial separation based on his wife's adultery with persons unknown.[31]

In 1938 Albert Piddington, who had been a justice of the High Court for 18 days in 1913, was knocked down by a motorcyclist in Phillip Street, Sydney. He was then aged 76. He sued the cyclist's employer but the jury found a verdict for the defendant. Piddington had no memory of the accident. A witness called in his case was asked how he came to be at the scene and replied that he had been at a nearby bank doing some business for a Major Jarvie. The trial judge permitted the bank manager to testify that Jarvie's account had not been operated on that day. In upholding Piddington's appeal, the majority of the High Court ruled that such a collateral attack on the credibility of a witness was impermissible. Latham CJ and Starke J dissented. Starke delivered a contemptuous backhander to his judicial colleagues that was characteristic save for its subtlety. After making plain his view that the appellant was guilty of contributory negligence (then a complete defence), Starke added that "friendship and sympathy for an old and distinguished member of the legal profession should not sway the judgment of the court".[32]

Thomas Ley's career in Australia included that of being a partner in the distinguished law firm of Norton Smith & Co, a member of the Legislative

---

30 The petition was served three days later, on the date when the Chief Justice certified that it had been presented: see *Molesworth v Molesworth* (1863) 2 VLR (IEM) 139.

31 Dean, *A Multitude of Counsellors*, pp 249-53.

32 *Piddington v Bennett and Wood Pty Ltd* (1940) 63 CLR 533 at 550.

Assembly of New South Wales, a stint as Minister for Justice between 1922 and 1925, and a member of the Commonwealth Parliament between 1925 and 1928. He then returned to his native England and got involved in various business deals, including a sweepstake in which he pocketed more than his fair share. In 1946 he arranged the murder of a man whom he believed, without any foundation, to be courting his estranged and aging mistress. He and the man procured to commit the "Chalkpit murder" were convicted and sentenced to death in a trial before Lord Chief Justice Goddard. To Goddard's great chagrin, the sentences were respited on the basis of medical evidence first produced after the trial that Ley always suffered from paranoia. He died of a stroke in Broadmoor Criminal Lunatic Asylum four months later. Ley's biographer makes a good case for believing that he had also murdered two political opponents before he left Sydney.[33]

Sometimes barristers or judges have been plaintiffs in a representative capacity, running a test case on a taxation issue for their professional brethren. In this capacity Cooper CJ,[34] Austin J[35] and Mr KR Handley QC[36] got their names into the law reports. After joining the New South Wales Court of Appeal, Handley JA was reminded of his earlier proceedings when the following exchange occurred:[37]

> Gleeson CJ: The submission you have made is the exact opposite of that made by the GIO and accepted by this Court in *Radnedge*.
> McAlary QC: ... Can I read a few notes that I wrote down and I wrote them down last night in bed so I apologise for the state
> Priestley JA: There is no need to go into the intimate details, Mr McAlary.
> McAlary: Your Honours, John Paul II could sit at the end of my bed these days.
> Priestley JA: His Honour Mr Justice Murphy has found that there is no tax deduction for such activities.
> Handley JA: I remember it well.

A judge has immunity from prosecution or civil action for words or actions in the course of judicial acts.[38] This, however, has scarcely stemmed the flood

33 Dan Morgan, *The Minister for Murder*, Hutchinson of Australia, 1979.

34 See further p 67.

35 See *Austin v Commonwealth* (2003) 215 CLR 185.

36 See *Handley v Federal Commissioner of Taxation* (1981) 148 CLR 203. In this case Mr Handley unsuccessfully sought deductions from his taxable income for a proportion of the borrowing expenses referable to the purchase of his home. The claim related to his study where he spent 20 hours per week for 45 weeks of each year. The High Court split three:two with the majority itself being divided as to their reasons. One of the majority was Murphy J who held that the expenses were entirely of a domestic nature. There is no evidence that the views of Mrs Handley about the accuracy of this description were conveyed to the High Court either before or after judgment.

37 *Saroukas v Sutherland Shire Council* (unrep, NSW Court of Appeal, 28 November 1991).

38 *Rajski v Powell* (1987) 11 NSWLR 522; *Yeldham v Rajski* (1989) 18 NSWLR 48.

of vexatious claims launched by litigants intent on punishing a judge or deterring him or her from sitting in a matter. Justices of the High Court have not escaped.[39] Surprisingly, judicial immunity was apparently overlooked by a magistrate, her lawyers and the Queensland Court of Appeal. In 2003 Ms Diane Fingleton, the Chief Magistrate of Queensland, was convicted and imprisoned for retaliating against a witness in a judicial proceeding. She was found to have threatened with effective demotion a fellow magistrate who had filed an affidavit supporting a third magistrate in judicial review proceedings over an ongoing industrial dispute. After she had served her imprisonment and lost an appeal to the Queensland Court of Appeal a successful point of law was taken for the first time in the High Court. The accused herself had a statutory immunity similar to that enjoyed by a judge of a superior court with reference to any judicial or administrative functions.[40]

In the 1840s a fiery Melbourne magistrate, Major Frederick Berkley St John, threatened a protesting litigant that, if he said another word, then "by God, he would be sent to gaol". A reporter who had been threatened with committal on an earlier occasion obtained a summons from another magistrate against St John for having used blasphemous language in public. The major appeared in answer to the summons and was fined 5s in his own court.[41]

Leading lights in the law have made their way into the law reports in mainstream civil cases that they have won or lost,[42] sometimes as litigants before their own court. Other lawyers have achieved distinction only through their involvement in what has become a "leading case", the most notable of them being the barrister Archibald Nugent Robertson who, having failed in the High Court and the Privy Council over claims arising out of his refusal to pay a one penny ferry fare, is Australia's patron saint of lost causes.[43]

Several high-flying lawyers have been brought to earth by proven charges of dishonesty, tax fraud or other professional misconduct, or fallen foul of the criminal law.

39 See *Gallo v Dawson* (1990) 64 ALJR 458.

40 *Fingleton v The Queen* (2005) 227 CLR 166.

41 Forde, *The Story of the Bar of Victoria*, p 17.

42 Examples include Edmund Barton who twice lost in the Privy Council during his career as a barrister and politician (see p 154 below), Piddington KC (see *Piddington v Bennett and Wood Pty Ltd* (1940) 63 CLR 533), Murphy J (see *Murphy v The Queen* (1989) 167 CLR 94) and Spry QC (see *Kennon v Spry* (2008) 238 CLR 366). See also *Cheeke v Commissioner of Railways* (1869) 8 SCR (L) 111; 9 SCR (L) 31 (despite gross negligence, Commissioner not liable for injury to valuable racehorses belonging to Cheeke J because of special condition in contract).

43 He is called Robinson in the High Court reports (*Balmain New Ferry Company Ltd v Robinson* (1906) 4 CLR 379) and Robertson in the Privy Council reports (*Robertson v Balmain New Ferry Company Ltd* [1910] AC 295).

Cattiness on and off the Bench

For judges, long years of sitting literally on a pedestal where counsel invariably laugh outwardly at one's jokes are poor training grounds for humility and frank self-assessment. Not all judges are blessed with partners who see it as their main calling to prick the inflated bubble or insist that (at home) the judge does not require assistance to get in and out of a chair.

Like all humans, judges can be catty and (when cattiness is not enough for the individual or the situation) can brawl openly. Some judges are just nasty by nature. Away from court, judicial nastiness will seldom be recorded or passed on. But there are still many titbits, especially from the era of diaries and letterwriting. Like most forms of humour it has the psychological function of releasing tension.

Membership of an appellate court allows a judge to pass instant asides about a colleague or counsel. Like the whispering and notes at the Bar table, they will seldom be heard or captured for posterity. But sometimes microphones are turned up or ears are sharp. Weigall KC, SG was fairly deaf when he used to address the Full Court in New South Wales during the era of Sir Frederick Jordan.[44] Once when he failed to hear what had fallen from the Bench he asked his instructing officer to tell him. The officer whispered the wise dictum of the judicial officer at which the law officer expostulated: "That's rubbish!" and went on with his submissions. When Barwick CJ whispered audibly to his colleague "Watch how long it takes for me to piss this bastard off", referring to the Solicitor-General for Victoria then addressing the court, the Victorian Bar was mightily affronted. For a generation, Victorian barristers reputedly advised litigants to take appeals to the Privy Council in preference to the High Court.

The idiosyncrasies of Boothby J are recounted elsewhere.[45] His judicial conduct towards Chief Justice Richard Hanson was discourteous, unprofessional and totally exasperating. But Boothby did not stop there. In 1863 he and other colonists persuaded the local Anglican bishop to carry a protest to the Governor against Mrs Hanson attending a ball at Government House. The Governor angrily rebuked the bishop for spreading slander and named the protesters in his report to London. Inquiry revealed that the lady had been Hanson's housekeeper before she married him and that all of their six children had been born in wedlock between 1853 and 1863.

In 1913 Sir Edmond Barton wrote to Sir Samuel Griffith, discussing the work of Higgins J who held a concurrent office as President of the Arbitration

44 An earlier Solicitor-General (John Kinchella) had such bad hearing that he could not attend to government business in the Legislative Council. He was then appointed to the Bench!

45 See pp 118-21.

Court.[46] "Higgins completes his seven years of 'stirring up peace' in 1914" was Barton's disparaging way of referring to Higgins' efforts, adding that "while opinions will vary as to the quality of his work in that field, there can be no doubt of its quantity".

Higgins' biographer observes that "more personal venom was reserved for Isaacs, the 'Jewling', on one occasion depicted as 'his jaws slavering for the devouring of some decision of ours'."[47] Isaac Isaacs was, by any standard, a bristly personality. He made many enemies in politics and the law. Some, but by no means all, of the antipathy displayed towards him was fuelled by anti-Semitism. Barton's correspondence with their Chief Justice, Sir Samuel Griffith disclosed significant hostility towards Isaacs. For example, in 1913, when there was talk of the creation of an Imperial Court of Appeal and of Griffith's possible appointment to it, Barton wrote:[48]

> It is plain to me, and I think to others, that Isaacs is building his hopes on your remaining in England and is trying to make such a big splash that he will make himself manifest as the right CJ ... His judgments are swelling to bigger proportions than ever – in fact they are very weighty – in respect of paper; and he has an oracular air in court that is quite laughable.

After their appointment in 1906, Barton perceived the new boys on the block, Isaacs and Higgins, as conspiring against him and Griffith, referring to one case as showing "the avidity with which two at least of our colleagues seize on a chance of doing some mischief while they can still command a majority". In a later missive he told Griffith:

> You will see how little decency there is about these two men – All the same, I think they hate each other, although they conspire. They had a little brush at consultation yesterday. Then Higgins said most offensively: 'You see, you men are only talking about words, but I have to do with things.' I gently pointed out that the words we were talking about were the words of an act of Parliament, which was apt to be a rather hard thing when people bumped against it. His manner, in his annoyance with Isaacs, was most offensive to all the rest of us.

In another letter to Griffith, Isaacs was depicted as "always trying to colloque with our colleagues apart from me".[49] Barton described his judicial colleague as "the malign influence" and observed that when he was not sitting "business gets along fairly well".[50] Isaacs could, of course, give as good as he got, but kept his fiercest language for his published judgments.[51]

46 See John Rickard, *HB Higgins*, George Allen & Unwin, 1984, pp 274, 279 for these statements and letters.

47 *Ibid*, p 274.

48 Cowen, *Isaac Isaacs*, p 116.

49 *Ibid*, p 279.

50 *Ibid*, p 116.

51 See eg *R v Snow* (1915) 20 CLR 315; *Wright v Cedzich* (1930) 43 CLR 493.

Sir Owen Dixon once remarked that "it wasn't until I heard Justice Powers deliver a judgement that I fully understood the meaning of the phrase *ultra vires*". Charles Powers was a barrister who had never argued a case before the High Court before his appointment there.[52] Dixon also once described a speech of Isaacs J as "a moving and meaningless flow of abstract nouns".[53] He described his colleague Evatt as having "an ever-widening circle of enemies".[54]

In his opening to a judgment written in 1928 Starke J observed that:[55]

> This is an appeal from the Chief Justice, which was argued by this Court over nine days, with some occasional assistance from the learned and experienced counsel who appeared for the parties. The evidence was taken and the matter argued before the Chief Justice in two days. This case involves two questions, of no transcendent importance, which are capable of brief statement, and could have been exhaustively argued by the learned counsel in a few hours.

This self-reflective humour contained a gentle jab at colleagues. But there is ample evidence of much greater disfunctionality during this era, much of it of Starke's making. Hayden Erskine Starke sat on the High Court between 1920 and 1950. He was abrasive, back-biting and uncooperative. According to Robert Menzies, "he would not temper the wind to the shorn lamb".[56] There were particular tensions with Evatt J and McTiernan J, and later with Rich J. Starke was the bane of successive Chief Justices, Gavan Duffy and Latham. The *Oxford Companion to the High Court*[57] records an occasion when, after a series of insults from Starke, the recipient of which is unknown, Gavan Duffy CJ adjourned the Court; but, due to a misunderstanding, Starke remained on the Bench alone. According to the Dixon diaries, Gavan Duffy confronted Starke about the incident years later. He asked Starke: "Is our misunderstanding to continue until I die?", to which Starke replied: "I see no reason why it should not".

Starke refused to have any consultation with Evatt, to exchange reasons for judgments and draft judgments with him, or even to supply him with final judgments. Evatt in turn refused to cooperate with Starke, leaving Latham in the invidious position of having to coordinate the work of two irascible, gifted lawyers who communicated only in the most stiffly formal terms.

The papers of Sir John Latham, Chief Justice between 1935 and 1952, reveal an appellate court in severe stress. Personal antipathies were not kept to

52 Three other justices were similarly placed (Griffith, Barton and O'Connor) but that was only because their careers as barristers had ended well before the establishment of the Court on which they would sit as founding members. Piddington and Evatt addressed the High Court before and after their terms on that Bench.

53 Dixon's diary 14 March 1936: see Ayres, *Owen Dixon*, p 56.

54 *Ibid*, p 200.

55 *Federal Commissioner of Taxation v Hoffnung & Co Ltd* (1928) 42 CLR 39 at 62.

56 Sir Robert Menzies, *The Measure of the Years*, Coronet Books, 1972, p 253.

57 "Personal relations" in Blackshield et al, *Oxford Companion to the High Court*.

the private musings of diaries, nor even to the tale-telling that is the inevitable lot of the presiding judge to receive. Even the customary civilities were abandoned. The High Court has always attracted lawyers of fierce independence, but Latham's experience was hopefully unique. The fighting is detailed in Clem Lloyd's article "Not Peace But a Sword – The High Court Under JG Latham".[58] Lloyd writes of a "web of bad relationships which enmeshed [the] judges" and a "deeply engrained personal antagonism which permeated the Bench".

Starke complained to Latham that Dixon dominated the Court, unduly influencing McTiernan and Evatt, savagely caricaturing this pair as "parrots". He contended that it was "gravely detrimental to the High Court and its independence that whenever a grave difference of opinion is disclosed, the 'parrots' always reache[d] the same conclusion as Dixon". On one occasion during the hearing of the *Bank Nationalisation Case* he asked Evatt: "Where does a long reading of generalities get us in this case?" Evatt replied: "The judgments of Mr Justice Dixon and Mr Justice Rich are precise and the conclusion is inescapable". Addressing Evatt, but seeking to wound the judges whose views Evatt relied on, Starke jibed: "Like Moses coming down the mountain with the tables of law".[59]

Starke greeted Rich J's appointment to the Privy Council in 1936 with the following missive to his Chief Justice:

> Rich will be like a dog with two tails ... but I thought the Privy Councillorship was reserved for those who had rendered distinguished political, judicial or other services. It is a pity to degrade the rank by such an appointment.

Starke once responded to Latham in the following terms:

> I resent your dirty insinuation that I stayed on in Sydney to make a bob out of the government, and also your silly schoolmaster attitude towards me. I think an apology is overdue and in future pray keep your criticisms of me to yourself unless I ask for them.

When Latham was absent, as he often was through illness in 1936-37, relations were even tenser because Starke acted as Chief Justice. In such circumstances, it seems remarkable that the Court functioned at all. Evatt reported to Latham that:

> I regret to say that Starke's behaviour as presiding justice towards colleagues – and I refer to McTiernan and myself – has been disgraceful. It is only one's sense of duty to the court that prevents scandal.

Starke's petty jealousies and unprofessional combativeness on and off the Bench catapults him easily into any list of Australia's top 10 worst appellate

58 (1987) 11 *Adelaide Law Review* 175.
59 Marr, *Barwick*, p 67.

judges of the 20th century even allowing for his relative competency in judgment writing. Effective membership of a collegiate court requires a lot more than that.

Kirby P and Meagher JA came from different backgrounds and had rather different personalities, but were always good friends on and off the Bench.[60] A few of their good-natured banterings on the New South Wales Court of Appeal have been preserved for posterity in their judgments. I would include the following.

Kirby P was in dissent in *Forgeard v Shanahan*.[61] Early in his reasons he addressed his colleague (in the majority) as follows:

> In my view, it is inappropriate to apply to the adjustment required, the supposed "rules" favoured by Meagher JA, in the exercise of the statutory discretion which was invoked, as it is to apply to personal relationships in today's Australian society, the epithets used by Meagher JA, such as "mistress" and "paramour". Principles of law, like language, must keep pace with the society that the law serves.

Sometimes a judicial side-swipe will be aimed concurrently at counsel and the judge's brethren who are seen to have given the barrister misguided encouragement. Thus Meagher JA gently rebuked Kirby P, Priestley JA and counsel (Mr Katz) when he delivered the following judgment in *Della Patrona v Director of Public Prosecutions (Cth) (No 2)*:[62]

> I have read in draft the judgment of Kirby P. The appeal raised the meaning of the word 'conviction' when used in the *Proceeds of Crime Act 1987* (Cth). On this matter I agree with Kirby P. On the hearing of the appeal the appellant sought to raise in addition a variety of constitutional matters which were not only not raised below but were inconsistent with the submissions which were raised below. Contrary to the principles laid down by the High Court ... my brethren permitted the appellant to do this. I dissented with as much vigour as I could muster. The majority sowed the wind, but the whole Court reaped the whirlwind. It now appears that all the additional constitutional arguments had the additional feature of being entirely unmeritorious, a fact which did not prevent learned counsel for the respondent discussing them at meticulous length and haud sine taedio. The appeal must be dismissed with costs.

Similarly, one judge's apparently hostile remark to counsel during argument may really be directed at the judicial colleague sitting alongside the rebuker. In the High Court Kirby J often tested the patience of his colleagues by lengthy interruptions of counsel on peripheral matters. Gleeson CJ gave the gentlest of

60 See Michael Kirby, "RP Meagher and I: The best of times. The worst of times" (2011) 35 *Australian Bar Review* 26.

61 (1994) 35 NSWLR 206.

62 (1995) 38 NSWLR 257 at 273.

swipes back during the hearing of the appeal in *Antoun v The Queen*[63] when there was the following exchange:

> Kirby J: Of course the Bench is made up of a myriad of different personalities and people have different ways of expressing themselves and some are more circumlocutious and longwinded than others. Others are given to more direct expression.
>
> Mr Byrne: Certainly.
>
> Kirby J: I think you would agree that the silent judge is the greatest menace of all.
>
> Gleeson CJ: One of the greatest.

Purists and pedants

In his paper on "Professional Conduct"[64] Sir Owen Dixon observed that "we have not with us now the judicial and forensic purists of the past". This was a truism, but even Dixon's intended point may be debatable. Nevertheless, his example is worth repeating:[65]

> When I was a young barrister the late Mr Gerald Pigott paid me a formal call for the purpose of reminding me that the word "first" was an adverb. But notwithstanding that elementary grammatical fact he had heard me say "firstly" in open court. The same authority refused to allow Mr Justice Isaacs to read him a passage from a judgment of Lord Birkenhead because it contained the spurious word "correctitude". "I cannot be bound," said Mr Pigott, "by the words of a Lord Chancellor who cannot express himself in English. There is no such word. His Lordship doubtless meant "correctness" but his mind must have been running very much on "rectitude".[66]

In similar spirit, Callaway JA laboured to make a point about plain English when he complained that certain provisions of the *Corporations Law* were:[67]

> drafted in the language of pop songs. Section 435A speaks of 'maximis[ing] the chances' and s 435C of '[the] normal outcome' and 'the deed's administrator'. Section 435C(3) begins with the word 'However' and a comma, a style that, at least until recently, has been eschewed by good writers. I am aware, of course, that there are those who believe that a statute should be drafted like a notice to quit or even a novel: their distinguished predecessors were the draftsmen of the Code Napoleon, later called the Code Civil: but an Australian Stendhal would not refresh his spirit or purify his style by dipping

63 [2005] HCATrans 823.

64 Reproduced in *Jesting Pilate and Other Papers and Addresses*, p 129ff.

65 *Op cit*, p 132.

66 *Lucas-Tooth v Lucas-Tooth* [1921] 1 AC 594 at 601.

67 *GM & AM Pearce & Co Pty Ltd v RGM Australia Pty Ltd* (1998) 4 VR 888 at 889.

> into legislation where the quest for simplicity pays the price of vulgarity and ends in obscurity.

Many 19th century and several early 20th century lawyers were highly proficient in both Greek and Latin. They could be scornful of those who lacked such accomplishments or were guilty of an isolated solecism. (In those days no one thought to blame the typist.) According to Sir Owen Dixon, "the credit of the most illustrious of our judges has suffered from rash excursions into Latin".[68] He certainly had his predecessor, Sir Samuel Griffith, in contemplation. Griffith prized himself on his ability with foreign languages given that he was fluent in Latin, Greek and Italian, publishing translations of Dante's *Inferno* in 1908 and the *Divina Commedia* in 1912. The latter was a feat of prolonged industry for so busy a man. Nevertheless, the work was satirised by an unnamed commentator who remembered that "Sir Samuel has succeeded in rendering the poetry of Dante into the language of a Parliamentary enactment".[69]

The same source also recounted[70] an exchange that Sir Julian Salomons claimed to have had with Billy Hughes, when the latter was Attorney General of the Commonwealth and a guest at Salomons' house. Salomons showed Hughes a copy of Griffith's translation of the *Inferno*. "Look at this book, Mr Hughes! Notice the inscription! 'From the author.' I was very careful to get that put in. You see I'm an old man now, and I don't know what may become of my belongings. I shouldn't like anybody who might pick up this book with my name in it to think that I had stolen it! *Still less, that I had bought it!*"

The Privy Council once laughed at Griffith's inaccuracy in Latin. In *Webb v Syme*,[71] he used the expression "*fons proxima non remota spectator*". Unfortunately "fons" is a masculine word. When the decision was under consideration in the Privy Council one of their Lordships asked counsel: "How do you account for the change of gender in the Antipodes?" Counsel deftly replied that it did not give cause for as much surprise as did the change undergone by legal principles.[72]

Sir Owen Dixon had the following exchange with Bernard Riley:[73]

> DIXON: I have recently heard a wonderfully amusing joke Riley, I suppose I can tell it to you in Greek?
> RILEY: No, it's one of the regrets of my life that I have no Greek.
> DIXON: Well then perhaps Latin will suffice.

---

68 "Professional Conduct" in *Jesting Pilate and Other Addresses*, p 132.

69 Piddington, *Worshipful Masters*, p 239.

70 *Ibid*, p 240.

71 (1910) 10 CLR 482 at 493.

72 Dixon, "Professional Conduct" in *Jesting Pilate and Other Addresses*, pp 132-3. Dixon also states that Sir Samuel Griffith was responsible for introducing the common error of describing the paragraphs of s 51 of the Constitution as "placita".

73 Recounted by JJ Spigelman when launching Phillip Ayres' biography of Dixon. Bernard Blomfield Riley QC practised at the Sydney Bar, was a Member of the Legislative Council and was appointed to the Federal Court of Australia.

RILEY: I regret that whilst I studied it at school, my Latin is very rusty.
DIXON: Well then, there's no point in telling you the joke.

The transcript of the recent appeal hearing in *Wicks v State Rail Authority of New South Wales known as State Rail*[74] shows that judges still get diverted by Latin infelicities. Justin Gleeson SC was in full flight before the High Court in a submission about a complex point of statutory construction. He drew attention to two critical paragraphs in the reasons of McColl JA which he proceeded to summarise and support. But he was stopped in his stride by Gummow J and French CJ when the following exchange occurred:

GUMMOW J: I hope you do not endorse line 18, is it, "they were not exposed to a danger which was a sequelae"?
MR GLEESON: Your Honour, the notion that underlies that, with respect – – –
GUMMOW J: I do not think you grasped my point either, anyhow, go on.
FRENCH CJ: It is the use of the plural.
MR GLEESON: Your Honour, underpinning this is a notion of a physical process by which the act or omission of the defendant is apprehended to work harm to the person of the victim. In that sense, we submit there is sound common sense in what her Honour has put ...

Gleeson SC who is very well educated in Latin has confirmed that his failure to "grasp" Gummow J's "point" was deliberate, because he was keen to have the case decided on a more substantive basis. High Court transcripts do not record stony expressions any more than laughter when that is the advocate's feigned or genuine response to judicial joke-making.

The Solicitor-General for the Commonwealth made a passing reference to "Lord Coke" before being brought to heel in the following exchange that would not take "sorry" for an answer:[75]

HEYDON J: His name is not Lord Coke.
Mr Gageler: I am sorry, your Honour.
HEYDON J: In what year was that lawyer given a peerage?
Mr Gageler: I do not have the answer to that question, your Honour.
GUMMOW J: He never was. He was just a knight.
Mr Gageler: I am sorry.
GUMMOW J: He was the last person James I was going to make a peer.
Mr Gageler: I will drop the Lord, your Honour.
GUMMOW J: It is causing an endless trouble in the Kings Bench.

Whew! Just as well the 20-minute special leave hourglass was not pouring out.

---

74 [2010] HCATrans 87 (13 April 2010).
75 *Australian Crime Commission v Stoddart* [2011] HCATrans 44 (1 March 2011).

Brushes with insanity

Mental illness is no laughing matter and it is alarmingly prevalent. Studies have shown that law students and legal practitioners are significantly more likely to suffer its ravages than other professions, which is not the same as saying that they will always seek treatment. For them, "presenteeism" may be more dangerous than absenteeism. Law has always attracted pessimistic, perfectionist types and imposed heavy stress on them. Many cope admirably, some do not. It is therefore unsurprising that the careers of a number of famous lawyers have been affected by bouts of mental disturbance. The fact that their numbers include men who rose to the top of their profession when psychiatry was at its infancy should be an encouragement never to forget that we are dealing with illnesses that are usually treatable.

Much has been written in recent years about the psychology of querulous and/or vexatious litigants some of whom evince signs of mental illness. Simon Smith has recently published a readable and rosy portrait of those who have been declared vexatious in Australia between 1930 and 2008.[76] It tells some fascinating tales, including one about Sir Isaac Isaacs' role in the creation of one of these "frequent filers" as he devised and assisted his brother in devious schemes to defeat the woman who had been married to the brother for a short period.[77] As often happens, a vexatious monster was created on the back of a litigious set-back that may well have entailed an initial miscarriage of justice. Smith's account (which largely confines itself to the handful of litigants declared vexatious) fails to capture the true impact on registry staff, opposing litigants, judges and court lists of the misguided or vicious souls who, as vexatious litigants, inflict incalculable[78] pain and cost on an already overburdened system.

Butler Cole Aspinall was a famous Victorian barrister of the 19th century who represented the Eureka rebels. He is attributed with many bursts of sparkling repartee, one of which found its way into a Mae West movie of the 1940s.[79] Aspinall was an alcoholic. In 1870, at the age of 40, his mind gave way and he was confined in an asylum, where it is said he spent much of his time addressing invisible juries. Sadly, he died at 45.

Hargrave J, who was New South Wales' first judge in Divorce, was peculiarly unsuited for the role and widely reputed as having a general bias against

76 Smith, *Maverick Litigants*.

77 The events took place after Isaacs' terms in public office, not that they were out of character.

78 In both senses of the word.

79 In response to a judge's "Mr Aspinall, are you trying to show your contempt for the court?" Aspinall retorted "No, your Honour, I was merely trying to conceal it". This may not have been the earliest sighting of this joke but it certainly preceded the 1940s Mae West movie *My Little Chickadee*. For other instances of Aspinall's wit, see Dean, *A Multitude of Counsellors*, p 80.

female suitors. Earlier in his life he had been involuntarily detained in a lunatic asylum on the application of his wife.[80]

Paris Nesbit KC was a leader of the South Australian Bar in the late 19th and early 20th century.[81] His relationships with the opposite sex were a mess by any standard. During a career at the Bar spanning over 30 years he was on four occasions detained in an asylum, each time having been certified "lunatic" according to the standards of the day. The first two occasions occurred during his manic pursuit of a young woman in Melbourne in 1885. The woman's father caught Nesbit in his home with the daughter late at night after he had been ordered to leave. The police were twice called and, on the second visit, took Nesbit to Kew Asylum where he was certified by two doctors. It would be three months before he was released into his brother-in-law's custody so that he could be taken back to Adelaide. Nesbit jumped the ship, swam to Williamstown and returned to the home of his lover. He was again apprehended and sent back to the asylum for some months.

Over 20 years later, Nesbit launched in the St Kilda Magistrate's Court a private prosecution against the certifying doctors. The press had a field day, especially when a principal witness called by Nesbit was the then Chief Justice of Victoria, Sir John Madden, who had consulted with Nesbit about some legal matter a day or two before one of the incidents at the young woman's home. Nesbit announced his intention to call as further witnesses Sir Samuel Way, the Chief Justice of his home state, and the federal Attorney-General, Sir Josiah Simon. Instead, as he probably intended all along, he closed his case at the end of the second day, declaring that he abandoned the prosecution because he had achieved his object of ensuring that the medical profession would take greater care in the future.

Two later episodes in Adelaide saw him again detained involuntarily. The South Australian cabinet got involved when it decided that he should be detained regardless of a technical problem with the warrant. Once again, Nesbit launched prosecutions against doctors and others. When the first case was dismissed by the magistrates he abused the Bench in the following terms:

> I withdraw the other informations. I will not make any more remarks to you. They would be simply lost on you. I shall have my informations heard by some men with sense in their heads, not fools like those on this bench. I shall go before a court with some sense of decency. You have warned me of contempt. Nothing can express the contempt I feel for this court!

Not surprisingly, he was sentenced to (seven days) gaol for contempt.

80 See further p 121.

81 Nesbit took silk in 1893. The following account is drawn from Graham Loughlin, "Paris Nesbit QC Lawyer, Libertine and Lunatic" (1977) 3 *Journal of the Historical Society of South Australia* 49. See also Castles and Harris, *Lawmakers and Wayward Whigs*, pp 217-20.

R v Pemble[82] is an oft-cited decision about directions as to recklessness in murder. The High Court held that Dunphy J had misdirected the jury with the result that a conviction for manslaughter was substituted. Ian Barker QC, who was Pemble's trial counsel, sought instructions for a plea of guilty to manslaughter and asked if he had anyone who could give character evidence for him. Pemble pulled out a missive written on the letterhead of an institution for the criminally insane. On inquiring about the author, Pemble said that he was a mate who had murdered a sheik.[83]

Judge Lloyd QC had to sentence a young man with a bad record. The shrewd prisoner, who had a passing acquaintance with *Dr Jekyll and Mr Hyde*, told his Honour that he was:[84]

> a split personality. I want to do the right thing; but there's another chap inside me who pushes me. I try to fight him, but he's too strong for me. It's really he that does all these things wrong, not me.

The kindly judge replied:

> Yes, I understand. As you say it's not your fault at all. But this other fellow, we'll have to do something about him, won't we? Now I am going to put him in gaol for two years — but don't let that upset you, he'll be doing the sentence.

82 (1971) 124 CLR 107.

83 Mildren, *Big Boss Fella All Same Judge*, p 183.

84 Holt, *A Court Rises*, p 238.

4 *Judicial Appointments and Disappointments*

Controversial appointments and non-appointments

Some judicial appointments have raised an immediate storm, because they were seen as motivated by political considerations and/or because of the protests of supporters of a disappointed rival. This is not to say that persons appointed in controversy necessarily turn out to be bad judges any more than the converse is true. The judicial career of Herbert Vere Evatt illustrates most of these propositions.

Herbert Vere Evatt

Evatt was twice appointed to high judicial office. Each event was controversial, indeed his second appointment was scandalous.

In 1930 he was appointed, together with Edward McTiernan, to the High Court of Australia. The Labor Cabinet acted when the Prime Minister and the Attorney-General were overseas urging the appointment of Isaac Isaacs as the first Australian-born Governor-General and in the teeth of their telegrammed opposition. Evatt was only 36 at the time, to this day the youngest appointment to the High Court. But he was academically brilliant and his standing in the profession justified the appointment. His term on the High Court saw him make lasting contributions in constitutional law and the law of torts. His dissenting judgment in *Chester v Waverley Corporation*[1] was a masterpiece that decades later would be accepted in Australia and abroad as good law. During this period he also published a work of outstanding scholarship.[2]

In 1940 "Doc" Evatt resigned to re-enter politics, serving terms as Attorney-General and Deputy Prime Minister in the Curtin and Chifley governments. He became the President of the General Assembly of the United Nations in 1948-49. He was Leader of the Opposition during Labor's disastrous split in the 1950s but it was not his finest hour. Indeed, it became clear over time that his leadership was an added burden to the Labor Party regaining office.

1 (1939) 62 CLR 1, discussed below pp 189-90.
2 *The King and His Dominion Governors*, Oxford University Press, 1936.

In 1960 a shabby deal was done whereby he was enticed away from his increasingly disastrous career in politics. Although far removed from the practice of the law and already showing signs of mental deterioration, he was made Chief Justice of New South Wales. According to one biography, the New South Wales Cabinet vote was at first evenly divided, the other candidate being Mr John Kerr QC. The highly respected Attorney-General of the day, Reg Downing MLC, opposed Evatt's appointment only to be overridden by the felt needs of political expediency amongst his Labor colleagues.[3]

Returning to the Bench after a 20-year interval, Evatt was unable to function at the most basic level. This put immense burdens on the senior judicial colleagues who daily covered for him.[4] Eventually the government was able to procure his resignation, with the collaboration of his wife. A relieved Attorney-General flew to Perth to get the papers signed after an episode of bizarre behaviour on board a ship that was taking Evatt on a prolonged overseas "study tour". The *Australian Law Journal* tersely recorded the "most widespread regret that illness prevented him from devoting his juristic talents to his work as Chief Justice".[5]

Other controversial judicial appointments are now considered.

John Kinchela

John Kinchela's extreme deafness hampered his performance as Attorney-General and prevented him from performing as well as he might as the Governor's nominee on the Legislative Council. Notwithstanding, he was appointed an acting judge of the Supreme Court of New South Wales in 1836. Governor Bourke pressed the home authorities to make the appointment permanent, at least in Van Diemen's Land. Lord Glenelg balked at the proposal, mainly out of concern at Kinchela's long-standing indebtedness. Kinchela retired from the Bench the following year to take up alternative legal jobs in the colony before being appointed Master in Equity, a second judicial post in which listening to counsel was not considered important.

John Nodes Dickinson

A controversy of a technical nature attended the arrival of John Nodes Dickinson at the Supreme Court of New South Wales in 1844, the last judge of that Court to be appointed in England.[6] Because he was then a barrister of less than five

3 Ken Buckley, Barbara Dale and Wayne Reynolds, *Doc Evatt: Patriot, Internationalist, Fighter and Scholar*, Longman Cheshire, 1994, pp 403-4.

4 One instance of this conduct is referred to below at p 104.

5 (1962) 36 *Australian Law Journal* 198.

6 JM Bennett and JK McLaughlin, "Sir John Dickinson. Almost a Chief Justice" (1970) 56 *Journal of the Royal Australian Historical Society* 315.

years' standing there was uncertainty as to his eligibility under the *New South Wales Act* (4 Geo IV c 96). The Crown law officers in England advised that the relevant provision applied only to appointment as Chief Justice, not as puisne judge. To avoid all doubt on the validity of his appointment Dickinson was furnished with two commissions differently worded. The Colonial Secretary advised him to present whichever was considered more appropriate after private discussion with the Governor, the colonial law officers and the other judges of the Supreme Court.

Dickinson served with distinction and acted as Chief Justice on occasions.

George Kerferd

George Kerferd had a modest practice at the Bar although he held office as Attorney-General in five conservative governments in Victoria between 1874 and 1885. His elevation to the Supreme Court Bench in 1886 illustrated the political jobbery accompanying many judicial appointments in the 19th century.

Having introduced a lengthy law reform Bill into Parliament, Kerferd allowed all but one of its clauses to be dropped after token resistance. That clause created a new judgeship that would be promptly filled by himself. Observers saw exactly what was happening. "A Barrister" wrote to *The Argus* in the following terms:[7]

> [He set out various details showing that there was no present need of an additional judge, and continued:] In face of these facts it is idle to contend that a sixth judge is wanted. Mr Justice Cope will act until the Chief Justice returns. Assuming that a sixth judge is wanted, there can be no doubt that the obvious intention of the Government is to appoint Mr Kerferd. Now, Sir, the bench should be stronger than the bar. A judge of the Supreme Court should be acquainted with all the latest decisions, both in substantive law and on the practice. It is well known that Mr Kerferd never had but a scant practice, and for the last two or three years has not appeared at all in the courts. Would those members of the Legislative Assembly who supported the appointment of Mr Kerferd prefer his opinion on some question of law affecting their own private rights and property, to that of some six or seven leaders of the bar whose names are familiar to me? If Mr Kerferd had forsaken a good practice at the bar in order to devote his time and attention to politics, I would be the last to oppose his appointment, but he sacrificed little or no practice in order to get a handsome salary as Attorney-General. It is quite true that members of the bar are to blame for neglecting politics, but is that any reason why the public should not have the services of the ablest men on the bench? Admitting that a sixth judge is wanted (which I deny) the Legislative Council is in duty bound to reject the bill in order to protect the bench.

7 *The Argus* Saturday, 28 November 1885, p 13.

The plea was in vain. The Bill passed and Kerferd was then appointed. The Bar gave him no formal welcome to the Bench.[8] Despite such a poor start in judicial life, Kerferd turned out to be a fairly sound judge. JL Forde, who wrote *The Story of the Bar in Victoria* in 1913, said of him that "as a judge, he disappointed those who disapproved of his elevation and predicted his failure".[9]

Edward Butler

The non-appointment to the chief justiceship of New South Wales of Edward Butler deserves to be recorded here.[10] Butler was Attorney-General in one of Henry Parkes' early administrations. On 12 June 1873 Sir Alfred Stephen (who had been Chief Justice for 29 years) sent his resignation, to take effect from 5 November. The delay left much time for speculation and intrigue. And the fixing of Guy Fawkes Day turned out to be prophetic because Butler was an Irish Roman Catholic.[11]

Well in advance of the date of Stephen's retirement Parkes told Butler that he would get the job. But word got around and there was extensive lobbying by Orangemen who were well represented in Parliament. Anti-Irish feelings had been aroused (and fomented by Parkes himself) by the attempted assassination of the Duke of Edinburgh at Clontarf, a Sydney beach. Sir James Martin was appointed in his stead. Dr Bennett's conclusion is that "the chief reason for Parkes' disingenuous conduct was that Butler was a Roman Catholic, and news of his likely elevation so outraged influential Protestants, in those days of sectarian passions, that Parkes feared his hold on the Premiership might suffer".[12]

William John Foster

In 1887 the Attorney-General, William Foster, created an uproar when he resigned from the government. He was upset at not being appointed to the Bench, despite the promise of this office if he declined nomination as the Speaker of the Assembly. The matter was rectified the following year.

---

8 Forbes, *Divided Legal Profession*, p 91.

9 Forde, *The Story of the Bar in Victoria*, p 278.

10 See generally Martha Rutledge, "Edward Butler and the Chief Justiceship, 1873" (1968) 13 *Australian Historical Studies* 207.

11 In 1844 Stephen himself had been appointed Chief Justice despite the competing claims of the highly respected Attorney-General John Hubert Plunkett. But this non-appointment preceded the politics of responsible government and Plunkett's Catholicism played no significant role. He was certainly well qualified, but so too, by the standards of the day, was Stephen who had already served as an Attorney-General in Van Diemen's Land and as a puisne judge in New South Wales. There is an excellent recent biography of Plunkett: see Tony Earls, *Plunkett's Legacy, An Irishman's Contribution to the Rule of Law in New South Wales*, Australian Scholarly Publishing, 2009.

12 Bennett, *Sir Alfred Stephen*, p 291.

Thomas William McCawley

The appointments in 1917 of Thomas William McCawley to the Presidency of the Queensland Court of Industrial Arbitration and as a justice of the Supreme Court of Queensland were highly controversial for several reasons.[13] The former Court was established in 1916 as the spearhead of a shift in social policies initiated under the premiership of Thomas J Ryan. Trade unions were for the first time given legal recognition and the Industrial Arbitration Court was armed with comprehensive powers to regulate industrial conditions. McCawley was a competent young public servant who had drafted the legislation as Crown Solicitor and Under Secretary for Justice. When E G Theodore, the Secretary for Public Works, defended McCawley's appointment to the Arbitration Court on the basis that he was "temperamentally fitted" for work of this kind, this remark was seized upon by McCawley's opponents, many of whom were opposed in principle to trade unionism and workers' compensation.

The accompanying Supreme Court appointment (at the age of 36) put additional noses out of joint, with extra heat fanned by McCawley never having practised as a barrister. There was also his Catholicism at a time when Australia was bitterly divided over conscription for service in the World War.

Special meetings of the Queensland Law Association and of the Bar Association opposed the Supreme Court appointment because senior members of the Bar were not chosen. Constitutional lawyers then got to work with the result that Full Court proceedings intended to be McCawley's swearing-in ceremony on 6 December 1917 were

> probably the most extraordinary event of the kind ever to occur in Australia. An occasion which is usually one of pure ceremony and professional bonhomie, even sycophancy, turned out to be the first day of intense and protracted litigation to have the appointment declared invalid. Two King's Counsel, Feez and Stumm, challenged the appointment on the grounds that McCawley, as a non-practising barrister, did not have five years' 'standing', that his tenure of office, not being life tenure, was unconstitutional, and that his addition to the court infringed the statutory limit upon the number of judges.[14]

Unusually, and pregnant with meaning, the additional chair at the Bench intended to seat the new judge when installed was placed *behind* that of the Chief Justice and not to his right. Immediately after the commission was presented and recorded Feez KC rose and announced:

---

13 See M Cope, "The Political Appointment of TW McCawley as President of the Court of Industrial Arbitration, Justice of the Supreme Court and Chief Justice of Queensland" (1976) 9 *University of Queensland Law Journal* 224; The Hon JB Thomas, "A Rocky Road; the Appointment of TW McCawley to the Bench" *Supreme Court History Program Yearbook 2005*, Supreme Court of Queensland Library, 1.

14 Forbes, *Divided Legal Profession*, p 166. The verbatim account recorded by Forbes is taken from the *Brisbane Courier* 7 December 1917, p 6.

> It was usual in the elevation of one of the profession to the Bench ... to felicitate the new judge on his appointment. They regretted that on this occasion they were unable to follow this time-honoured practice. In saying this he was able to speak for the whole profession, both Bar and solicitors.

The sole member of the profession to dissociate himself from these remarks was Mr Ryan who, as Premier and Attorney-General, had been responsible for the appointment. He protested that Feez and those whom he represented had no right to make "such attacks in such a place". Cooper CJ threw oil on the flames by challenging Ryan to name one lawyer who approved the appointment. Real J, the Senior Puisne Judge,[15] interjected that "no sane man" would suggest that the Supreme Court required an additional judge. McCawley exclaimed: "Does the court propose to permit a personal attack upon me?", to be answered by Real J: "This must be very disagreeable for Mr Justice McCawley to sit here and listen to". (Acute observers might have noticed the appellation "Mr Justice". As it turned out, only Real J would uphold the validity of McCawley's appointment to the Supreme Court.[16])

McCawley requested that the two customary oaths should be administered. The Chief Justice countered that the Court should give a pro forma decision against the validity of the appointment to enable the matter to be taken in some appropriate manner to a court of appeal, presumably the High Court of Australia. But McCawley pressed for the matter to be treated as an ordinary point of law coming before the Full Court. As his lone supporter, Ryan voiced the legal proposition that eventually won the day: the Supreme Court appointment was expressly authorised by the *Industrial Arbitration Act 1916*.

The Court heard full argument, reserved judgment, received supplementary written submissions and announced its decision the following February in the form of a reasoned judgment given by Cooper CJ[17] for the whole

---

15 See further pp 71-2.

16 The report of the original proceedings arising directly out of the swearing-in ceremony (see *In re McCawley* [1918] St R Qd 62) shows Real J sharing the opinion of his colleagues that McCawley's appointment to the Industrial Arbitration Court was invalid due to the failure to fix any salary pertinent to that office. But this problem was trumped, in his (minority) view (see at 97), by a provision enabling a Judge of the Arbitration Court to be appointed to the Supreme Court, a provision that Real J alone held to be valid. In the subsequent quo warranto proceedings Real J dissented from the judgment in ouster.

17 Ironically, the principal authority applied by Cooper CJ was *Sir Pope Cooper v Commissioner of Income Tax (Qld)* (1907) 4 CLR 1304, a decision in which the Chief Justice (as litigant) had contended that a State income tax did not apply to him and his fellow judges because the taxing Act implicitly but not directly contradicted a provision in the Queensland *Constitution Act* about judicial salaries. In *Cooper*, the High Court held that the *Constitution Act* could not be ignored in such an indirect manner, although this did not help the Chief Justice because the Court also ruled that there was no inconsistency between the constitutional provision and the generally expressed taxing statute. When the McCawley matter went (via the High Court) to the Privy

Court, recording within its four walls the reasons for dissent of Real J.[18] McCawley was spectacularly unsuccessful in this initial foray before the Court over which he would later preside as Chief Justice. His appointment was held invalid because the Executive Council Minute did not fix the salary for that office prior to the commission being issued, despite it being intended by the Executive (and McCawley himself) that his salary as President of the Industrial Arbitration Court would suffice for both offices. The Supreme Court appointment was also declared invalid because McCawley's appointment was implicitly annexed to his seven-year term of office as President of the Industrial Arbitration Court and thus of more limited duration than the appointment for life during good behaviour stipulated in the Queensland *Constitution Act of 1867*.

McCawley immediately applied for leave to appeal to the High Court, to be met with a ruling on 25 February 1918 that the Full Court decision was not a "judgment" against which any appeal could lie. On 6 March 1918, McCawley swore and subscribed the oaths of office and of allegiance in the presence of a District Court judge.[19] This highly contumelious action laid the foundation for proceedings on which an appeal could be taken to the High Court. I find it difficult to fault McCawley in this matter, although it is not so easy to justify his defiance in continuing to sit (throughout 1918, 1919 and 1920) as President of the Industrial Court, notwithstanding the Full Court having specifically declared that his commission was void.

The Supreme Court subsequently granted leave to Mr Feez KC and other relators to file an information in the nature of quo warranto challenging McCawley's purported assumption of the Supreme Court judicial office. To this McCawley demurred. The demurrer was overruled (Real J dissenting) and judgment in ouster was entered by the Full Court on 22 August 1918, apparently without issuance of further reasons for judgment.[20]

Thus, belatedly armed with an appealable order from the Supreme Court, (Mr) McCawley then went off to the High Court of Australia where he was again represented by his Premier and Attorney-General, TJ Ryan. There he lost by 4:3. The majority justices produced a scattergun of reasons. Characteristically,

---

Council, that tribunal overturned the High Court and declared that the Queensland Constitution was uncontrolled, like the British Constitution (see *McCawley v The King* [1920] AC 691).

18 Among the protests and other steps taken by the Queensland judges who were forced to retire by the *Judges' Retirement Act of 1921* Real J appeared before the Bar of the Parliament contending that the Bill was detrimental to the public interest because it proposed to deprive the present members of the Supreme Court of rights on which they had accepted office. He attempted to enlist the sympathy of the government by drawing attention to his favourable dissent in the *McCawley Case* (Cope, *op cit*, p 240).

19 See the advice of the Privy Council: [1920] AC 691 at 699; 28 CLR 106 at 111; Thomas, *op cit*, p 9.

20 Ibid.

Isaacs J recorded his dissent with hyperbolic certitude and Rich J lent his name to joint reasons obviously penned by another.[21]

McCawley appealed to the Privy Council. His victory there notched up an eight to nil success rate for the Queensland government between 1915 and 1919. Several of these cases were argued by Ryan himself.[22] Ironically, he was absent on this occasion in what would have been his greatest triumph as a constitutional advocate. McCawley's interests in his ultimate appeal were nevertheless represented by two of the best possible teams of lawyers. His own counsel were a team led by Sir John Simon who would later become Lord Chancellor. In addition, the Solicitor-General of England, Sir Ernest Pollock S-G ("Sir Gordon Hewart A-G and Branson with him"),[23] intervened in McCawley's interest and adopted Simon's arguments. The reason why Hewart left it to his junior law officer to address the Board is not disclosed. He was clearly a better advocate than he turned out to be a Chief Justice.[24]

The Privy Council overturned the High Court's reasoning in both *Cooper* and *McCawley*, holding that the Queensland *Constitution Act* was uncontrolled in the sense that it could be amended expressly or impliedly by a later enactment, just like an ordinary statute. Accordingly, it was open to the Parliament to pass the *Industrial Arbitration Act 1916* even if it entailed a seven-year term appointment of McCawley to the Supreme Court, to coincide with the term of his appointment as the President of the Industrial Arbitration Court. In a further irony, it appears that this was never what Ryan had intended[25] and the matter was quickly put right by legislation passed in 1921 (*Supreme Court Act of 1921*). That Act retrospectively declared McCawley's original Supreme Court commission to have been both permanent and independent of his seven-year tenure of office as a judge of the Court of Industrial Arbitration. Presumably as a political sweetener, McCawley's pension rights referable to his Supreme Court office were removed. This provision would produce a nasty sting in the tail for McCawley, as we shall see.

21 See 26 CLR 9 at 48 ("notwithstanding the wealth of argument that has been showered upon the case, we regard the law as affecting the present case to be simple and unattended with any real difficulty. The words of both the Imperial Act of 1865 and the Queensland Constitution of 1867, so far as they affect the present case, are so plain, in our opinion, that but for the respect we feel for the opinions from which we have the misfortune to differ, and but for the enormous importance of the question, our duty would be very briefly performed"). As to Rich J and ghostwriting, see pp 103-4.

22 See McPherson, *The Supreme Court of Queensland*, p 248.

23 See [1920] AC 691 at 695.

24 Lord Devlin, *Easing the Passing; the Trial of Dr John Bodkin Adams*, Bodley Head, 1985, p 92, said of him that "Hewart … has been called the worst chief justice since Scroggs and Jeffreys in the seventeenth century. I do not think that this is quite fair. When one considers the enormous improvement in judicial standards between the seventeenth and twentieth centuries, I should say that, comparatively speaking, he was the worst chief justice ever".

25 See Cope, *op cit*, p 236.

In 1921 Queensland also passed the *Judges' Retirement Act*, a controversial measure that required three incumbent members of the Supreme Court (Cooper CJ (aged 75), Real J (aged 74) and Chubb J (aged 76)) to retire on a proclaimed date, all being then older than the newly mandated retiring age of 70, even though they had been appointed for life. This represented an extreme flexing of the constitutional muscles given to Parliament by the Privy Council decision in *McCawley*. In all probability it would have been struck down in the High Court had the Privy Council not declared in the clearest of terms that the State Constitution was uncontrolled.

The following year McCawley was appointed Queensland's fifth Chief Justice at the age of 41. Four years later he was dead, felled by a cerebral haemorrhage running to board a train to the Ipswich sittings. In death, as in life, McCawley represented the truth of the biblical maxim "Put not your trust in princes".[26] The *Judges' Retirement Act of 1921* that removed three of the Supreme Court judges who had found against McCawley in 1918 preserved their pension rights but abolished pensions in respect of all future judicial appointments. This provision fell heavily on McCawley because his appointment as Chief Justice occurred the day *after* the legislation commenced. Despite his later protests, the Cabinet did nothing to restore the pension rights he had acquired under the original Supreme Court commission that he had fought all the way to London to uphold but laid down when he moved to the chief justiceship. "For one who had served the Government so loyally and well, it was a reward made more bitter by his death only two months later".[27]

Frank Tennison Brennan

Brennan J was the father of Sir Gerard Brennan, Chief Justice of Australia. His, the father's, career was dogged with controversy, some of it of his own making.

Brennan snr was a Labor politician in Queensland between 1918 and 1925 during which time he urged the fusion of the two branches of the profession, a sticky business in any generation of Australian legal history. In 1921 he supported an amendment to the *Supreme Court Act* (later known as the "Brennan Clause") which allowed solicitors of five years' standing to be admitted as barristers. When he took advantage of it a few years later it would cause him double embarrassment.

In 1922 Brennan reported an attempt to bribe him into voting with the Opposition on a no confidence motion. Two men were subsequently convicted when Brennan alerted the police and corroborative evidence was secured by placing two stenographers in a specially constructed cavity in the room where the men came to finalise their corrupt plan.[28]

26 Psalm 146:3 (KJV). For judicial invocation of this proposition, see p 195.

27 McPherson, *The Supreme Court of Queensland*, p 306.

28 See Elvery, *In My Opinion*, pp 89-90. The Brennan family retains a photo of the room.

Brennan's appointment to the Bench in 1925 was controversial on several fronts.[29] When the Premier Theodore resigned to seek federal election, Brennan gave effectively the casting vote in favour of an ineffectual contender, Gillies, and against the leading contender, McCormack, against whom Brennan had strong feelings. A short time later Brennan was appointed an acting judge of the Supreme Court although the announcement was delayed by several days. It turned out that Brennan, by now a barrister, did not satisfy the statutory minimum of five years' standing as a barrister. He was forced to seek his own disbarment and readmission as a solicitor before he could be appointed to the Bench in reliance upon his own "Brennan Clause". He was appointed an acting judge on 10 March 1925 and, on 1 July 1925, was permanently appointed to replace Shand J, whose retirement took effect the preceding day. Brennan's commission mistakenly appointed him to Brisbane, so within three weeks he resigned in order to be appointed Central Judge at Rockhampton as intended. His demands in the ensuing years for transfer to Brisbane were steadfastly refused until 1947, only two years before his death.

The selection of Brennan as a judge was condemned by the press, the Bar Association and the Law Society. Although he turned out to be a fair judge and a man of wit and honesty, his judicial career tended to reinforce the views of his critics. His judicial unorthodoxy in some matters and his financial problems gave food for those who continued to criticise him after judicial appointment. He also brawled with the press and used the Bench as a platform for his political views, and not just in the course of disposing of cases. This aspect of his career is addressed in a later chapter.[30]

Disappointed senior puisnes

Not all judges aspire to rise higher. Some realise their own limitations or the pitfalls of the higher office that strangers assume to be universally coveted. Since, however, lawyers seldom practise their own preaching about not being a sound judge in their own cause, there have been several instances of high pique, and at times extreme unprofessionalism, when an aspirant for appointment or promotion has been disappointed.

The judges other than the Chief Justice in a superior court are sometimes referred to as puisne judges. Other things being equal, the longest serving at any point of time will automatically assume the mantle of senior puisne judge (not that such title has been very much in vogue in the south-eastern States). In Queensland and Western Australia there is a statutory office of Senior Puisne Judge ("SPJ").

Other things are never equal in Queensland as we shall see.

29 This account is taken from McPherson, *The Supreme Court of Queensland*, pp 328-9.
30 See p 99.

The office of senior puisne judge (with or without capital letters) does not guarantee appointment to Chief Justice in the event of a vacancy. Nevertheless, there have been some extreme reactions when the senior puisne was passed over for the top job. Some of those thus disappointed have borne their chagrin with complete professionalism, leaving it to friends and supporters to vent spleen. Some have been more vocal in their own right. Others have gone into a prolonged sulk.

William Westbrooke Burton

After the retirement of John Stephen J in 1832, Dowling J became the next senior judge after Forbes CJ in New South Wales – or so he thought. He had not allowed for the claims of the thrusting William Westbrooke Burton. Burton had been a judge of the Supreme Court of the Cape of Good Hope. When he arrived in Sydney to take up appointment as a judge of the Supreme Court of New South Wales, he claimed seniority to Dowling on the basis of his earlier nomination to the Bench in the Cape and the rule prevailing in the courts of Westminster Hall where, if a judge of one court translated to the Bench of another court, he took rank according to the date of his original patent. Burton was generally supported by Governor Bourke who had been Governor at the Cape and had formed a favourable impression of him there.

When Forbes took lengthy leave of absence Governor Bourke reluctantly appointed Dowling Acting Chief Justice and sought a ruling from England. Burton bombarded Bourke, pressing his claim, and he furiously lobbied support in England. He told the Under Secretary to the Colonial Office, James Stephen, that he (Burton) had been "cheated by one of my brother judges [Dowling J] and ... the other [Forbes CJ] was an accessory to it".[31] Dowling in turn sought the assistance of Lord Brougham who was still a force in English politics despite having recently relinquished the Lord Chancellorship. Dowling also had newspaper connexions in England that were used to good effect.

The Colonial Office ruled that Burton's claim based on alleged priority of commission in another British colony was untenable. More to the point, the Office denied that any right to succession to chief justiceship rested on seniority. When Forbes resigned in 1837 Dowling became the second Chief Justice of New South Wales, despite further machinations by Burton who still enjoyed the support of Governor Bourke and colonial "exclusives" like James Macarthur. Dowling wrote to his son that "Mr Burton is sadly cut at his disappointment. However he sought promotion by unfair means, so I don't pity him".[32]

---

31 See Bennett, *Sir James Dowling*, p 91.

32 *Ibid*, p 108.

Benjamin Boothby

Benjamin Boothby's reaction to being passed over for the chief justiceship of South Australia in favour of Richard Hanson was extreme enough to deserve mention here.[33] He greeted the arrival of his new Chief Justice with a challenge to the validity of his commission and subsequently lost no opportunity to snub him both publicly and privately. Boothby also petitioned the Queen about Hanson's appointment. The matter was referred to the Judicial Committee of the Privy Council which advised that Boothby was at liberty to prosecute an appeal on the matter to itself *at his own expense*. Hanson stated in open court that Boothby's continuing obstruction was designed to induce a private litigant, or the government itself, to underwrite that venture by launching a separate appeal that would raise the same issue. An allegation to this effect was made and found proved against Boothby in his dismissal proceedings before the Governor in Executive Council.[34]

Alfred James Peter Lutwyche

Alfred Lutwyche suffered double appointment disappointment in his judicial career.[35]

In early 1859 he was appointed to the New South Wales Supreme Court so that he could become the judge at Moreton Bay (modern Brisbane). The *Sydney Morning Herald* lambasted the decision, announcing that a "political judge is only less mischievous to a community than a profligate one". Later that year, when the separation of Queensland was imminent, he claimed a seat on the Sydney Bench, arguing that continued residence in Brisbane would be incompatible with his post as a New South Wales judge. The government of the day[36] ruled that Lutwyche could either become a judge of the Supreme Court of Queensland or resign. Lutwyche publicly denounced this decision but elected to hang on to the judicial post now fixedly relocated in Queensland.

In July 1861 Lutwyche petitioned the Queen to disallow an Act which provided for a second judge in the Supreme Court of Queensland but which did not name him as Chief Justice. He also threatened refusal to execute all legislation of the session because two members of the Assembly had taken their seats unlawfully. These actions provoked Governor Bowen to inquire whether

33 For other aspects of Boothby's misbehaviour, see pp 118-21.

34 See pp 120-1 and AJ Hannan, "Mr Justice Boothby" (1957) 58 *Proceedings of the Royal Geographic Society of Australasia South Australian Branch* 24.

35 See generally BH McPherson, "The Case of Mr Justice Lutwyche. Removing a Judge of the Supreme Court of Queensland" *Quadrant* September 1986, p 48.

36 Lutwyche had been involved in New South Wales politics throughout the 1850s, holding the offices of Attorney-General and Solicitor-General in various short-lived administrations.

he could remove Lutwyche under Burke's Act.[37] He was told that he could, but he ultimately decided not to take the action. Instead, James Cockle was sworn in as "additional Judge and Chief Justice".

Before this happened, the government through its Attorney-General launched a prosecution against the *Courier* for seditious libel. The newspaper had published an editorial in strong terms attacking the Legislative Council for its "brazen mendacity" and "utter disregard for the truth". What was the subject matter of the editorial? It concerned an attack on the Council for having passed a resolution condemning Lutwyche for his "political partisanship calculated seriously to impair confidence in the administration of justice". Heady times to be testing the boundaries of free speech. There were even rumours that Lutwyche had penned the editorial. Who should preside at the sedition trial but the only judge then in office, Lutwyche J? Lutwyche instructed the jury to acquit on the basis that sedition could not be directed at a legislative body. According to the advice of the English law officers that was published shortly afterwards, this ruling was wrong in law, but the acquittal was received rapturously by the public.[38]

Lutwyche's prominent role in delivering unpalatable constitutional advice about a blunder that disenfranchised one third of the electors in the newly created colony, and his prickliness in asserting his rights about precedence, status and salary, put him decidedly at odds with the Herbert ministry. Lutwyche insisted on keeping his (New South Wales) salary of £2000 even though this far exceeded what the government wanted to pay and what it would in due course pay his incoming Chief Justice. Both Houses of Parliament carried resolutions against Lutwyche's "political partizanship". Lutwyche countered with a public attack on the government during a general election. He denounced Herbert's administration as "despotism cloaked in the guise of responsible government". As parliamentary knives were being sharpened for his dismissal, Cockle CJ took Lutwyche aside and persuaded him to publish an undertaking not to participate in politics during the remainder of his judicial career. It was an undertaking that he scrupulously honoured until his death in 1880.

The brawl between judge and government attracted the attention of the teenage Samuel Griffith, who would later become the Queensland Chief Justice and then the first Chief Justice of the High Court of Australia. Griffith published an amusing poem on the matter under the pen name Charley Chalk.

Edward Castres Gwynne

Gwynne J who was appointed in 1859 as a counterweight to the obstructive Boothby J was (after Boothby's dismissal) the senior judge of the Supreme

37 See generally p 108.

38 See McPherson, *The Supreme Court of Queensland*, pp 31-3.

Court of South Australia for eleven years. In 1876, Samuel Way, the Attorney-General, recommended his own appointment as Chief Justice. Gwynne served on as senior puisne judge for another five years. After he died, Way wrote that he "must have sworn a mighty oath never to speak to me in private, for he never did".[39]

Edmund Sheppard

In 1874 Edmund Sheppard was appointed to the office of Northern Judge in the Supreme Court of Queensland. When Lutwyche J died in 1880, Sheppard (who by then was the longest serving Supreme Court judge in Queensland) claimed that, in 1874, he had been given a "distinct promise" that he should in due course become the Senior Puisne Judge of the Supreme Court of Queensland. This office had the added attractions of enabling him to return to Brisbane generally and also to sit on the Full Court. Sheppard J announced his claim publicly in the Full Court immediately after Pring J had been sworn in as Lutwyche's successor, surviving a protest by Griffith QC in relation to the validity of his (Pring's) own commission. Represented before the Full Court by (the future Chief Justices) Griffith QC and Cooper, Sheppard nevertheless saw his claim rejected. Lilley CJ (with the concurrence of Harding J who stood directly to gain if Sheppard J's claim was rejected) ruled that the Supreme Court had been divided into two branches since 1874, with a limitation of the Southern judges to the south, and of the Northern Judge to the north; that, as the Senior Puisne Judge *in Brisbane*, Harding J (appointed in 1879) was the Senior Puisne Judge of the Court; that Sheppard J had no right to come to Brisbane and participate in the deliberations of the Full Court; and that he (Lilley CJ) was in possession of an Executive minute ordering Sheppard J to return to his duties in the north.[40] Pow!

Patrick Real

When Sir Pope Cooper succeeded Sir Samuel Griffith as Chief Justice of Queensland in 1903 he administered to himself the oaths of allegiance and office. The historian of the Supreme Court of Queensland explains the reason for this Napoleonic gesture:[41]

> The reason ... was revealed when Real J spoke,[42] which he did with characteristic vigour and at considerable length ... Real made little secret of his belief that the position of Chief Justice should have been

39 Castles and Harris, *Lawmakers and Wayward Whigs*, p 204.

40 *Re Justice Sheppard's Claim, Brisbane Courier*, 14 July 1880. As will be seen immediately below, equality between north and south was restored by legislation in 1895 that produced its own share of grief to Real J.

41 McPherson, *Supreme Court of Queensland*, pp 253-4.

42 For another instance of untimely and inappropriate remarks by Real J, see p 67.

> his. He began by saying that, apart from the 'small circumstance' of having himself been appointed Senior Puisne Judge, he 'could not sit on this Bench other than under a feeling of absolute insult ... The tenor of Real J's remarks was that he had lost his seniority through a draftsman's slip in ... *The Supreme Court Act of 1895*, which retrospectively placed the judges in the north on a footing of equality with those in Brisbane; and also by his having refrained from having the slip corrected ' in the full belief that it would best serve the interests of the country if I took no step in the matter'. It was only the combination of these circumstances, he said, that now persuaded him that no slight was intended, and so enabled him to accept Cooper's seniority and his appointment as Chief Justice 'with friendship and warmth'.

Justices Williams (father and son)

Edward Eyre Williams and his son Hartley Williams were each the senior puisne judge of the Supreme Court of Victoria. And each was considerably put out on failing to attain the chief justiceship when it fell vacant.

Mr Justice Edward Eyre Williams was the senior puisne when (to his great chagrin) William Stawell, the Attorney-General, was appointed Chief Justice over him in 1857. In 1892 Frank Gavan Duffy (who many years later rose to become Chief Justice of the High Court of Australia) published a poem under the nom de plume "Vie Manquee". Its full text is set out elsewhere.[43] In the following verses, the author mentions Williams' snr's upset in the context of referring to his son, himself the senior puisne judge at the time of writing:[44]

> ... turning I appealed
> To one that stood beside.
>
> But he, with sick and scornful looks averse,
> To its full height his stately stature draws –
> "My prime," he said, "is blasted with a curse,
> And this man is the cause.
>
> I am cut off from hope in dull despair,
> A wretched puisne who should be a chief,
> My father suffered so, and now I bear
> Hereditary grief.
>
> And much it chafes me that I cannot bend
> His will, nor stir the calm propriety
> Of my slow, solemn colleague ..."

When this poem was published, the younger Williams J was the senior puisne judge, hence the reference to him as one "that stood beside" Higinbotham

43 See pp 35-8.
44 As to CJ Ahern's notes on this passage, see p 36.

CJ who had just been referred to. At the time of writing, Williams' attributed grief stemmed from his Chief Justice (Higinbotham CJ) being considerably younger than him and in apparently good health. Williams had been appointed in 1881 at the age of 37. But the lines would contain a deeper irony. Only seven months after their publication, Higinbotham died unexpectedly and Williams was passed over for the Chief Justiceship in favour of John Madden QC who was appointed directly from the Bar.

Williams let fly in a letter to the *Argus* that made it plain that he, not Madden, should have received the appointment. According to Sir Arthur Dean,[45] Williams' reputation "has suffered" as the result of the letter which is bizarre enough to merit repetition in full:[46]

> Dr Madden has not for many years been engaged in politics, nor can he be regarded as a supporter of the present Government. The reasons, therefore, why he has been selected to be Chief Justice, as successor to Sir William Stawell and Mr George Higinbotham, can only be because as an advocate he, conjointly with Mr Purves QC, occupies the foremost position at the Bar as it is now constituted.
>
> Let me briefly examine the weight and cogency of this reason. Firstly, in what capacity does Dr Madden occupy this foremost position, and secondly how came he to fill it? As lawyers Mr Mitchell, Mr Box, Mr Isaacs, Mr Topp, and Mr Higgins are undoubtedly sounder and superior. As advocates, they are equally clearly his inferiors. It is therefore, as an advocate, and not as a lawyer, that Dr Madden holds at the Bar the position he now does. But I apprehend that an essential qualification for those sought to fill vacancies on the Supreme Court Bench is that they should be sound lawyers, and not brilliant or effective advocates.
>
> It is only within the past eleven years that he has done so. When the late Chief Justice, Mr Justice Holroyd, and I were at the Bar, Dr Madden's practice was of a very insignificant description. The best practising solicitors of those days will readily substantiate this. It was only the rapidly-succeeding elevation to the Bench of the three whom I have just mentioned which enabled Dr Madden to push his way to the front rank and into a better class of business. Though Dr Madden started at the Bar before me I was 'standing counsel' for nearly every bank in Melbourne, for many of the insurance offices, leading mercantile firms, the Corporation of Melbourne, the *Argus* and the *Age* newspapers, and for many private individuals, and was making thousands a year when Dr Madden did not, I venture to say, hold one 'general retainer', and was making hundreds.
>
> When the late Chief Justice, Mr Justice Holroyd, and I were rapidly, the one after the other, elevated to the Bench, the great gap so caused

45 Dean, *A Multitude of Counsellors*, p 138.

46 It is reproduced from Dean, *op cit*, pp 153-4. JRS Forbes, *Divided Legal Profession*, p 123, describes the letter as "somewhat acidulous" (surely an understatement). According to Forbes: "Somehow Williams and Madden found a *modus vivendi* for ten years: judicially speaking, they were brothers until 1903".

was filled by other men who hitherto had occupied comparatively obscure positions. Amongst these, I do not, of course, include Mr Purves QC, as he had been before the time I mentioned in the front rank with Mr Higinbotham, Mr Holroyd and myself.

As regards large pecuniary sacrifices, every one of my colleagues and I have, for the honour of the position, made very large pecuniary sacrifices. Every present occupant of the Supreme Court Bench is nothing if not a lawyer. Each one of us has in turn been elevated because each in his turn was supposed to be, not the best advocate, but the best lawyer, though he has justly been regarded as a successful and brilliant advocate; but I take it that we do not require forensic powers on the Bench. I have now been nearly twelve years on the Bench, doing considerably more than my duty, and taking a keen interest in expediting the work of the Court. The treatment which I have just received is not such as to encourage me for the future to do more than my bare duty. I have felt constrained to depart from my usual custom and to write to the press upon this subject, for the purpose of reminding the public that, because Dr Madden happens to hold a prominent position at the Bar as at present constituted, it does not follow that the present five occupants of the Supreme Court bench are not at any rate his equals in point of legal knowledge and attainments. In conclusion, so keenly do I feel the injustice of this latest appointment, and the insult that was cast by it upon the present occupants of the Bench, that had I left the Bar only five years ago instead of twelve I should unhesitatingly have resigned my Judgeship and returned to the Bar,

I am etc.
HARTLEY WILLIAMS
Gracedale-House, Healesville. Jan 7.

The statement in the letter that Williams would thenceforth do only his "bare duty" gave rise to a story. Alfred Deakin and a friend were at Point Lonsdale and, as they emerged from the sea after their morning swim, they were surprised to see a naked figure coming out of the water. "Good gracious", said Deakin's companion, "Who is that?" "Oh", said Deakin, "that is Williams doing his bare duty".[47]

Leapfrogging Queensland style

In 1926 Queensland legislation enabled the Executive to decide which of the judges might be appointed Senior Puisne Judge whereupon the government immediately appointed the then most junior judge, Hugh Denis Macrossan. HD Macrossan served as Senior Puisne Judge for 14 years until his appointment as Chief Justice in 1940 to succeed Blair CJ. Macrossan CJ died 37 days later to be succeeded as Chief Justice by the then SPJ, William Webb.

47 Dean, *A Multitude of Counsellors*, p 138.

Philp J (who had only become a judge in 1939) was then invited to accept appointment as the Senior Puisne Judge. He was next in seniority to EA Douglas J and he declined until satisfied that a similar offer had been made to Douglas, who was then the senior judge of the Queensland Supreme Court after the Chief Justice. Unfortunately, the government held a grudge against Douglas stemming from a decision he had made in 1938 in the *Ithaca* election case.[48] In declining appointment, Philp acted without consulting Douglas, who later expressed disappointment that his friend and colleague had not accepted a post that would not have been given to himself. The Premier, Forgan Smith, would not agree to Douglas' appointment because of the *Ithaca* ruling. The Senior Puisne position was then offered to and accepted by Neal Macrossan, the brother of the recently deceased Chief Justice. Neal Macrossan was appointed a judge of the Court on 29 June 1940 and elevated to the Senior Puisne Judgeship two days later, leapfrogging everyone else, as his brother had done 14 years before.

When Neal Macrossan SPJ became Chief Justice in 1946 following the appointment of Webb CJ to the High Court, EA Douglas was only eight months from statutory retirement. Nonetheless, Philp J again refused appointment as SPJ because Douglas had not been approached. The next in seniority, Mansfield J accepted the SPJ position and later went on to become Chief Justice in 1956. Philp J became SPJ at this stage and remained in that position until his death in 1965. Philp and Mansfield did not speak to each other again during this final decade of Philp's distinguished judicial career: they communicated in writing between their associates.[49]

James Archibald Douglas

This judge had a legitimate sense of grievance relating to the circumstances in which he was passed over for appointment as Chief Justice of Queensland and as Senior Puisne Judge in 1982. Unlike some of the others discussed in this section, he left it to others, including family members, to "maintain the rage".

In late 1981, the then Chief Justice, Sir Charles Wanstall, and the Senior Puisne Judge, Mr Justice Lucas, were due to retire. The Minister for Justice and Attorney-General, a member of the Liberal Party in the Coalition government headed by Sir Johannes Bjelke-Petersen, recommended that Mr Justice Douglas be appointed as Chief Justice. Douglas was the next most senior judge after those retiring; he had the overwhelming support of his fellow judges, the Bar

48 Sitting as the Elections Tribunal Judge, EA Douglas J ruled against the valid election of the sitting member for Ithaca, EM Hanlon. An appeal to the Full Court was upheld by a majority, one of whose members was Douglas' brother, RJ Douglas J. See *The Ithaca Election Petition. Webb v Hanlon* [1939] St R Qd 90.

49 See the book review by Francis M Douglas in (1990) 6 *Australian Bar Review* 181.

and the Attorney-General; and he was a man of unquestionable ability and integrity. Yet, according to the findings of the Fitzgerald Royal Commission:[50]

> Bjelke-Petersen would not accept [the Attorney-General's] recommendation of Mr Justice Douglas, whom it was rumoured had voted for the Australian Labor Party in a previous State election. Instead he advocated a more junior judge, Mr Justice Dormer George Andrews, a friend of Lyons,[51] who had discussed the appointment with Bjelke-Petersen. Bjelke-Petersen's refusal to appoint Mr Justice Douglas and his nomination of Mr Justice Andrews met with determined opposition from the Liberal members of his Cabinet. On 12 January, 1982, the matter was resolved when Cabinet unanimously decided that Sir Walter Benjamin Campbell, then a puisne judge of the Supreme Court, be the next Chief Justice. At the same time, Mr Justice Andrews was appointed Senior Puisne Judge. Liberal ministers noted their objections to the latter appointment on the Cabinet minute. Superimposed upon the other factors were the influence of Lyons and Bjelke-Petersen's wish to have his way and not to yield to the junior coalition partner. The respective merits of the prospective appointees and other considerations were subordinated to Bjelke-Petersen's determination to show his support for Lyons and the appointee whom he desired and that he and his party were pre-eminent in the Government of Queensland.

It is widely believed that the Premier discovered by some means that Douglas had voted for the Australian Labor Party at the 1972 State election when Douglas cast a postal vote. Douglas bore his rejection with highly professional fortitude.

The creation of the New South Wales Court of Appeal

The New South Wales Court of Appeal was established (for the second time)[52] in 1965. There would be, after the Chief Justice, a President and six permanent Judges of Appeal. The creation of a permanent appellate court was generally supported by the legal profession and the proposal had had a long gestation period. The legislative drafting was, however, complicated because the Australian Constitution placed the Supreme Court in a special relationship to the High Court in the judicial hierarchy, so the Court of Appeal had to remain part of that same Supreme Court.[53] Had the government simply translated the seven senior judges (after the Chief Justice) into the Court of Appeal there

50 See *Report of a Commission of Inquiry Pursuant to Orders in Council*, 3 July 1989 (GE Fitzgerald, Chairman), p 97.

51 Sir Edward Lyons was described by Commissioner Fitzgerald as having an extraordinary influence on the Premier.

52 The first was the Governor's Court of Appeal, established in each of the colonies in earliest times, and continued in South Australia until 1936.

53 See generally *Stewart v The King* (1921) 29 CLR 234.

would have been little gnashing of judicial teeth. But judges are not the only guardians of sound policy and there were ample reasons to justify selection on merit and not seniority in the new Court.

The Court of Appeal replaced an institution that had operated for well over a century. Under that system, the Chief Justice selected any three judges of the Supreme Court to constitute a Full Court in a civil or criminal appeal. In practice, the senior judges exercised this role, thereby getting relief from an unbroken diet of trial work that had been their lot for many years. It was these judges who became most anxious about possible non-appointment to the Court of Appeal if and when the long-discussed new system came into being. The process and its impact are reviewed by Justice Michael Kirby in an article titled "Judicial Supersession: The Controversial Establishment of the New South Wales Court of Appeal".[54] "Supersession" is what happens when existing seniority arrangements are displaced within a single court.

Because he was appointed to the newly created office of President, the promotion of Gordon Wallace did not strictly involve supersession, but it ruffled many feathers for different reasons. As a puisne judge, Wallace J was 16th in the order of seniority out of the 26 Supreme Court judges. And he had close political links with the recently elected Liberal government under Robert Askin which got to implement the proposal that had had its lengthy gestation under the predecessor Labor government. Kirby observes that the "pain of the creation was anticipated by the successive governments that planned the innovation". But the prolonged anticipation tended in this case to intensify the disappointment of the men who were passed over. Deep divisions emerged that affected relationships within the Supreme Court of New South Wales for at least 20 years.

As soon as specific proposals about the structure of the new Court began to circulate, some senior judges communicated their concerns to the Chief Justice or directly with the Attorney-General or the Premier. A "Memorial" protesting the proposed abolition of the Full Court system was discussed by most of the judges in circumstances of great acrimony, heightened by the rumours about the likelihood that Wallace J and Asprey J would leap up the ladder, as it turned out that they did. The Memorial was presented to the President of the Legislative Council, the Premier and the Attorney-General. As often happens in similar situations, some of its signatories acted out of solidarity with their soon to be disappointed brethren and against their own self-interest. But the government had made up its mind about the creation of a fresh Court to be manned[55] by those considered most meritorious, and not on a seniority basis. The outcome,

54 (2008) 30 *Sydney Law Review* 177.

55 There would be no female Judges of Appeal in New South Wales until Beazley JA was appointed in 1996. In 1999 she sat with Justices Simpson and Bell to constituted the first all-woman Bench of the New South Wales Court of Criminal Appeal.

showing seniority vis-à-vis the Chief Justice, as depicted in a Table produced by one of the newspapers was as follows:[56]

SEESAW	BEFORE	AFTER
Wallace [P]	15	2
Sugerman	2	3
McLelland	3	4
Walsh	9	5
Jacobs	16	6
Asprey	21	7
Holmes		8

Apart from being leapfrogged by Wallace P, Sugerman and McLelland JJ could have had no objection. The other four newly appointed Judges of Appeal were highly eminent on any reckoning. Walsh JA, who would shortly depart for the High Court, was probably the most gifted and sound judge ever to sit on the Supreme Court of New South Wales.[57] Jacobs JA would later preside over the Court of Appeal before himself being appointed to the High Court in 1974, a position from which he retired following the diagnosis of a life-threatening disease in 1979. (He is still living.)

The puisne judges of the Supreme Court who were bypassed in the appointments responded in different ways, but Russell Le Gay Brereton J and some others were, in Kirby's diplomatic understatement:

> profoundly disappointed by the disturbance of ... seniority and loss of participation in civil appeals ... The disappointment for the individual judges affected was real and, in some cases, probably justified ... [T]he issues were not solely narcissistic. They presented institutional questions that went beyond the disgruntlement of a few elderly judges. Theirs was certainly more than a storm in a teacup. However, in the end, the prediction of Chief Justice Herron proved accurate. The legal profession came to accept and welcome the change.

Extremely short appointments

Before the 20th century judges held office for life during good behaviour. Yet some appointees were gone before the ink was dry on their commissions.

John Jeffcott

Sir John William Jeffcott was appointed founding judge of the new colony of South Australia in May 1836.[58] He arrived in April 1837 and established the Supreme Court in October that year. The administration of the colony was in disarray due in large part to the incompetence of Lieutenant-Governor

56 Reproduced by Kirby, *op cit*.

57 He had three university medals, for English, Philosophy and Law.

58 He had previously been tried and acquitted of murder: see p 47.

Hindmarsh, a man described by one of his officials as being incapable of writing "two sentences of grammar or commonsense".[59] Jeffcott sought leave to travel to Hobart Town, telling the Governor that he needed to obtain new clothes and other supplies. His real motives were to visit his fiancée, to seek financial assistance from his intended father-in-law, and to sound out the authorities in Van Diemen's Land about getting an official position in the island colony.[60] He stayed away from Adelaide for seventeen weeks. Only months after his return, he was off again to Hobart Town, this time on the pretext of consulting people there about certain legal matters troubling him. While awaiting a ship to take him to Van Diemen's Land he was drowned when a whaleboat was capsized at the mouth of the River Murray. His body was never found. He had been "on the job" for less than a year although he only sat as a judge twice. "In all he spent little more than three months in the colony; and the greater part of that time his anxiety was to be quit of the place as soon as possible".[61]

John Fletcher Hargrave

Hargrave was a judge of the District Court of New South Wales in 1859 for a mere 14 days before he resigned in order to enter politics. Unfortunately for Stephen CJ, on whose Supreme Court he sat between 1865 and 1881, he did not stay in politics.[62]

Edmund Sheppard

In 1873 the judges of the Supreme Court of Queensland were Cockle CJ and Lutwyche J. Lutwyche became ill. The Chief Justice sat as the Full Court, but (after hearing argument) ruled that he could not alone constitute the Court in Banc. Sheppard DCJ was hurriedly commissioned as acting judge "until the return of Mr Justice Lutwyche, or the appointment of his successor, during good behaviour". Appearing as amicus curiae, Lilley QC submitted that the appointment was invalid, not for its qualified duration, but because it would increase the number of judges beyond the limit of two imposed by the *Supreme Court Act of 1867* (Qld). The Chief Justice upheld the validity of the commission.[63] Sheppard was sworn in and took his seat on the Bench. But the following day he tendered his resignation as an acting judge and the Court sitting was abandoned.[64]

59 Castles and Harris, *Lawmakers and Wayward Whigs*, p 31.

60 *Ibid*, pp 65-7.

61 Hague, *Sir John Jeffcott, Portrait of a Colonial Judge*, p 126.

62 See pp 121-3.

63 *Re the Appointment of a Deputy Judge* (1873) BCR Mar 12.

64 See generally McPherson, *Supreme Court of Queensland*, pp 42, 55-6. Apparently no one thought of the possibility that Sheppard AJ's commission in the Supreme Court had voided his commission in the District Court due to the doctrine of incompatible offices

Richard Annesley Billing

Judge Billing died nine weeks after his appointment to the County Court Bench in Victoria in 1882.[65]

Julian Emanuel Salomons

Julian Salomons was Chief Justice of New South Wales for 16 days in 1886 and he resigned without being sworn in. On 29 November 1886 his successor Darley's appointment was gazetted "*vice* Mr JE Salomons, QC, resigned".[66]

Salomons was called to the Bar at Gray's Inn, London before commencing practice in New South Wales in 1861. He held office as Solicitor-General for a brief period in 1869-70 and he was counsel of choice for the State in many leading cases. According to Suzanne Edgar in the *Australian Dictionary of Biography*, "a certain emotional brashness and vanity did not retard his mounting eminence" at the Bar. In the words of Wilfred Blacket,[67] Salomons was "the most brilliant man of his generation, and the most voluble ... His faith in his own powers knew no limits". Dr JM Bennett has concluded that Salomons' "forensic style, scathing and fearless, marked him out as a man whose regard for decorum was suspect".[68] Salomons' brash exterior masked an inner insecurity. His frenetic approach to work also brought him to nervous breakdown on more than one occasion.

In 1886 the chief justiceship was refused by WB Dalley QC and FM Darley QC. Salomons accepted the office, "being assured by those most qualified to guide me ... that my appointment will be acceptable to the public and to both branches of the profession". In fact, there was a mixed reaction to the appointment in the press. The Attorney-General's proposal for a welcoming dinner by the Bar elicited many indications of unwillingness to attend, so the idea was abandoned. Salomons then displayed irresolution by calling on Windeyer J, the only judge of the Supreme Court who had not visited to welcome him

---

(see generally *Wilson v Minister for Aboriginal and Torres Strait Islander Affairs* (1996) 189 CLR 1 at 15). As indicated above, Sheppard J was given a permanent appointment in 1874 as the Northern Judge of the Supreme Court. That appointment proved more permanent than he wanted (see p 75).

65 Hewitt, *Judges Through the Years*, p 27.

66 This is early evidence of the view, contested in Victoria, that appointment to a superior court caused a commission as Queen's or King's Counsel to fall dormant, and not to lapse altogether, with the consequence that retirement enabled it to revive. See further pp 142-3.

67 Blacket, *May it Please Your Honour*, p 36. See also Piddington, *Worshipful Masters*, p 201.

68 JM Bennett, "Sir Julian Salomons – Fifth Chief Justice of New South Wales" (1972) 58 *Journal of the Royal Australian Historical Society* 101 at 103. Several instances of clever but sarcastic remarks attributed to Salomons are recounted elsewhere in this work.

formally.[69] He copped it with both barrels. According to Salomons' record of the event, Windeyer "said that [his] appointment was outrageous (and other like insulting terms)". He taunted Salomons that he was ignorant of public opinion, at least of the "public whose opinion [was] worth regarding". Windeyer said:

> 'Why are you always breaking down mentally ... Faucett is much stronger than you.' I answered, 'Faucett! Why he is quite an old man.'[70] To this he responded. 'He is much stronger than you.'

Although Windeyer J published a letter in the *Telegraph* on 20 November 1886 denying any "personal feeling of hostility", such a backhanded republication of opposition would have rubbed further salt into Salomons' wounds. Appointed Chief Justice on 12 November 1886, Salomons resigned on 27 November without being sworn in. Although the profession met and urged him to reconsider, he refused. His portrait appears in the gallery of portraits of Chief Justices in the Banco Court at Sydney. The chief justiceship was then offered a second time to the reluctant Darley who this time accepted.

Salomons returned to the Bar. His pivotal role in an even greater drama, involving Richard Denis Meagher and the legal and political establishments of New South Wales in 1895, is recounted elsewhere in this work.[71]

Albert Bathurst Piddington

Albert Piddington[72] was appointed a justice of the High Court in 1913 but 18 days later, alone of all the High Court justices, resigned before taking up his position. Before his appointment he had been sounded out on behalf of Prime Minister Hughes and had rashly sent a telegram stating that he was "in sympathy with supremacy of Commonwealth powers". He accepted the offer of appointment on the understanding that he had "complete independence". But, shattered by the intensity of the opposition from the New South Wales and Victorian Bars he gave up the office on the ground that he had compromised himself. Hughes was on his way from Sydney to Melbourne for the swearing-in ceremony when he read of Piddington's resignation in the newspapers. An attempt to persuade his protégé to weather the storm having failed, Hughes

69 According to Dr Bennett, *op cit*, Salomons' decision to make such a formal visit to Windeyer "was an extraordinary action, by itself indication of hesitancy, diffidence and inferiority. [Salomons] thereby placed himself at such a tactical disadvantage that he could not recover from the shock that awaited him". Bennett also states that there is no evidence that anti-Semitic feeling influenced events.

70 Faucett J had been a Judge of the Supreme Court since 1865 and he was then aged about 73.

71 See pp 146-51.

72 See generally David Ash, "Albert Bathurst Piddington" *Bar News*, Summer 2009-2010, p 45.

turned to attack, describing Piddington as having "resigned from his great office like a panic-stricken boy".[73]

In 1922 Piddington opposed Hughes for a seat in a federal election, and the circumstances of Hughes' abortive attempt to appoint Piddington became a bitter issue in the campaign that Hughes would win narrowly.[74]

Hugh Denis Macrossan

HD Macrossan waited 14 years as Senior Puisne Judge of the Supreme Court of Queensland before being appointed Chief Justice on 17 May 1940.[75] Five weeks later, he died suddenly, to be succeeded as Chief Justice by Webb SPJ. The ensuing vacancy on the Supreme Court was filled by his younger brother Neal who was immediately catapulted into the office of Senior Puisne Judge and became Chief Justice six years later when Webb was appointed to the High Court.

Charles Stumm

Mr Justice Stumm was a leader of the Bar when appointed to the Queensland Supreme Court Bench in 1929.[76] A little over three weeks later he was killed when struck by a car as he descended from a tram. The driver of the car was acquitted of manslaughter after evidence that the tram was moving when the judge alighted.[77]

The young, the old and the stayers

In response to an observation that "the best time to go to the Bench is when you are fifty" a wit responded that "the best time to go is when you are asked".[78]

It would appear that the youngest person to be appointed an Australian judge was Henry Walter Parker who was appointed, by royal warrant, to be the founding judge in the Supreme Court of South Australia in 1835. He was aged 26 and had been a barrister only three years. He resigned before setting off for the colony over a dispute about whether his salary commenced from

73 Contrast the attitude of the High Court itself, when Piddington announced his appointment as King's Counsel a few months later (see p 141).

74 Piddington would later serve with distinction on the Inter-State Commission and the Industrial Commission, resigning (and abandoning pension rights) in protest at Governor Game's dismissal of Premier Jack Lang. Other aspects of Piddington's eventful career in the law include his controversial yet effective role as counsel in the Kisch saga and his own situation as litigant in the High Court (see p 48).

75 See above, p 78.

76 He had played a part in the public opposition by the Queensland Bar to the appointment of Thomas McCawley: see p 66.

77 McPherson, *The Supreme Court of Queensland*, p 334.

78 Beanland, *A Court Apart*, p 202.

embarkation or arrival.[79] John Kinchela jnr was 22 when, on his father's prompting, he was appointed police magistrate at Bathurst. Because of his inexperience other magistrates refused to sit with him.

Thomas McCawley was only 36 when appointed to the Supreme Court of Queensland in October 1917 and 40 when made Chief Justice in 1922.[80] He died at the age of 43. Herbert Vere Evatt was (to date) both the youngest to arrive at the High Court of Australia (aged 36) and to depart from it (aged 46). Sir Frank Gavan Duffy was 79 when, as senior puisne judge of the High Court, he was appointed to be its Chief Justice. Recognising that this was not his first judicial appointment, I believe it to be the oldest age at which an Australian judge has been appointed.

Records for lengthy judicial service that were set in the era when appointment was for life are unlikely to be passed.

Alfred Stephen served as a judge of the Supreme Court of New South Wales for five years then as its Chief Justice for another 29 years.

Queensland has seen some real stayers. Sir Alexander Pope Cooper sat on the Bench for over 39 years, 21 of them as Chief Justice. Charles Chubb served an unbroken term on the Supreme Court for 32 years from 1889, just shaving Real J's 31 years. Judge George Paul was a member of the District Court of Queensland for 35 years around the turn of the 20th century.

The South Australian record is held by Sir Mellis Napier who was on the Bench for 43 years, 25 of them as Chief Justice. He narrowly pipped Samuel Way who was Chief Justice for almost 40 years, having been appointed at the age of 39 in 1876. Indeed, South Australia is remarkable for the paucity of its Chief Justices. Between the appointment of Way in 1876 and the retirement of King CJ in 1978 there were only five Chief Justices. By contrast, each of New South Wales and Queensland saw at least twice that number come and go through the same period.

The Victorian record for judicial service is held by Lowe J who was on the Supreme Court Bench for 37 years. Sir Robert Menzies is reported to have said of him that: "No man could be half as wise as Sir Charles Lowe looks".

William Pidgeon's term of nearly 31 years as a judge on the District Court and then the Supreme Court of Western Australia was a record for that State.

Sir Edward McTiernan served on the High Court between 1930 and 1976. He retired at the age of 84, apparently in response to Barwick CJ's refusal to permit alteration of the High Court accommodation to provide for a judge in

79 Hannan, *The Life of Chief Justice Way*, p 34; Hague, *Sir John Jeffcott, Portrait of a Colonial Judge*, p 54. Judge Advocate Ellis Bent was 28 when appointed, as was Judge Arthur Noel of the District Court of Queensland. Algernon Montagu was about 30 when he went onto the Bench in Van Diemen's Land. Roberts J was 32 when appointed as the judge of the Northern Territory in 1921.

80 See above pp 66-70. Robert French, the current Chief Justice of Australia, was only 39 when he started his judicial career as a judge of the Federal Court.

a wheelchair. McTiernan had broken his hip chasing a cricket in the Windsor Hotel, Melbourne. His 46-year record will never be broken given that a retiring age of 70 was introduced in 1977.

Retiring (or failing to retire)

Judge Severin Woinarski, the editor of Sir Owen Dixon's *Jesting Pilate and Other Papers and Addresses*, retired after 11 years' service on the County Court of Victoria. Woinarski took pains to maintain the secrecy of the impending retirement. He wanted no official farewell and the retirement would be announced by the Attorney-General. Yet, a week before the judge stepped down, a young barrister said at the conclusion of a case, "Your Honour, this will be the last time I shall be appearing before you". The judge replied, "What! Are you leaving the Bar?"[81]

When the Queensland Parliament legislated to force three Supreme Court judges who had been appointed for life to retire because they were already past the newly mandated age of statutory senility they departed most reluctantly. One of them (Real J) addressed Parliament in opposition to the legislation before it was passed.[82]

Although there is now a compulsory retiring age for judges, the decision about when a judge should draw stumps often remains a very difficult one. All judges may share Sir Alfred Stephen's vision that "it is better for him to leave the law before the law left him".[83] But, whether or not they subscribe to the maxim that none should be a judge in his or her own cause, they may not be the best judges of their own performance. Friends and foes will usually keep their views to themselves, for opposing reasons. Even the judge's spouse may be conflicted. Mrs Foster was no doubt delighted to see more of her husband when a few years back he eventually retired after a most distinguished career as a Supreme Court judge, a Federal Court judge and an acting judge of the Court of Appeal. This was conveyed when she reportedly told friends that "having Michael at home was like having a grand piano in the kitchen".

Heydon J recently commended Bayley J for the length of his service after qualifying for a judicial pension. "How different, how very different, from the mercantile, even mercenary, retirement policies of some modern Australian judges."[84] His Honour refrained from identifying those he had in contemplation.

James Lang Campbell's appointment to the Supreme Court of New South Wales in August 1922 was criticised because of his age – he had been born in 1858 in Scotland. He was no great shakes as a lawyer or a judge and is probably

81 Hewitt, *Judges Through the Years*, p 88.

82 See p 68.

83 Bennett, *Sir Alfred Stephen*, p 293.

84 *Australian Crime Commission v Stoddart* [2011] HCA 47 at [86].

best known for the problems that arose out of his failure to stand down on reaching the statutory retiring age of 70. He had publicly given the date of his birth as 1860 but, in *Celebrity Pictures Pty Ltd v Turnbull*,[85] it was alleged that he had already attained his seventieth birthday and that his participation in the case rendered the outcome void. A summons was brought before another judge to set aside the verdict. A Scottish birth certificate was tendered and Campbell was called as a witness. The summons was nevertheless dismissed on the ground that the date of the judge's birth had not been proven (a fitting verdict for a Scot), but Parliament was persuaded to legislate to validate Campbell's judicial acts.[86] Sir Owen Dixon has demonstrated that the legislation was unnecessary having regard to the doctrine of de facto officers.[87]

Mr Justice Campbell was not the last Australian judge to turn a blind eye to matters of age. In 2002 a magistrate in Western Australia, Deborah Bennett-Borlase, was forced to step down in a hurry. In 1987 she had put her birth date on her application form as seven years earlier than it was. Three years after she had passed the mandatory retirement age someone tipped off the Chief Magistrate who alerted the Attorney-General. The Attorney-General announced that it was not proposed to do anything about the cases heard and determined by the magistrate during her superannuated years.

Life tenure was abolished for High Court and other federal judicial appointments in 1977. The retiring age is now 70. But it has been the practice of the handful of justices who have chosen to go full term in the High Court to deliver outstanding judgments on the day that is two days earlier than their birthday. Section 72 of the Constitution now states: "The appointment of a Justice of the High Court shall be for a term expiring upon his attaining the age of seventy years ...".[88] One might think that time would be up for the judge at midnight on the day before his or her 70th birthday. But, in 1961, the High Court reminded the unlearned that the common law has its own technical rule about when a person attains majority or any other milestone measured by the effluxion of years. In *Prowse v McIntyre*[89] it was held that an action for damages was statute-barred because it was commenced on 27 November 1957

85 Unreported, NSW Supreme Court, 1929. One interlocutory ruling in the case is, however, reported: see (1929) 46 WN (NSW) 121. The Attorney-General had claimed Crown privilege in answer to a subpoena for the production of a birth certificate (presumably Campbell's) forwarded from the United Kingdom. The ground was that "it was contrary to public policy, and against the public interest that the document should be produced"! Halse Rogers J ordered production on the basis that the claim for privilege was obviously based on a misconception.

86 Act No 29 of 1929 (NSW).

87 Owen Dixon, "De Facto Officers" (1938) 1 *Res Judicatae* 285. The article is reproduced in *Jesting Pilate*.

88 The provision further stipulates that 70 is the maximum age for justices of any court created by the Commonwealth Parliament and that the Parliament may fix a lower maximum age for any court created by it.

89 (1961) 111 CLR 264.

by a person born on 28 November 1930 in respect of injuries sustained during infancy. The *Limitation Act 1623* (Imp) allowed such a claim to be brought within six years "after ... coming to or being of full age" and the High Court ruled that this occurred at midnight on 26 November 1957, not later, even though the plaintiff celebrated his majority on the 28th. Windeyer J observed:[90]

> The birth of a man is an event. His attaining twenty-one is not, in the same sense, an event. It is merely a way of saying that a certain period of time, twenty-one years, has passed since he was born.

Although legislatures across Australia rushed to overturn this arcane pocket of common law[91] such provisions could not touch the meaning of the federal Constitution which is an Imperial statute. The possibility of a *female* justice arguing that the amended retiring age provision does not apply to her at all because it uses "his" and because the common law as understood in 1900 did not contemplate the appointment of a woman to a public office[92] lies yet in the future. If upheld, the argument might invalidate the justice's own appointment, along with that of her sister justices.[93]

Justice Deidre O'Connor, of the Federal Court of Australia, had a difficult litigant in person before her. He was obviously finding it hard to believe that a woman could be a judge. Finally, he asked how he could be sure that she was indeed a judge. Thinking to put a swift end to a possibly genuine (but probably cheeky) inquiry, O'Connor J had her associate bring into court the commission by which she had been appointed. The litigant scrutinised it carefully, pondering over the statement about the term of office coming to an end when the judge turned 70. Looking directly at her Honour, the man asked, "But how do I know that you're still under 70?".

Death in harness

Sir James Macfarlan was a judge of the Supreme Court of Victoria between 1922 and 1949, resigning from the Bench in his late 70s. He had the unusual experience of reading of his own death in *Debrett's Peerage*, surviving for another five years to recount the tale.

Many Australian judges have died in office, some "in the course of their employment" as a worker's compensation lawyer would put it. Sir Douglas

90 *Ibid* at 278.

91 For example, s 25E of the *Acts Interpretation Act 1901* (Cth) provides that, "for the purposes of any Act, unless the contrary intention appears, the time at which a person attains a particular age expressed in years is the commencement of the relevant anniversary of the date of the birth of that person".

92 See *Chorlton v Lings* (1868) LR 4 CP 374; *Rhondda's (Viscountess) Claim* [1922] 2 AC 339. The issue would prove a test for any committed originalist in constitutional matters.

93 Cf *Edwards v Attorney-General for Canada* [1930] AC 124.

Menzies of the High Court collapsed and died at a Bar Dinner. Wearing J of the Supreme Court of South Australia perished at sea when the ship in which he was returning from circuit in Palmerston (now Darwin) struck a reef off the coast of Queensland in 1875. McCawley CJ was felled by a cerebral haemorrhage running to board a train to the Ipswich sittings. Jeffcott J's drowning at the mouth of the Murray River was probably in the same category although his true reasons for travelling from Adelaide to Hobart Town were more personal than professional.[94] David Opas, a Family Court judge, was murdered in 1980 in an as yet unsolved crime.[95] Milner Stephen J's sudden death while a jury was out reputedly prompted a characteristic response from Sir Frederick Jordan.[96]

The hearing of the Privy Council appeal in the *Bank Nationalisation Case* spanned 37 days with Evatt QC AG speaking for 18 days. Two members of the Bench, Lords Uthwatt and du Parcq, died during the hearing.

All of the evidence in a contested divorce case had been received when the judge (Edwards J) died. At a further hearing before Clancy J, the parties agreed to tender the transcript and allow the new judge to decide if he wished any of the witnesses to be recalled for cross-examination. The losing party then complained unsuccessfully to the High Court that the open justice principle had thereby been breached.[97]

Starke J accompanied Sir George Rich (then aged 85 and still on the Bench) to the funeral of Isaac Isaacs in 1948. Legend has it that, as they passed by the open grave, Starke leant over to Rich and asked him: "George, are you sure it's worth your while to go home?" Starke's assessment of Rich's life expectancy obviously did not match that of the lady who married him two years later and who survived him after six years of marriage.

Murphy J delivered judgments in the High Court on the day that he died from a prolonged illness. There have even been incidents of judgments penned by a judge being delivered after his demise, usually by a colleague on an appellate court who adopted them. Fullagar J tried a case and then prepared his judgment, dying before it could be delivered. By agreement of the parties, Dixon J delivered the reasons and pronounced orders without further hearing. The orders were set aside on appeal, but not due to any problem raised on account of the trial judge's demise.[98] In September 1977 Ward J heard a personal injuries action. He had prepared his judgment but died before being able to deliver it. The judgment was delivered posthumously by Forster CJ.[99]

94 See pp 82-3.

95 The wife of another Family Court judge, Watson J, was killed around this time when a bomb was detonated at their home.

96 See p 16.

97 *Brennan v Brennan* (1953) 89 CLR 129.

98 See *Carter Bros v Renouf* (1962) 111 CLR 140.

99 *Kidney v Janides* (1977) 18 ALR 113.

Other judges have fallen asleep on the Bench in a more literal sense. The late Justices Hutley and Meagher sometimes struggled to stay awake during appeal hearings, and (if they succumbed) they left counsel in the gentle hands of their colleagues. The narcoleptic jurists always ensured that any (adverse) thoughts were conveyed to counsel before they nodded off and they had an uncanny knack of waking suddenly in response to a jarring submission or crashing law report. Appellate courts have generally insisted that there is no automatic miscarriage of justice when a judge or juror momentarily doses off and that, in general, it is the duty of counsel to raise the point rather than keep it in reserve for an appeal.[100] But when a District Court judge fell asleep on a number of occasions during a drug trial, causing some members of the jury to be amused and distracted, the ensuing conviction was set aside by the High Court.[101]

---

100 *Stathooles v Mount Isa Mines Ltd* [1997] 2 Qd R 106 esp at 113. See also PWY, "Sleeping barristers" (2001) 75 *Australian Law Journal* 4.

101 *Cesan v The Queen* (2008) 236 CLR 358.

5 *Judicial Shenanigans*

Judges getting political

The Council of Chief Justices of Australia warns Australian judges that they are expected, on appointment, to sever all ties with political parties as well as any appearance of continuing ties: and that a judge must avoid involvement in political controversy, unless the controversy itself directly affects the operation of the courts, the independence of the judiciary or aspects of the administration of justice.[1] This proclaims a standard that was frequently ignored in earlier times.

It is hardly surprising that judges are, at times, drawn into political controversy. The fate of governments or their policies may turn on the outcome of a case. Governments reversed in high-profile cases have been known, even in modern times, to attack the judges fiercely and at times personally. Both law and politics attract men and women who are themselves comfortable with the exercise of power and experienced in brawling. Until comparatively recently in our legal history, it was very common to have leading lawyers (even judges) moving in and out of politics.

During the time when New South Wales was a penal settlement, the men who held office as (Deputy) Judge-Advocate were closely involved in the politics of Sydney Town, as litigants, judges and participants in political debate or governmental decision-making. Since much of the politics of the day touched upon the institutions of law, their involvement was hardly surprising. Of course, judges did not always line up on the same side of any debate. Thus, Judge-Advocate Wylde sent Commissioner Bigge a rambling representation favouring jury trial. In the other camp, Mr Justice Barron Field "vehemently attacked the emancipist class, drawn as it was from 'the overindulged and vicious mass of transported people' and insisted that the jury be withheld from them. Those persons, he assured the Commissioner, 'can have no such ardent admiration of an institution that has convicted them; it is *trial by convicts* they mean; and then the lion would be the carver'."[2]

1 The Council of Chief Justices of Australia, *Guide to Judicial Conduct (Second Edition)*, 2007, pp 10 and 23.

2 Bennett, *A History of the Supreme Court of New South Wales*, pp 80-1.

In the infant colonies, the Chief Justice was invariably *ex officio* a member of the Governor's Executive Council and (after its establishment) his Legislative Council. In the latter role, the Chief Justice debated, and sometimes drafted and sponsored, legislation. He was also required to certify as to the constitutionality of local enactments. All hell broke loose when the judges of the Supreme Court of Van Diemen's Land (Pedder CJ and Montagu J) ruled against the validity of the *Dog Act* which they had earlier intimated was in order. The story is recounted elsewhere.[3]

During his shortish term of judicial office in Western Australia,[4] Judge McFarland also sat *ex officio* as a member of the Legislative Council. His frequent clashes with other members, including Governor Kennedy who presided, offered great public entertainment. McFarland quit Western Australia after three years and quickly assumed office in the District Court of New South Wales where he spent his considerable energy (when not on the Bench) drafting legislation, proposing law reform, teaching law, fighting public battles and private creditors.[5]

With the advent of responsible government it might have been thought that the judges would retire to the Bench. But for a time in New South Wales three of them exercised an additional role as legislators in a non-elective upper house, with Stephen CJ becoming the first President of the Legislative Council after responsible government in 1856. Their involvement was openly criticised "not without justification as the risk of conflict of interests was considerable".[6] After two years the judges resigned from the Council, Dickinson J first, Stephen CJ and Therry J shortly afterwards. (Stephen would have to wait until he retired from the Bench before returning openly to the political fray as an appointed member of the Legislative Council between 1875 and 1890 where he became embroiled in many good causes, most notably the press for a workable divorce law.)

Thomas Horne was concurrently a judge of the Supreme Court of Tasmania and the elected member for Hobart in the Legislative Council where he was the President. He also took an active role in debates, including strongly opposing the remarriage of divorced persons. When the incongruity of his dual appointments was realised an Act was passed which prevented him from drawing two salaries.[7]

When Richard Hanson became Chief Justice of South Australia in 1861 one of his first duties was to inquire into the validity of local legislation, much

---

3 See pp 114-15.

4 1858-61. McFarland later became a judge of the District Court of New South Wales, serving between 1865 and 1891.

5 See Holt, *A Court Rises*, pp 78-84.

6 JM Bennett & JK McLaughlin, "Sir John Dickinson. Almost a Chief Justice" (1970) 56 *Journal of the Royal Australian Historical Society* 315 at 327.

7 Henry Finlay, *To Have But Not to Hold*, Federation Press, 2005, p 65. Other aspects of Horne's stormy career are discussed at pp 117-18.

of which he had drafted when in politics. One of them was the *Real Property Act* that Hanson had redrafted, believing that Torrens' "clumsy and unprofessional attempt to improve the law" needed some fixing to ensure its validity.[8] Hanson recommended various amendments "not because he considered them necessary but merely to set the minds of people at rest".[9] Hanson's judicial colleague, Boothby J, entertained no doubts about the invalidity of the *Real Property Act* and much else besides. For a time the third judge on the Court, Gwynne J, hovered into Boothby's camp. Ultimately (supported by the explicit terms of s 7 of the *Colonial Laws Validity Act 1865* (Imp)), he too fell in line and upheld validity.[10]

The late 19th century saw the judges getting out of the political frontline,[11] but this did not mean that the politics got out of the judges (or at least some of them). Men do not change character simply because they don a wig and gown in their middle to late years. And very many of the men who went to the Bench in the late 19th and early 20th centuries had spent most of their adult lives on the hustings. At least six Chief Justices from this era were Premiers of their colony before being appointed to judicial office.[12] Many other judges went to the Bench in this era after and because of successful careers as Attorneys-General.[13] The notion that politics might in itself be a disqualifying factor was not even voiced until the late 20th century and it still lacks much currency, beyond the squawks from the Opposition benches accompanying particularly controversial appointments.

I do not imply that all of these men bore the political torch onto the Bench. But some certainly did, most notably George Higinbotham, who was for a time Attorney-General in Victoria before becoming Chief Justice in 1880. Higinbotham carried into his judicial writings strong and as yet unorthodox

---

8 By this time, Torrens himself had ceased to be Premier of South Australia. He had become the member for Cambridge in the United Kingdom Parliament in 1868 but was unable to persuade the British to adopt his system of land title registration.

9 'Hanson, "Sir Richard Davies (1805 1876)", *Australian Dictionary of Biography*, National Centre of Biography, Australian National University, <http://adb.anu.edu.au/biography/hanson-sir-richard-davies-3710/text5821>.

10 See p 119.

11 Although Bevan J's combined roles (about which he complained) as Supreme Court judge and legal adviser to the Administrator of the Northern Territory were aspects of controversies that overwhelmed his judicial career: see p 127 and Mildren, *Big Boss Fella All Same Judge*, pp 39-63.

12 I include among the ex-Premiers Chief Justices Martin (NSW), Hanson (SA), Smith (Tas), Lilley, Griffith (Qld) and Irvine (Vic). Wade J and Bavin J had been Premiers in New South Wales before their appointment to the Bench. Two of the first three justices of the High Court had been colonial Premiers before federation.

13 These included (Alfred) Stephen, Way, Higinbotham, Griffith, Isaacs and Menzies. Nigel Bowen was Attorney-General for the Commonwealth before his appointment as the founding Chief Justice of the Federal Court of Australia. Five justices of the High Court served as federal Attorney-General before their appointment (Isaacs, Higgins, Latham, Barwick and Murphy). Evatt held that office *after* his term on the Court.

views about the relationship between colonial governments and the Home authorities that were still pulling strings through their Governors.[14] At the time of his elevation, he told the Chief Secretary that he considered it his "duty, in [his] judicial capacity as well as personally as a Victorian politician" to uphold Victoria's public law. Five years later, he was writing to a friend stating that "I claim the right of still calling myself a Victorian politician".[15]

In the 20th century, a number of Australian judges have retired from the Bench to become Governors-General, State Governors or the Administrator of the Northern Territory. Isaac Isaacs blazed the way, as it were, given that his appointment as Australia's first native born Governor-General was highly controversial. Chief justices and other judges have also served as Lieutenant-Governor or administrator during the absence of the Governor.

I know of two instances when judges were confronted with determining the validity of their own vice-regal acts. I imply no irregularity given that such acts involved no resort to reserve powers but were the simple function of carrying into effect the advice of Cabinet conveyed through the Executive Council.

In the first case, the judge had the validity of his vice-regal conduct shored up by a controversial later enactment that he would declare (with considerable hesitation, not shared by his colleagues) to be itself valid, thereby putting beyond doubt the legal efficacy of that earlier conduct. In the second case, the judge ruled that his earlier vice-regal conduct was valid, only to be overturned on appeal. As will be seen, both situations occurred in comparatively recent times.

The *Industrial Arbitration (Special Provisions) Act 1984* authorised the government to cancel the registration of a single trade union, the highly combative Builders Labourers' Federation (BLF). The trigger was to be a declaration made by the Governor that the Act applied with respect to the union. According to the New South Wales Government Gazette of 11 January 1985, such a declaration was made by "His Excellency the Governor, with the advice of the Executive Council" on 2 January 1985. In truth (and there is no suggestion of misleading), the vice-regal act was done by the Lieutenant-Governor, Sir Laurence Street.[16] The validity of this administrative act came to be challenged on natural justice grounds. That challenge failed at first instance[17] and the BLF appealed to the New South Wales Court of Appeal. As it happened, the author was at that stage briefed to support the judgment below. Such was the government's confidence in his forensic capacities that (without his knowledge)

14 See *Toy v Musgrove* (1888) 14 VLR 349.

15 Charles Parkinson, "George Higinbotham and Responsible Government in Colonial Victoria" (2001) 25 *Melbourne University Law Review* 181 at 191.

16 This matter has been confirmed by correspondence in 2011 from the Official Secretary and Chief of Staff of the Office of the Governor.

17 *Building Construction Employees and Builders' Labourers Federation of New South Wales v Minister for Industrial Relations* (1985) 1 NSWLR 197.

special legislation was rushed through on the eve of the hearing purporting to put the matter beyond all doubt[18] and stipulating that the parties to the pending appeal should each bear their own costs.

This latter statute was the *Builders Labourers' Federation (Special Provisions) Act 1986*. The focus of the litigation in the Court of Appeal therefore shifted to profound constitutional issues concerning the power of the State Parliament to kill blue eyed babies (and not so blue eyed trade unions). The legislative power to interfere with pending litigation was also challenged. A Bench of five senior judges would rule that the 1986 Act was valid, but for the Chief Justice, Sir Laurence Street, it was a near-run thing.[19]

The author did not emerge with such flying colours in the second vice-regal encounter, one in which the Deputy Commissioner of the Police Service had been removed from office by himself acting as Administrator.[20] In *Commissioner of Police for New South Wales v Jarratt*[21] the author and his colleagues in the New South Wales Court of Appeal upheld the validity of his vice-regal conduct. The Court concluded that Simpson J below had erred when she found that the Deputy Commissioner of the Police Service had been invalidly dismissed. The High Court disagreed and reinstated both the first instance decision and the senior police officer.[22]

There have been several judges who chose to embroil themselves in matters political in ways that they would definitely have disapproved of in lesser mortals and which, by modern standards of judicial ethics, attract armchair censure.[23] Being good at one's profession has never been a universal antidote to double standards and personal failings of the widest variety, oftentimes of the sort visible to colleagues but apparently hidden to oneself. Wherever the line of rectitude for non-involvement is drawn, some judges of note have crossed it. Many of them crossed it voluntarily and publicly, some did so quietly behind the scenes, and some were dragged by force of events beyond their control.

Until late in the 20th century senior judges were apparently untroubled with assuming concurrent executive roles, especially in wartime. Nor did those

---

18 Section 3(2) of the 1986 Act provided that the registration of the union "shall, for all purposes, be taken to have been cancelled on 2 January 1985 by the operation of, and pursuant to" the 1984 Act.

19 See *BLF v Minister for Industrial Relations* (1986) 7 NSWLR 372 at 385-7. When concurring with Kirby P in a later case, Meagher JA teasingly added that he subscribed to the "perhaps surprisingly conventional" views expressed by Kirby P in the *BLF Case*: *Galea v NSW Egg Corporation* (unrep, NSW Court of Appeal, 21 November 1989).

20 See *Constitution Act 1902* (NSW), s 9B.

21 (2003) 59 NSWLR 87. The author's vice-regal role came to everyone's attention (including the forgetful author) early in the appeal hearing but no objection was taken to him continuing to sit.

22 *Jarratt v Commissioner of Police (NSW)* (2005) 224 CLR 44.

23 For a general discussion about this topic, see Laurence Maher, "Tales of the Overt and the Covert: Judges and Politics in Early Cold War Australia" (1993) 21 *Federal Law Review* 151.

whose views were sought hesitate to give confidential advice to Governors-General or Governors about the exercise of reserve powers or other hot political potatoes. Griffith, Dixon, Herring and Barwick were four Chief Justices who did so. By today's standards, such a crossing of the constitutional lines would be scandalous. In part, this is because so much more of political life is now viewed as potentially justiciable. Nowadays, too, we are more prepared to attack our tallest poppies for their double standards and much more likely to find out about them. But it is just another of many illustrations of how some things have changed between "Then and Now".

In 1863 Lutwyche J published in the Brisbane *Courier* an address to electors inviting them to vote against the Herbert Ministry, denouncing it as "despotism cloaked in responsible government". An uproar ensued with Parliament entertaining a motion to establish a select committee to prepare his removal from office. This was abandoned only after Cockle CJ secured from his colleague a written undertaking to refrain from further public comment during his term of office. Both letters were published in the *Courier*.[24]

Towards the end of his term of office "Lilley CJ's public utterances on political questions showed that the enforced detachment of judicial life was becoming irksome to him, and he was increasingly tempted to influence the course of political events".[25] His views advocating an Australian republic and decrying the Imperial connexion particularly angered those of a conservative bent.

Sir Samuel Way became Chief Justice of South Australia in 1876 after a career at the Bar culminating in the office of Advocate-General (then the local equivalent of Attorney-General). He would hold the chief justiceship until his death in 1914. In the 1890s South Australia came out strongly in favour of federation. Way went way beyond exercising his vote at the various referendums. He made a last minute direct intervention, sending the British government a secret memorandum which urged the retention of appeals to the Privy Council for all matters. His membership of the Privy Council did not justify such an intervention at this critical point in our national history, particularly on the topic most likely to stall the final step in the constitutional process in London. According to Alex Castles and Michael Harris,[26] it is possible that:

> [Way] may not really have understood how inappropriate was his action, given an unshakeable belief in his own rectitude and an inflated view of his capacity to know better than others, even though his view conflicted with the combined opinions of some of the best minds in the country as expressed in the final draft of the Constitution.

---

24 McPherson, *Supreme Court of Queensland*, p 38.

25 McPherson, *ibid*, p 190, refers to statements on federation, republicanism, workers' rights etc.

26 *Lawmakers and Wayward Whigs*, p 237.

In his push to clip the future High Court's wings in this manner, Way anticipated the attitude he would come to adopt after that Court was set up under Griffith CJ to sit in judgment over Way's own Supreme Court. Way considered Griffith "narrow as well as cold" and he refused a justiceship under him when Prime Minister Deakin offered it in 1906. Officially, Way wrote to the Prime Minister that the prospect of "long and frequent journeys and absences from home" was an important bar to taking up the appointment. More candidly, he told friends that he did not want to forego the roles of Lieutenant-Governor and university chancellor in Adelaide. He also had no wish "to tramp about the continent as a subordinate member of the itinerant tribunal".[27]

The controversies surrounding Frank Tennison Brennan's appointment to the Queensland Supreme Court have been discussed elsewhere.[28] After his arrival, Brennan brawled frequently with the Fourth Estate. He commenced his judicial career as Northern Judge by warning the press of the Court's powers over contempt. On another occasion he denied court room press facilities to the *Rockhampton Bulletin* because of what he considered to be misreporting. In 1945 he publicly condemned the Soviet Union, embroiling him in heated altercation with Barrister FW Paterson MLA and the communist press. They had disinterred complaints about the judge's conduct in a Labor Party pre-selection case in 1926, in which Brennan from the Bench advised the plaintiff how to overcome a problem with *locus standi* and then adjourned the proceedings to enable the plaintiff to do so before ruling in his favour. Over the ensuing days mutual recriminations followed as verbal blows were exchanged, Brennan denouncing Paterson from the Bench and Paterson denouncing Brennan in the press, daring him to prosecute for contempt. During these public exchanges of discourtesies Paterson branded Brennan a 'third-rate lawyer" and Brennan branded Paterson a "callous liar".[29]

Parts of Sir John Latham's dissent in the *Communist Party Case* read more like an historical diatribe than a piece of judicial reasoning.[30] When Attorney-General for the Commonwealth in the Bruce and Lyons governments, Latham had introduced *Crimes Act* provisions designed to suppress the Communist Party of Australia as a revolutionary organisation. After his appointment as Chief Justice he gave much confidential advice to Menzies, Casey and other ministers in conservative administrations.[31] None of these matters disqualified him from sitting on the case. However, the language of his dissent indicated that he had passed the line between having an open and an empty mind on the key issues with which the High Court was confronted. Zelman Cowen

---

27 *Ibid*, p 331.

28 See pp 70-1.

29 See McPherson, *Supreme Court of Queensland*, p 330; Maher, *op cit*, pp 159-66.

30 See *Australian Communist Party v Commonwealth* (1951) 83 CLR 1.

31 Fiona Wheeler, "Sir John Latham's Extra-Judicial Advising" (2011) 35 *MULR* 651.

described Latham's reasoning as "almost incredulous"[32]. The long diatribe of self-elevating judicial rhetoric poses a series of dichotomies, choices between right and wrong, action and inaction, fighting or retreating, subversion or survival of the Commonwealth, as if the answers were self-evident. "According to Latham, the 1950 Act was valid because the Government had to be absolutely free to make such obvious choices if the Commonwealth was to survive."[33] The idea that one had no choice but to be for or against communism mirrored the political rhetoric of the Menzies government, but it told nothing about whether a proportionate legislated response might suffice, let alone anything about the constitutionality of the Act before the Court.

Latham was satisfied that his "Court may ... allow itself to be sufficiently informed of affairs to be aware that any peace which now [in 1951] exists is uneasy and is considered by many informed people to be very precarious".[34] But history would prove him wrong. And the sharp divisions within the Australian community about the response to communism show that he was no more in a position to take judicial notice of what he believed than the Menzies government was entitled to recite itself into using the defence power in the way that it had done in the 1950 Act. The striking down of the 1950 Act was an amazing vindication of the rule of law in Australia. And the rejection of Menzies' 1951 referendum proposal on the topic showed the confidence of Australian democracy. It also aided Menzies in keeping the communist bogey in play throughout the 1950s to great political effect.

Herring CJ made several extra-judicial interventions in favour of conservative political interests, including a Remembrance Day speech as part of a Menzies-government led *Call to the Nation*. While it is difficult to get inside the mood of the times, one can see at this distance that he "was at the centre of a conservative campaign hatched in secret and deliberately aimed at whipping up widespread community measures to combat the supposed evils of Communism".[35] Herring also declined to make EA (Ted) Laurie a QC despite his eminence at the Bar and his large constitutional and industrial law practice. Laurie was a communist.[36] In so acting, he may have been no more a man of his times sitting towards the extremity of a political spectrum, just as Justice Jim Staples, discussed below, erred on his side of the fence.

32 Zelman Cowen, *Sir John Latham and Other Papers*, Oxford University Press, 1965, p 43.

33 Maher, *op cit*, p 179. Maher discusses Latham's rhetorical dichotomies at pp 178-83.

34 (1951) 83 CLR 1 at 155.

35 Maher, *op cit*, p 188.

36 Laurie represented the Communist Party in the *Communist Party Case*. Silk was granted soon after Herring retired and was replaced by Sir Henry Winneke as Chief Justice. Winneke also remedied Herring's refusal to appoint Joan Rosanove as Victoria's first female silk: see Robert Coleman, *Above Renown. The Biography of Sir Henry Winneke*, Macmillan, 1968, p 295.

Justice Jim Staples exhausted the goodwill of his Chief Justice and his judicial colleagues on the Conciliation and Arbitration Commission when he publicly attacked the legislation under which they functioned. He also set his own opinions above the appellate structure of the Commission. He was a deputy president of this peak federal body, joining it shortly before the Dismissal of 1975. Staples was well read, outspoken and of decidedly leftist views, none of which qualities were themselves disqualifying for the office to which he was appointed. But he also lacked the essential qualities of tact, discipline and even-handedness. And he was not a team-player. He spoke publicly on a range of social and political issues "often alienating politicians and powerful figures in the business community, and sometimes the unions".[37] The President of the Commission, Sir John Moore, had a quiet word in his ear reminding him that he was a judge and not a political agitator but this failed to have the desired effect.

Staples' manner of handling a maritime dispute involving the Broken Hill Proprietary Company Ltd (BHP) as employer saw him removed from the relevant panel by the President. He had castigated BHP's application to transfer the proceedings to a Full Bench for review.[38] Moore removed Staples from the maritime industry panel considering that his impartiality was compromised. When Staples returned from a 12-month "study tour" that had been arranged by the incoming conservative government, he found that he had been allocated no work at all. The legality of this contentious step by the President was never tested. However, by 1979 Staples was again allocated a full panel of industries.

Staples then came into conflict with the Fraser government when his letter attacking proposed amendments to the *Conciliation and Arbitration Act* was leaked to the press. There were other incidents, including a controversial speech defending his decision to award a wage rise to wool store workers despite it having been overturned on appeal. In the speech, he criticised the Full Bench and laid the blame on the employers of the country and, by implication, on the legislation that created the guidelines under which the Full Bench had acted. He asserted that "[t]he employers of this country have been reduced to cowardice by the guidelines and the government, a state of ignobility which fortifies, however, their material interest".[39] A letter signed by eight deputy presidents[40] was delivered to the President. It condemned Staples' conduct of publicly criticising his own Commission, describing his speech as "an unprecedented breach of a fundamental convention [that] threatens the appeal structure in the Commission and the standing of Full Bench decisions".[41]

37 Burton, *From Moree to Mabo*, p 152.
38 (1975) 171 CAR 711 esp at 723-4.
39 (1980) 22(3) *Journal of Industrial Relations* 354.
40 There were 14 deputy presidents at the time.
41 Burton, *From Moree to Mabo*, p 170.

President Moore informed Staples that he had lost the confidence of his colleagues and that he would henceforth be confined to Full Bench duties. Staples' colleague and previous supporter, Mary Gaudron, while adhering to the sentiments of the joint letter, wrote privately to the President expressing disappointment about the decision to deprive Staples of his panel responsibilities and announcing her own resignation from the Commission.[42] Staples continued in office, without much to do, until the Commission was itself disbanded in 1988. All other judicial members were appointed to the successor Commission, but Staples was not. He was thereby forcibly retired, on a full judicial pension.

For some modern judges, political activity confines itself to entirely uncontroversial topics like supporting or opposing an Australian republic, a Bill of Rights, the ordination of women as priests, the preservation of the environment or attacking the judicial activism of fellow judges.

The Hon Michael McHugh AC once described Gummow J as "a great judicial politician", putting the remark into context by observing that he "always had three votes". By contrast, McHugh said of his former colleague Kirby J that "he never did any alliance building. His work methods excluded it".[43]

Ghostwriting

Lawyers are not the only literary species who have published anonymously. Authorship can be suppressed for many reasons. The quality of the product may be doubtful. Even if it is not (at least, in the author's eyes) its linkage to the author may be embarrassing. Or the author may believe that a thing of quality may still cause personal embarrassment, or worse, if connected with the author.

Shortly after he was moved to Port Phillip in 1841, Willis J formed a close relationship with the editor of the *Port Phillip Patriot*. The Sydney-based judges of the Supreme Court of New South Wales suspected Willis of writing articles for the paper disparaging their decisions.[44]

During the time that he was a judge in Port Phillip, William a'Beckett contributed poems to the *Port Phillip Herald* under the pseudonym "Malwyn" until the *Argus* revealed his identity.[45] In 1862 the 16-year-old Samuel Griffith, who attended Parliament regularly, wrote 25 articles on local politics for the

42 She would return to the private Bar for a short period before being appointed Solicitor-General for New South Wales. She served in that office with conspicuous distinction and, in 1987, became the first woman to be appointed to the High Court.

43 David Marr, "Now History will be the judge" *Sydney Morning Herald*, 31 January 2009.

44 McLaren, *Dewigged, Bothered and Bewildered*, pp 182-3. Willis certainly disparaged his brethren in open court: see pp 116-17.

45 JM Bennett, *Sir William a'Beckett, First Chief Justice of Victoria 1852-1857*, Federation Press, 2001, pp 92, 122.

Queensland Guardian, using the pen name *Charley Chalk*. Griffith's biographer remarks on the effrontery of the tone and content of these articles.[46] Griffith sketched the member for Warwick, JG Jones, referring to his "downright stupidity ... egregious vanity, unfinished gentility, garrulous inanity, mock dignity". He also published a long, amusing poem on the dispute between the Queensland government and Alfred Lutwyche, the first judge of the Queensland Supreme Court.[47] Griffith considered Lutwyche's judicial power to be oppressive, and wrote of "the easy way in which the Judge appears to twist every member of the Queensland bar around his finger".[48]

Lutwyche was not beneath some ghostwriting of his own. The *Moreton Bay Courier* published an anonymous article supporting his right to express radical views. This spurred the Attorney-General to launch a seditious libel prosecution against the publisher. In his capacity as a judge, Lutwyche acquitted the *Courier*. It was widely believed at the time that the article had been largely written by Lutwyche himself.[49] Sir Alfred Stephen wrote anonymously to the press, expressing his liberal views on divorce at a time when controversy on the subject was raging.[50] The youthful exploits (under the *nom de plume* "Vie Manquee") of Frank Gavan Duffy have already been discussed.[51]

Sir Owen Dixon's exploits are probably the most infamous instances of ghostwriting on the job. They reveal one of the complex contradictions in this most human of jurists as well as toleration for something in one era that would, if exposed, lead to public censure (if not dismissal) in another. In *R v Brislan; Ex parte Williams*[52] Dixon J dissented on the issue whether the Commonwealth Parliament had power to regulate radio broadcasting, but this did not prevent him from helping his judicial brother, Rich J, compose his non-dissenting judgment in the case "like a debater momentarily changing sides".[53] This type of assistance is excusable, even commendable, assuming that Rich's writer's block was holding up the disposition of the case. But it was not an isolated instance, because Dixon's diaries reveal him regularly helping Rich with his judgments (even when Dixon had not sat on the case).[54]

46 Roger B Joyce, *Samuel Walker Griffith*, University of Queensland Press, 1984, p 12.

47 See generally pp 73-4.

48 *Queensland Guardian*, 18 January 1862.

49 Gregory, *The Queensland Law Society Inc*, p 12; McPherson, *Supreme Court of Queensland*, p 32.

50 Bennett, *A History of the Supreme Court of New South Wales*, p 149.

51 See pp 34-5.

52 (1935) 54 CLR 262.

53 Ayres, *Owen Dixon*, p 73.

54 Blackshield et al, *Oxford Companion to the High Court of Australia*, "Dixon Diaries", p 223. According to Dixon's biographer, the practice of ghostwriting for Rich commenced from the outset: Ayres, *Owen Dixon*, p 57 ("One of Dixon's first judgments for the High Court was written for a case on which he had not even sat").

In *Sun Newspapers Ltd v Federal Commissioner of Taxation*[55] Rich J sat at first instance. Dixon recorded in his diary that had had spent all day working on Rich's judgment only finishing it at 2.15 am. It was therefore hardly surprising that an appeal to the Full Court (on which Dixon sat) was dismissed. Dixon's judgment in the Full Court is unlikely to have been subcontracted back to Rich.

However, Rich's own role in another matter (as recorded in Dixon's diary) was misconduct of an entirely different order. If true, it was quite scandalous. Justice "Sammy" Clyne was the Federal Judge in Bankruptcy and a close friend of both Dixon and Rich. *Isaacs v McKinnon*[56] was an appeal from Clyne himself to the High Court. The Court dismissed the appeal with Dixon in lone dissent. While judgment stood reserved, Latham told Dixon that he had been convinced by Rich's draft. This would have been unusual given Rich J's general reputation within the Court, but Dixon was incensed because he had good reason to believe that Clyne himself had written Rich's judgment. Dixon's plea for Latham to list the matter for re-argument fell upon deaf ears.[57]

Dixon's diary also reveals that he penned McTiernan J's closely reasoned recantation on the scope of s 92 of the Constitution in *Hughes and Vale Pty Ltd v New South Wales (No 2)*.[58]

I was told the following story by the late Hon Athol Moffitt QC. Herbert Vere Evatt was already displaying signs of mental imbalance by the time he was appointed Chief Justice of New South Wales.[59] He once sat in an appeal in a work injury case with Herron J and Owen J each of whom circulated a draft judgment in favour of the employer not long after the appeal was argued. Evatt had indicated to his brethren that he favoured the worker, but he long delayed preparing any reasons. Owen J eventually offered to write the dissenting reasons for him, with the proposed conclusion favouring the worker. In the course of this exercise Owen J convinced himself that the worker should win and switched his own vote and the result of the appeal.

Ghostwriting of a different sort occurs when a judge borrows an unattributed slab from another person's judgment or a legal textbook. In recent years a Federal Court judge and a federal magistrate attracted criticism for what would have been plagiarism in an academic community. Their reasons for judgment included substantial unattributed "cut and paste" borrowings from legal texts (not of their own authorship).

Sometimes judges have been embroiled in trouble because of a *false* attribution of authorship. In 1856, while he was still a barrister, Alfred Lutwyche sued John Fairfax for libel. The claim was based on an anonymous report in the

---

55 (1938) 61 CLR 337.

56 (1949) 80 CLR 502.

57 Ayres, *Owen Dixon*, pp 191-2.

58 (1955) 93 CLR 127 at 183. See pp 246-7.

59 See further p 63.

Sydney Morning Herald alleging that he was the author of a piece in another newspaper that reflected on Australian women. Although the *Herald* published Lutwyche's rebuttal he sued for libel but recovered only £2 damages.

In 1851 a Presbyterian minister, the Revd Dr James Fullerton, was acquitted on a charge of having illegally solemnised a marriage. The issue was whether the officiant had duly inquired whether the bride was of lawful age. The *Sydney Morning Herald* criticised the governing law as a "miserable patchwork" that needed reform. It expressed pleasure that Fullerton had escaped conviction and described his prosecution as "one of the most melancholy spectacles that our Courts of Justice have ever presented". *The Press* was a short-lived newspaper that had been launched by the Presbyterian firebrand, the Revd John Dunmore Lang, who had clashed with the Chief Justice, Sir Alfred Stephen, on a number of occasions. John Clayton who was the editor and publisher of *The Press* was convinced that Stephen himself had written the *Sydney Morning Herald* article. He published in *The Press* an article entitled "The Honour and Charity of Political Judges". This depicted the *Herald* article as emanating 'from the pen of a Puseyite Political Judge" who, "occasionally, when he forgets, or does not get the opportunity of indulging his abuse by spewing forth his prejudiced verbiage from the bench, takes to the pen and evacuates his spleen". Among other unpleasant things, the article asked "were political Judges ever known to be honest?".

Instead of hailing the editor for contempt before the Supreme Court, the Chief Justice commenced a private prosecution for criminal libel. At the committal proceedings Stephen appeared in person as both prosecutor and leading witness. He called John Fairfax, one of the proprietors of the *Sydney Morning Herald*, to testify that he, Stephen, was not the author of the editorial about Fullerton. And he went into the witness box on the issue of identification, stating on oath his reasons for believing he was the "Puseyite Political Judge" referred to. Stephen deposed that his judicial colleagues on the Supreme Court were Mr Justice Therry, a Roman Catholic, and Mr Justice Dickinson, who had taken no part in the Church of England in the colony. Stephen's commitment to the Church of England was well known, meaning that he must be the judge defamed. In his biography of Stephen, Dr Bennett further records:[60]

> In resisting the further imputation that he could not look an honest man in the face, Stephen gave an interesting account of his own demeanour on the Bench. It was:
>
> > 'my common habit of either looking at a paper from which I read my notes, or shutting my eyes or looking upwards in order to prevent distraction of my thoughts. These peculiarities in my manner do not apply to either of the other Judges.'

60 Bennett, *Sir Alfred Stephen*, p 181. This work is the source of the earlier stages of the matter recounted above.

In light of this evidence, counsel for the defendant, James Martin (who would himself become Chief Justice of New South Wales some years later) then conceded that the article referred to Stephen and that it was libellous. Clayton was committed for trial. He later pleaded guilty and, despite Stephen's letter to the court urging that the matter be taken no further, was sentenced to one month's imprisonment by Dickinson J.

Trouble in post-retirement activities

Some judges have returned to successful practice at the Bar after retiring from the Bench. The 19th century saw at least Salomons, Wrenfordsley and Rogers doing so. It has become relatively commonplace since then, although judicial pension schemes in some jurisdictions and professional ethical restrictions on appearing before one's own former court for a period[61] may be added to the usual barriers to re-entry. Former judges can expect to have, at least, the advantage of a clean claims record when taking out professional indemnity insurance. Dr Evatt returned to appear before his old Court in the *Bank Nationalisation Case*. He was untroubled by any of these modern problems, but (for a number of reasons) encountered a very hostile reception.[62] (Justices Evatt and Piddington were the only two persons to appear as barristers in the High Court both before and after their term of office there.)

Other senior judges have suffered the embarrassment of having their post-retirement conduct as arbitrators, mediators and royal commissioners set aside for misconduct or bias and severely criticised by much younger jurists.

In 1988 the former Reynolds JA suffered the indignity of being removed as a court-appointed referee (27 days into the hearing) for words and conduct that conveyed to a fair-minded observer that he had strongly adverse views about the plaintiff's case and of the credit of a key witness.[63] Reynolds had always demonstrated a "vigorous" style on the Bench, in keeping with the standards of the Court of Appeal of his era. He may have assumed that such behaviour would be tolerated in other venues.

In *Carruthers v Connolly*[64] Thomas J ruled that there was "overwhelming evidence of ostensible bias" on the part of his erstwhile senior judicial colleague. "Mr Connolly" was a former judge of the Supreme Court of Queensland who was appointed to a Commission of Inquiry into the Criminal Justice Commission of Queensland and the conduct there of the Honourable KJ Carruthers QC

61 The validity of the professional ethical restrictions must be doubtful, but they have never been tested.

62 See Marr, *Barwick*, pp 63-7.

63 *Pimas Constructions Pty Ltd v Metropolitan Waste Disposal Authority* (unrep, NSW Supreme Court, Brownie J, 4 August 1988).

64 [1998] 1 Qd R 339.

(himself a former judge of the Supreme Court of New South Wales). Thomas J's stinging assessment that found actual bias in everything but name culminated in the following summary:[65]

> When all the relevant factors are brought into account I venture to think that there is overwhelming evidence of ostensible bias against Mr Connolly with respect to matters that his Commission had to consider. The picture would include all of the following perceptions in the mind of a fair-minded and informed member of the public: that shortly before the Commission was set up, Mr Connolly had given an opinion to Mr Cooper concerning the Memorandum of Understanding such that Mr Connolly's view might be thought to be that the Carruthers Inquiry (still running) was a waste of time and money; his acceptance of the Commission to investigate the conduct of the CJC in circumstances where his former client Mr Cooper was sorely aggrieved by the CJC's conduct; his publicly insulting Mr Carruthers; his public reinforcement of his opinions; his expression of political alignment while the Commission was current; his participation in hearing, with a view to making final recommendations based thereon, numerous politically driven and politically sensitive complaints that the CJC was favouring one side of politics; his difficulty in effectively fencing himself off from what was called the "Inquiry into the Carruthers Inquiry"; his conduct of hearings in a manner apparently more supportive of witnesses adverse to the CJC than those favourable to it; his frequent display of rancour, without apparent cause, against the CJC and those representing it; his willingness to participate in determining the validity of complaints such as the two complaints of Mr Beanland and at least to some extent the wide-ranging complaints of his former client Mr Cooper and other politically contentious issues; his uneven conduct in relation to the important issue of alleged impropriety by Mr Le Grand including a refusal to receive evidence that would support Mr Le Grand's defence; and finally, the consistency of the above pattern and of the direction in which all these matters point.

Later in the reasons Thomas said that the facts included a perception of the Commission's "continuing favour for one side of politics".[66]

65 *Ibid* at 374.
66 *Ibid* at 393.

6 *Judges: The Good, the Bad and the Sacked*

Tenure for judges

In Australia judges are appointed by the government, which takes collective responsibility to parliament and the people for the wisdom of its choices. Judges in turn enjoy tenure "during good behaviour",[1] which means that they can expect to outlast the government that appointed them. At times there have been unfortunate appointments because care was not taken in the selection process.[2] Sometimes the most careful choices have disappointed both the appointors and the public interest. Sometimes highly competent judges buckle under the impact of illness, aging, family or financial troubles.

As will appear, a handful of delinquent judges were dismissed or threatened with dismissal by colonial Governors reliant on *Burke's Act of 1782*.[3] This statute ended the practice of colonial appointments that permitted the office holder to auction the deputyship to the highest bidder and stay put in London. Henceforth, offices had to be exercised in person and during good behaviour. The colonial Governor was empowered to "amove" for misbehaviour or wilful absence without cause, subject to a right of appeal to the Privy Council. The Crown (in London) retained a parallel right to remove at pleasure except in relation to offices given statutory tenure.

Jeffrey Hart Bent was removed by the authorities in London in 1816. Three later colonial Supreme Court judges were dismissed locally under *Burke's Act*: Willis, Montagu and Boothby. Willis' amoval by Governor Gipps was set aside by the Privy Council, on the ground of denial of natural justice, but he did

---

1 This is the modern translation of the British *Act of Settlement of 1701* guarantee "*quamdiu se bene gesserint*" that is found in most jurisdictions. In the Commonwealth and New South Wales judges may be removed upon address by Parliament on the ground of "proved misbehaviour or incapacity".

2 Taking care and leaving a record of it can create its own difficulties, as Prime Minister Hughes discovered in his selection of Albert Piddington for the High Court: see pp 85-6.

3 22 Geo III c 75. In 1896 it was given the short title of the *Colonial Leave of Absence Act 1782*. The Act remained on the English statute book until 1964. Its status as regards Australian colonies (and later, States) both before and after 1964 is a very nice constitutional question (see Selway QC, *The Constitution of South Australia*, p 122) with the answer possibly varying from jurisdiction to jurisdiction.

not return to New South Wales for the hearing to which he would have been entitled. Instead, he went off to be appointed a judge in another colony, only to be dismissed a second time for further misconduct.

Perceiving contested amovals to be a growth industry, the Privy Council published in 1869 a Memorandum outlining procedures, including a process for suspension pending amoval or confirmation of amoval.[4] But this came just when the quality of appointments to the Supreme Court benches turned upwards. There appears to have been no further use of the procedure in this country although it looked for a time that the Privy Council might in the 1890s get involved in determining the fate of the Chief Justice of Western Australia, Alexander Onslow. No one dreamed of using *Burke's Act* after the 19th century.

After attaining responsible government the colonial parliaments followed English law on the tenure of Supreme Court judges, providing that they were removable for misbehaviour, but only on address of both Houses of Parliament.[5] Judges of inferior courts and magistrates did not enjoy similar protection until it was conferred (in some places) by late 20th century legislation. For example, when District Courts were established in New South Wales in 1858, their judges would hold office during ability and good behaviour, subject to liability to removal by the Governor in Council after being given the opportunity of being heard in their defence.

On 8 January 1878 the Victorian Government Gazette announced the dismissal of all persons holding office as judges of County Courts, magistrates, coroners and numerous other public servants. This event, known as "Black Wednesday", was a culmination of a prolonged struggle between the two Houses of Parliament that drained the government of money. The Full Court held (Stawell CJ dissenting) that each judge held his office at pleasure of the Governor-in-Council and was liable to be removed without cause assigned.[6] After several conferences between the Houses some, but not all, of the dismissed judges and magistrates were re-appointed, with pensions and compensation being later paid to those who were not. Judge Lewis refused reinstatement because the government declined to pass legislation giving County Court judges the tenure of their Supreme Court brethren. He returned to the Bar and is believed to have been one of a handful of persons to have taken silk *after* being appointed to full-time positions on the Bench.[7]

Stipendiary magistrates were regarded primarily as civil servants until well into the 20th century. When the Attorney-General for New South Wales, Henry

4 See *Memorandum of the Lords of the Council on the Removal of Colonial Judges* (1869) 6 Moo PC (NS) 9, 16 ER 827.

5 See generally Selway, *The Constitution of South Australia*, p 122.

6 *R v Rogers; Ex parte Lewis* (1878) 4 VLR (L) 334.

7 Another was Henry Wrenfordsley (below, p 123) who took silk in 1889, "a recognition he ill deserved" (JM Bennett, *Sir Henry Wrenfordsley, Second Chief Justice of Western Australia*, Federation Press, 2004, p 92). For others, see pp 140-1.

Manning KC, represented the Commonwealth before a New South Wales stipendiary magistrate at one stage of the Kisch proceedings,[8] Kisch's counsel Piddington had a backward swipe at him (at least according to Justice Nicholas Hasluck's semi-fictional account):[9]

> Unlike the conduct of counsel for the Crown who stands before you as the state Attorney-General. Your employer, sir! He claims to be relieved of the conflict of interest because he holds a Brief from the federal government.

New South Wales gave tenure to its magistrates in 1982.[10] But some were thought unworthy of this status and simply not appointed to the new Local Court. This generated litigation that went to the High Court twice.[11]

The good and the bad

In 1999 Gleeson CJ opined that Jeffrey Hart Bent was probably Australia's worst judge, followed by Willis J. This prompted Justice Peter Young, the editor of the *Australian Law Journal*, to call for nominations for the third spot, promising to publish the results by the beginning of the following year.[12] For "self-protection and ... reasons connected with the defamation laws" he confined eligible nominations to the already deceased. Sadly, nothing was heard again of the project. A later piece from the editor reported a judicial popularity poll conducted by *Justinian*, a legal gossip magazine that is less concerned about defamation of the living than the *Australian Law Journal*. Young J disclosed that he and some (unnamed) colleagues had the distinction of being on both *Justinian's* list of the best judges and its list of the worst judges in Australia.[13]

It would be hard to overlook the following in any list of Australia's worst judges.[14]

Jeffrey Hart Bent

Jeffrey Hart Bent, whose brother Ellis Bent had served as Judge-Advocate, was a judge of the Supreme Court of Civil Judicature of New South Wales that was created by Letters Patent in 1814. His going out (from England) and his coming in (to New South Wales) presaged much of what was to follow.

---

8 *R v Wilson; Ex parte Kisch* (1934) 52 CLR 234 at 238.

9 Nicholas Hasluck, *Our Man K*, Penguin Books, 1999, p 328.

10 *Local Courts Act 1982* (NSW).

11 *Macrae v Attorney-General (NSW)* (1987) 9 NSWLR 268 (special leave to appeal to the High Court was refused); *Attorney-General (NSW) v Quin* (1990) 170 CLR 1.

12 (1999) 73 *Australian Law Journal* 469.

13 (1999) 73 *Australian Law Journal* 855.

14 See the recently published McLaren, *Dewigged, Bothered and Bewildered*, for further information particularly about the Bent brothers, Montagu, Willis and Boothby.

Bent quarrelled with the Colonial Secretary, Lord Bathurst, about not receiving a knighthood before he set sail. On arrival in the Colony, he refused to land or proceed to Government House unless and until greeted with a formal salute. He declined to open his Court for over four months because no fitting venue had been provided for it in Sydney. Bent used his leisure time to write denunciatory letters home about the Governor. The new Court House was ready by the end of 1814, but this time Bent's excuse for inaction was because the two attorneys he had nominated to migrate to New South Wales, Moore and Garling, had not yet arrived. Bent would have no truck with convict attorneys, including Crossley on whom the Governor relied extensively.[15]

Then, for some undisclosed reason, Bent decided to open his Supreme Court on 1 May 1815. As required by the Letters Patent, the Governor nominated two magistrates to complete the Court's composition. The fact that the two could vote against the judge, leaving him with a right of protest and an inside running if there were an appeal to the Governor's Court, set the scene for the storms that quickly followed. The magistrates ruled that fairness to litigants dictated that "convict attorneys" should be admitted to practise, at least pending Garling's arrival. Bent was furious that, as "a barrister of near ten years' standing", he should be outvoted by the magistrates. He insulted them grossly and refrained from taking his seat rather than be faced with a majority decision against his views. The Supreme Court remained closed although the judge continued to draw his salary.

The next big fight involved the port regulations. Ellis Bent had previously approved them. Now, with brother Jeffrey in town, he took the opposite view when asked to check the technicalities of a revised set. He claimed that most of the rules were unnecessary and some were illegal. Despite being required to obey Macquarie's orders, Ellis refused to budge, supported to the hilt by Jeffrey. Macquarie told Lord Bathurst that he would have to choose between him or the Bent brothers. In January 1816 Bathurst decided to remove both of the judges. They seemed, he wrote, "too much disposed to resent the authority of the Governor and to withhold from him that cordial co-operation without which the business of the colony could not be satisfied". Bathurst based his dismissal of Jeffrey on the latter's closing of his court. Although sympathetic to the problem of convict attorneys, the Colonial Secretary viewed the suspension of justice as the more serious evil.

Ellis Bent died before he got notice of his dismissal. Jeffrey used the time to wreak further havoc on Macquarie's initiatives. He helped draft a petition to the House of Commons craving relief from the Governor's "oppressions". Then, in a remarkable turnaround, Bent announced that he would open his Supreme Court, despite having by then received notice of dismissal from London. Macquarie countered with the cancellation of the appointments of

15 See further pp 129-30 for the struggle on this matter.

the two accompanying magistrates, declining to appoint others in their stead. Bent issued a warrant for the arrest of one of the magistrates and then sought to attach (ie imprison) the Provost-Marshall when he refused to execute the warrant. Finally, Macquarie issued a Government Order which declared Bent to be "positively and absolutely removed from his appointment" and proclaimed that he had "no jurisdiction or authority whatever in" the colony, forbidding him "at his peril ... to assume or exercise" any such authority.

Bent returned to England intent on securing Macquarie's recall and another judicial appointment. He even floated the idea that he might replace Macquarie as Governor. This offer was ignored along with any other proposal involving his return to the colony. Was this the end of the line? No way. Such was the quality control for colonial judges that Bent secured appointment to an impending vacancy in the chief justiceship of Grenada in 1819! Assured of this post, he tarried in England for another 12 months in the hope that he might pick up something more attractive in India. Failing in this endeavour, he repaired to the West Indies where his conduct matched the standards he had set in New South Wales.[16]

Alexander Macduff Baxter

Alexander Macduff Baxter was close enough to being a judge, and certainly bad enough, to merit inclusion in this rogues' gallery. A Scottish-born barrister admitted in Lincoln's Inn in 1819, he was nominated for the post of Attorney-General in New South Wales in 1826. He married a Spanish heiress and set sail for Sydney. Within two months after his arrival, Governor Darling was reporting to the Colonial Office that "Dandy" Baxter had never had a brief in his life, was totally inexperienced as a lawyer, incapable of addressing either court or jury, and helpless against Robert Wardell and William Charles Wentworth whose effrontery and talent kept the Court and Bar in subjection.[17] Baxter leaned heavily on his Solicitor-General and, at times, left it to the Chief Justice and the Colonial Secretary to draft bills for the Legislative Council.

In spite of, perhaps because of, Darling's laments, Baxter was nominated for the post of second judge in Van Diemen's Land. When confirmation reached New South Wales, he tendered his resignation as Attorney-General. He also walked out on his wife and took refuge under the *Insolvency Act* about the same time. On his arrival at Hobart Town, Lieutenant-Governor Arthur "found him in a high state of neurotic excitement and such an habitual sot that it would have been a violation of all public decency to have suffered him to take his seat on the Bench". Baxter sailed back to Sydney. Then he returned to Van Diemen's

---

16 See McLaren, *Dewigged, Bothered and Bewildered*, pp 235-44.

17 "Baxter, Alexander Macduff (1798–1836)", Australian Dictionary of Biography, National Centre of Biography, Australian National University, <http://adb.anu.edu.au/biography/baxter-alexander-macduff-1756/text1955>.

Land, presenting his credentials along with a request for leave of absence with advance of salary so that he could go off to London to recoup his health and rebut Darling's charges against him. Arthur welcomed the chance to be rid of him even at the cost of the salary advance. He nevertheless took the precaution of entrusting the money to Daniel Cooper, a Sydney merchant, who sailed with Baxter from Hobart Town.

In May 1832, the Hobart Town newspapers announced that Baxter had died on the voyage. But, to adopt Mark Twain's words, these reports were "greatly exaggerated". In fact, Baxter was back in London claiming that ill health had prevented him from taking judicial office, and seeking appointment in some other colony. He spent over a year in Marshalsea prison for debt in 1832-33 and died in about 1836 without returning to Australia.

Algernon Montagu

Algernon Montagu[18] was appointed Attorney-General for Van Diemen's Land in 1828, thereby outraging the youthful Alfred Stephen. Stephen as Solicitor-General had acted in the position and had three years' seniority to Montagu at the English Bar. The two men took an instant dislike to each other. They were unable to agree on key matters of constitutional law advice. To add salt to the wound, Montagu kept proposing to return to England, but not doing so. Each of these combative worthies was in his 20s at the time.

At the tail of Lieutenant-Governor Arthur's term of office, a dispute erupted between the two men that could easily have ruined both their careers. In 1833 Montagu had been appointed the puisne judge of the Supreme Court, joining Pedder CJ. This made way for Stephen to become Attorney-General, but his long apprenticeship appeared to have rendered him both imperious and fractious. Stephen provoked the Bench by habitually appearing late in court, often without his silk gown, and by eating sandwiches at the Bar table during trials. There were also disputes about his right as Attorney-General to act as the exclusive filter for instituting and prosecuting serious criminal matters.

The stage was set for a huge brawl with Montagu, a spat described by Professor AGL Shaw as a "childish but complicated dispute between ... two opinionated, forensic fighting-cocks".[19] Childish maybe, but Montagu's outburst ranks as one of the most virulent attacks ever made on a Crown Law Officer in open court. In July 1836 the judge called a trial on for hearing, not caring that it originated from an *ex officio* indictment which Stephen was not yet ready to have tried. Arriving late (as usual), and finding the matter already

18 See generally L Robson, *A History of Tasmania*, vol 1, pp 468-72; McLaren, *Dewigged, Bothered and Bewildered*, pp 160-170. For a generally sympathetic portrait, see BA Keon-Cohen, "Mad Judge Montagu: A Misnomer?" (1975) 2 *Monash University Law Review* 50.

19 AGL Shaw, *Sir George Arthur, Bart*, Melbourne University Press, 1980, p 175.

in progress, Stephen protested that the discretion, when to proceed with an *ex officio* indictment, rested solely with him. The enraged Montagu responded:[20]

> Mr Attorney-General, your conduct throughout has been most unwarrantable: I come here today, and the jury are here, and we find the prosecutor is not ready to try the case, and why? – no reason is given, but that it does not suit the royal pleasure of His Majesty's Attorney-General that the trial should take place today ... really, Sir, I cannot imagine anything more monstrous ... Sir, in your official capacity I shall always treat you with the courtesy and respect due to you. Were you elsewhere I should treat you after your conduct with even less courtesy than a dog or a cur as your conduct richly deserves. I say this, Sir, as an English gentleman, and only as such.

In the jury's presence, Montagu went on to accuse Stephen of insulting the court, of treating judge and jury with "such indignity as I have never before witnessed in any Court of Justice" and of committing a gross contempt. The accused was a solicitor charged with libel who was an associate of Montagu. After further diversions involving Stephen, the trial got underway. The jury found the defendant guilty.

The enraged Stephen then called on Lieutenant-Governor Arthur to take action against "Mr Montagu". The judge responded with 76 pages of justification and 22 pages charging Stephen with professional misconduct. The British authorities were dragged into the unsavoury affair by the despairing Lieutenant-Governor. (His own despatch spanned 82 double-sided pages.) The Colonial Office eventually reprimanded both Stephen and Montagu, visiting greater blame on the judge.

Montagu was constantly in financial troubles, but the Lieutenant-Governor constantly refused him leave of absence. In 1841 Montagu made a deal with the Attorney-General, Edward MacDowell, to swap jobs so that he could boost his income by taking briefs. Lieutenant-Governor Franklin refused to go along, not out of principle but because of his lower opinion of the Attorney-General.

In 1847 the autocratic Lieutenant-Governor Denison got into a serious spat with both of his judges, Pedder CJ and Montagu J. They had ruled that a law for dog licences imposed taxation and was therefore invalid because it did not apply the money to a nominated appropriation.[21] Denison signalled to the Colonial Office his intention to dismiss the judges for failing to bend to his will and accept the alternative view of the constitutional point favoured by his Attorney-General. Fortunately for the rule of law, the Colonial Office thought that it would be a poor precedent to remove a judge for an honest opinion on a legal point. But the Office was happy to see the back of Montagu, whose dismissal would be based on a firmer ground. This was the incompatibility of

---

20 Bennett, *Sir Alfred Stephen*, pp 84-5. These and the following pages are the source of the summary that follows.

21 See Castles, *Lawless Harvests*, pp 198-9.

continuing to hold judicial office while ruling as a member of the Court that his own creditors could not sue in that Court! Montagu's indebtedness dogged him to the last minute: when boarding his ship he was halted by legal process issued by his butcher whom he owed £60. His application to the Executive Council to pay the debt and allow him to leave was declined, but a private subscription, to which the Lieutenant-Governor himself donated £20, enabled him to depart the colony.[22] The Privy Council rejected Montagu's appeal.[23] Montagu would be replaced by Thomas Horne who turned out to be little better, as we shall see.[24]

In 1894, long after he had retired as Chief Justice of New South Wales, Sir Alfred Stephen penned a remarkable document called *A Trio of Judges*. He described three instances of "Judicial Delinquency or Incompetency ... occurring in my own time, and affecting vitally the interest of suitors, as well as my own tranquillity and position, terminating in my retirement from the Bench". Each was an instance of "a character so flagrant, that I am astounded at the recollection of such men having been permitted to continue in office so long". Stephen's remarks about "Judge Montagu" and "Judge Willis"[25] descended into no greater detail than recording that:[26]

> after a mischievous and unworthy career extending over many years, [the careers of these two] ended by the removal of both Judges from the Bench by the Governor and Executive Council: confirmed in each case by the Privy Council on appeal.

John Walpole Willis

John Walpole Willis,[27] a member of the Chancery Bar in London and the author of two legal text books, was appointed a judge in Upper Canada in 1827. He was dismissed from that office the following year for failure to attend to his duties. In reality, he had fallen foul of the local Attorney-General. His appeal to the Privy Council was rejected, but Willis was given a second chance by the incoming Secretary of State, Lord Goderich. He was appointed a judge in British Guiana. There he quarrelled with everybody and was pipped in his ambition to become Chief Justice, with the Colonial Office favouring Jeffrey Hart Bent! Returning to England in 1836, he was appointed to the Supreme Court of New

22 Keon-Cohen, *op cit*, pp 76-7.

23 *Montagu v Lieutenant-Governor and Executive Council of Van Diemen's Land* (1849) 6 Moo PC 489, 13 ER 773.

24 See p 117.

25 Willis' career is discussed immediately below.

26 As indicated below, Stephen was in error as regards Willis. Although the Privy Council ruled that the Governor had power to amove Willis and the facts gave sufficient grounds for amoval, the order was invalid and set aside because of want of procedural fairness: see *Willis v Gipps* (1846) 5 Moo PC 379, 13 ER 536.

27 See generally McLaren, *Dewigged, Bothered and Bewildered*, pp 170-89.

South Wales the following year. Willis' stay in British Guiana badly affected his health and this provides limited explanation for his continuing unpleasantness.

In Australia he continued his obstructive behaviour on several fronts. Dowling CJ found it impossible to live in amity with him despite considerable efforts to do so. "I am a peaceable person", he wrote, "but even a lamb will flinch from the knife". Dowling wrote to his son in 1838 describing Willis as:[28]

> a fidgety restless conceited self-opinionated fellow and it requires a good deal of forebearance and caution on my part to go smoothly with him. Some people have the opinion that he is cracked.

In 1839, Willis "in a spirit of kindness and friendship" invited his Chief Justice to resign on the basis that the latter's appointment was invalid. The English law officers disagreed. Willis published a contrary opinion by his friend Serjeant Merewether and he pressed for the matter to be resolved by a Bench of 15 English judges entertaining a test appeal from any conviction previously pronounced by Dowling in the Vice-Admiralty Court.

A short time later Willis was sitting with Dowling CJ and Stephen J in *Walker v Hughes*, an action for damages for breach of contract to sell a sheep station. Willis J, in dissent, considered that a provision that would have permitted the purchaser temporary use of the vendor's convict shepherds vitiated the contract because it purported to recognise a practice akin to slavery.[29] To the astonishment of all in court, and to a wider public thereafter, Willis announced:[30]

> I believe the His Honour Chief Justice Dowling has been and is the assignee of the services of very many convicts, or transported offenders ... I have ever considered the provision of His Majesty's Orders in Council ... to be most wise in prohibiting the judges from being the owners or in any wise interested in slaves, or their labour ... I will never permit the possibility of insinuation, that my private interest can in any wise interfere with the honest discharge of my judicial duties.

Willis' quarrelsome attitude saw him relocated to the Resident Judgeship at Port Phillip in 1841. Dowling wrote to his son: "The detestable Willis is going tomorrow to Port Phillip ... where I pray he may stick and that I may never see his face again".[31] According to Sir Arthur Dean (writing about Willis in Port Phillip):[32]

> Willis, despite his legal ability, soon proved to be unfitted for judicial office. It is easy to apply derogatory epithets to him. He was vain and

28 Bennett, *Sir James Dowling*, p 111.

29 Cf Lord Atkin in *Nokes v Doncaster Amalgamated Collieries Ltd* [1940] AC 1014 at 1026.

30 Bennett, *Sir James Dowling*, p 116.

31 Letter to son James, 14 February 1841, quoted in Forbes, *Divided Legal Profession*, p 74.

32 *A Multitude of Counsellors*, p 12.

> conceited, quick-tempered and quarrelsome, vindictive in action and violent in language. He quarrelled with all those with whom he had to do: the Bar, the attorneys, parties, witnesses and the press. Well-known and respected citizens, such as Mr JB Were, were committed for contempt of Court. The administration of justice suffered from Willis's eccentricities. In his Court one day he made some offensive remarks to Croke who bowed and left the Court, followed by the other barristers present.

On receipt of a judgment of the Full Court reversing him, Willis read it aloud in Court adding derogatory remarks and ridicule for those who were parties to it.[33] This was too much for the authorities, and on 24 June 1843 Governor Gipps amoved him from office. Willis appealed to the Privy Council, choosing not to serve the process on the Governor. Perhaps this was a tit for tat for Gipps' own denial of natural justice when he dismissed the judge without a hearing.[34] The appeal dragged on until 1846 when the Privy Council held that there had been good reasons for Willis' suspension and that the Governor had power to act as he did, were it not for the fact that procedural fairness was denied since Willis should have been heard in his own defence.[35] By this stage, Willis had gone to London in high dudgeon (never to return), but the success meant that he received his arrears of salary.

Some doubt was felt about whether the appointment of Willis' successor, during the period of the suspension, was invalid. In consequence, all death sentences during the period of uncertainty were commuted to imprisonment for life.

Thomas Horne

Thomas Horne was a Supreme Court judge in Tasmania in the mid-19th century. Due to his constant financial difficulties and Governor Grey's preference for the Attorney-General Valentine Fleming, Horne was passed over when Fleming was appointed Chief Justice in 1854. For a period Horne held concurrently the offices of Supreme Court judge and (elected) member (and President of) the Legislative Council.[36] In 1860 he was attacked in the Legislative Council in light of the judgment of Molesworth ACJ in Victoria in the case of *Horne v Gilles* which found that Horne and his cousin had exerted undue influence

33 For another instance of judicial recalcitrance towards appellate correction, see *Baxter v Commissioner of Taxation (NSW)* (1907) 4 CLR 1087 at 1099.

34 This was no mere oversight. According to Forde, *The Story of the Bar of Victoria*, p 95, Gipps wrote to Sir Roger Therry stating: "Had the law officers advised me to give Mr Willis a hearing before the Executive Council – or, in other words, to bring him up to Sydney, and, in fact, try him before the Executive Council – I would not have followed the advice".

35 See *Willis v Gipps* (1846) 5 Moo PC 379, 13 ER 536.

36 When the incongruity of his dual appointments was perceived, an Act was passed which prevented him from drawing two salaries.

on the cousin's father in the execution of his will. (An appeal was later upheld, clearing Horne of any fault but imprudence.) In the meantime, a litigant named Solomon had come forward alleging that, while a plaintiff before Horne J, he had been approached by the judge for a loan of £500 which he had refused. To prevent his amoval, Horne resigned.

Benjamin Boothby

Benjamin Boothby was appointed a judge of the Supreme Court of South Australia in 1853. He was the last such judge to be appointed by the Colonial Office in London and, as we shall see, he placed great store on the fact that his commission was issued by Queen Victoria under royal warrant.

One of the many extreme positions he adopted was that his fellow judges in South Australia were legal usurpers because they were "mere attorneys" whose appointments by the Governor of the colony were invalid. When Richard Davies Hanson presented his commission as Chief Justice at a formal sitting, in the presence of Boothby J and Gwynne J who had also been appointed locally in 1859, Boothby, in the language of the official record, "made objection thereto that the same had no legal validity and is void and of no effect, as being contrary to law". Gwynne joined his new chief in ruling in favour of Hanson (and inferentially himself), but such majority determinations carried no weight with Boothby who continued to take formal objection to the validity of his two colleagues' commissions.[37] In open court, he referred to them as "unlawful Judges", "assumed Judges" and "those who call themselves my colleagues, but have no more right to the name than you who stand upon the floor of the Court".[38]

Boothby took a related point about the Attorney-General of the colony, arguing that because he had not been admitted as a barrister in England, Ireland or Scotland, his appointment was invalid. This led Boothby, in 1866, to discharge all the prisoners in the Criminal Court on the ground that the informations against them were not signed by a (real) Attorney-General. Since no appeal lay from this order, several prisoners walked free, to the consternation of the public and Boothby's judicial colleagues.

Boothby also declared invalid many statutes passed in South Australia, including the *Real Property Act*, the *Registration of Deeds Act* and the

---

37 Since judges of all people should follow the law, the problem of a judge who carries a dissent beyond the original case is a particularly serious challenge to the rule of law. It is one thing for a judge bound by a precedent of his or her own or a higher court to keep on saying that the majority are wrong, it is another to decide a case on that basis. See generally Keith Mason, "The Rule of Law" in Paul Finn (ed), *Essays on Law and Government, Vol 1, Principles and Values*, LBC Information Services, 1995, pp 136-9. See also *CSR Ltd v Bouwhuis* (1991) 7 NSWCCR 223 at 243 (Samuels JA).

38 Hannan, *The Life of Chief Justice Way*, pp 65-6, quoting from Way's summing up in Boothby's amoval proceedings.

legislation confirming the Governor in Council as the Court of Appeals in South Australia.[39] For a time, Boothby's views about the capacity of the local legislature to repeal or vary English common law were tentatively shared by one of his fellow judges, Gwynne J. But after the *Colonial Laws Validity Act 1865* was passed by the Imperial Parliament Boothby J found himself in a minority on the Full Court in having any remaining concerns about validity. But, as a Queensland taxi driver once proudly remarked about his beloved Premier Joe Bjelke-Petersen, Boothby's endearing quality was that he stuck to his guns even when he was wrong. He continued to attack the validity of the local appointments of his fellow judges and to speak publicly and privately against the validity of legislation passed by the South Australian Parliament.

The reporter of the 1867 *South Australian Law Reports* recorded the impasse within the Court in these terse observations:[40]

> His Honour Mr Justice Boothby ... uniformly declined to recognise or take part in any proceedings under 'The Equity Act, 1866.' His Honour refused to give effect to that Act as law on the ground principally that it was *ultra vires* and illegal, as professing to introduce a new practice in Equity which varied in many respects from the English practice, and as repealing prior colonial legislation on the same subject, which his Honour contended had the force of an Imperial statute within the province. His Honour had further stated that he could not recognise his colleagues as Judges legally appointed; and objected to all proceedings which came before him tested in the name of the Chief Justice, on the ground that there was no lawful holder of that office, and that the colonial Parliament had no power to confer that title upon any one. It would be very difficult and is unnecessary here to set out his Honour's reasons at any length, – they were constantly repeated; and whatever weight may have been due to them, the practical result was that the business of the Court – both in Equity and Common Law – was brought to a stand-still.

In 1867 Hanson CJ appears to have called Boothby's bluff by sitting all three judges in a run of the mill equity case, *England v Coulthard*.[41] Hanson CJ, Boothby J and Gwynne J heard the arguments of counsel and reserved judgment. The following day, Gwynne J announced the reasons of himself and the Chief Justice, disposing of the issues in the proceedings and stating that the plaintiff should have the decree sought, leaving to the defendant any advantage she might have under the Statute of Limitations to be made available before the Master on inquiry. Gwynne J observed that "as things exist we are peculiarly situated, and we think that is the best order at present". The reporter added by way of footnote to this remark the commentary set out above.

39 This was a court of superior status to Boothby's own Supreme Court and Boothby stuck to his guns even when overruled on the point by that superior tribunal.

40 (1867) SALR 9 at 11.

41 (1867) SALR 9.

The law report abbreviated Boothby's lengthy reasons for dissent as follows:

> Boothby J was of opinion that, on the merits of the case, the plaintiff was not entitled to the decree asked for. He dissented from the judgment of the Court, on other grounds.

The three judges convened the Court the following day, when the following events occurred. The Chief Justice read this statement on behalf of himself and Gwynne J:

> After the rising of the Court yesterday, I conferred with my learned colleague Mr Justice Gwynne as to the course which it was expedient for us to adopt in view of the line of conduct of His Honour the Second Judge. We both felt that a repetition of such proceedings as marked the sittings of the Court yesterday and Friday could not but lower the dignity of this Court, and weaken the confidence of suitors and the public in the administration of justice; and at the same time we felt that, however painful – and in some sense degrading – such scenes might be, we must be prepared to encounter them if no means could be devised for the purpose of preventing their recurrence. We have had already under our notice a representation, addressed by some members of the profession to the Hon the Attorney-General, calling his attention to the necessity of taking some steps to enable the Court to exercise more satisfactorily its Equity jurisdiction; and we had invited His Honour the Second Judge to meet us for the purpose of considering the reply that we should give to that communication. It seemed therefore to us that the same opportunity might be taken of bringing under his notice the effects of the mode which he had adopted of enforcing his peculiar views – in the hope that something might be agreed upon to prevent the time of the Court and the Bar being wasted, and the respect due to this Court being diminished or destroyed. Until such an attempt is made, it, however, appears to us inexpedient to continue the sittings of the Court, and they will therefore be adjourned until the first day of Term.

Boothby J announced:

> I dissent from that order, and I shall still continue to sit here as the Full Court.

The Chief Justice then directed the Master to adjourn the Court and he and Gwynne J left the Bench. Boothby J stayed in his seat, then inviting the three barristers seated at the Bar table, one by one, to make an application. Each declined to do so and Boothby J solemnly directed the Master to record this. The Master was also directed to record that Boothby J himself was adjourning the Court until the first day of Term. Waiting until this was read over to him, Boothby then left the Court.

This was the final straw. Following a letter from the Chief Justice and Gwynne J, proceedings for the "amoval" of Boothby were instituted by the Attorney-General. Boothby's fellow judges gave evidence against him at what must have been a very sad and uncomfortable event at Government House.[42] Boothby attended accompanied by his son. He made no attempt to contradict the overwhelming evidence tendered, his defence really being that the Governor in Executive Council had no jurisdiction to try him. He was dismissed for misbehaviour, with all five charges proffered against him being found established. He lodged an appeal to the Privy Council but died before it could be prosecuted to completion.

John Fletcher Hargrave

In his early years at the English Bar, Hargrave suffered from mental illness, probably through overwork.[43] His wife, who was his cousin, committed him to an asylum, for which he never forgave her nor womankind in general. When he recovered his health and moved to Sydney she accompanied him, but he could not bear her presence in his house, and she eventually returned to England.

After practising in Sydney, Hargrave became a judge of the New South Wales District Court and Chairman of Quarter Sessions. He resigned after 14 days in order to enter politics. Later he became Solicitor-General and Attorney-General in various short-lived administrations during the early days of responsible government.

Hargrave was appointed to the Supreme Court of New South Wales at the same time in June 1865 that Judge Cheeke was elevated from the District Court. At the swearing-in ceremony all chairs at the Bar table were empty. Only two barristers were present, one of them sitting robed with the attorneys, the other being in mufti. The press criticised the boycott and suggested that it had been organised by RM Isaacs and P Faucett, who considered that they had been passed over. In Hargrave's case, the appointment was a clearly political one: it so enraged the Attorney-General (JB Darvall) that he immediately resigned and returned to England.[44]

Hargrave was a judge of the Supreme Court between 1865 and 1881. His prickly, uncooperative nature so outraged his aging Chief Justice, Sir Alfred Stephen, as to persuade him to bring down the curtains on his record term of 29 years in that office. Stephen devoted most of his unpublished *Trio of Judges* to a lament about Hargrave in the following terms, never once identifying him by name:

> I select here the most recent example, with sorrow rather than anger. I believe that the unhappy individual had nothing really spiteful or

42 See Hannan, *The Life of Chief Justice Way*, ch 4.

43 Among other things he edited a new edition of *Blackstone's Commentaries* and produced a commentary on the *Thellusson Act*.

44 According to Dr Bennett, Darvall was upset that Hargrave and Cheeke were raised to the Supreme Court over his head: JM Bennett, "Of Silks and Serjeants" (1978) 52 *Australian Law Journal* 264 at 271.

> malevolent about him, but was simply incapable of seeing things and subjects – where they crossed his own painful impressions – in any light but the one which lunacy presented to his view. It is true that he has said many rude things to me, and that (so far as I know and believe) he rarely, if ever, failed to express a different opinion judicially from my own, whatever the question. Verses were commonly in circulation at the time, ending with the lines "No matter what the case may be, I differ from the Chief". A notable instance of the former class was his reply to my request, on one occasion, that he would meet me in Chambers to consider the draft of an outstanding Judgment. He told his Associate that it would be useless for him to attend; as he could never understand my Judgments.
>
> But the most painful example of the Judge's mental obliquity was his habit of deciding against married women in any application of theirs before him ... The Judge's painful history is, that having unhinged his mind by incessant laborious study, he was placed by his wife, after the usual necessary examinations, in the Lunatic Asylum at Colney Hatch, where he remained some years. He then came to this Colony; and was, I know not on whose recommendation, appointed Lecturer on Law at the University. A year or two afterwards he was selected by the then Prime Minister to be his Attorney General ... [T]he Judge's elevation to the Bench ... [an] event disastrous for women suitors, and some others, took place in June 1865, on the lamented death of Mr Justice Milford. The meditated appointment had been denounced by Sir James Martin, in his place in Parliament, and afterwards by Sir James William Macleay. But the reins of power were then in hands of iron. The fiat had gone forth, and remonstrance was idle.
>
> I now resume the Judicial history. The unfortunate gentleman never believed that he had been rightly placed under restraint, but was the victim of either a conspiracy, or of his wife's culpable mistake, not to be forgiven. Hence he seem to have thought ill of, if not to have hated, all women, for her sake ... He looked with suspicion, apparently, on all medical certificates imputing lunacy to any one; and he occasionally scrutinized them with care. On one occasion, having received from the patient perfectly sensible answers, it is said that he discharged the man – saying "You may go; you are as sane as I am" – It would have been well, had all his utterances been equally harmless ...

Historians are divided as to the complete accuracy of this assessment.[45] Any unpublished rant needs to be kept in perspective and this was the untested testimony of a deeply involved witness, himself in his 91st year. Hargrave's judicial conduct was unbalanced, and its replication towards Stephen's successor showed that it was not the personal vendetta that Stephen observed. Nevertheless, there is a lot of evidence that Hargrave had a real bias against female litigants and that he was peculiarly unsuited to have been made the

45 For an alternative view to that of Stephen, see Holt, *A Court Rises*, pp 45-6.

colony's first Divorce Judge. In Dr Bennett's assessment, Hargrave's responsibility for divorce matters was "so inappropriate that it smacked of jest".[46]

Henry Thomas Wrenfordsley

Henry Wrenfordsley became Chief Justice of Western Australia in 1880. He had failed in law and politics in England, but he had powerful political connections whose faith in him never waned throughout his career as a wandering colonial judge. According to his biographer,[47] "whatever his position, and wherever he occupied it, his career from beginning to end was disgraceful". Wrenfordsley's "undistinguished career was driven by ambition, self-interest, contempt for the duties of office, and surmounting all by the quest for an easy living". He made so many moves – to Western Australia, Fiji, Tasmania, Victoria, a second term in Western Australia and finally to the Leeward Islands – that he got the name of the "journeyman judge, who carries his robes in a carpet bag".

Wrenfordsley served as Chief Justice of Western Australia until 1883 when the Colonial Office despatched him to Fiji. Despite his obvious shortcomings, the colonists in the west were desperate enough to entice him back to act in the position in 1890-91 when Onslow CJ took 12 months' leave of absence whilst his own future hung under a cloud.[48]

Frederick William Meymott

Frederick Meymott became a barrister in London in 1847. Being completely at home in the musical and literary life of mid-century London and an intimate friend of celebrities such as Dickens and Thackeray,[49] his reasons for choosing Sydney over London in 1850 are obscure. He served for a time as a Crown Prosecutor before being appointed a judge of the District Court for the Southern Highlands in 1863. A brush with the bushranger Hall did nothing to make him a lenient sentencer.

Meymott moved to the Northern District in 1865. As the years went by he became increasingly autocratic, drawing criticism from the citizenry of Grafton and the press. A petition complaining of his conduct in 1873 was not taken up. But in 1876 Meymott was called upon by the Executive Council to show cause why he should not be removed from office because of neglect of duty,

46 Bennett, *A History of the Supreme Court of New South Wales*, p 148.

47 Dr JM Bennett, *Sir Henry Wrenfordsley, Second Chief Justice of Western Australia 1880-1883*, Federation Press, 2004. The second quotation is from Dr Bennett's biography of Wrenfordsley's predecessor, *Sir Archibald Burt, First Chief Justice of Western Australia 1861-1879*, Federation Press, 2002, p 115. For an example of Wrenfordsley's judicial work, and the rebuke he received from the Privy Council, see *Sherwood v Thomas* (1883) 9 App Cas 142.

48 See p 126.

49 Holt, *A Court Rises*, p 73.

particularly for not proceeding to Grafton in proper time to hold Quarter Sessions there. In the meantime he was suspended.[50]

Meymott attended and addressed the Executive Council. But the Council was dissatisfied with his explanations and admonished him as to his future conduct. The amount of £126 paid to an Acting District Court judge was to be deducted from his salary as the expenses incurred in his neglect of duty. Meymott then sued the government for his full salary. The Crown's defence was that he had not in fact rendered his services as a judge so as to entitle him to any more than he had been paid. A majority of the Supreme Court (Martin CJ and Faucett J) held that it was not open to the government to choose the milder penalty of reduction of salary instead of dismissal. Hargrave J characteristically dissented.[51]

Meymott's conduct on the Bench got worse. He bullied and insulted jurors and displayed partiality in his dealings with offenders. He was attacked in parliament by the Attorney-General and responded by writing to the *Murrurundi Times* and the *Sydney Morning Herald* denying the allegations and challenging the Attorney-General to repeat them outside the privilege of parliament. This only strengthened the resolve of his accusers. Charges were drawn up alleging particularly that the judge was influenced in his verdicts by presents of valuable horses and other inducements. A barrister was then appointed to inquire into the judge's conduct. His report exonerated the judge from the allegations of bribery, corruption and unscrupulousness. But its other findings discredited Meymott. The Minister for Justice gave the Executive Council his opinion that the judge had been guilty of misbehaviour, including repeated and unjustified rudeness to practitioners as well as improper interference with juries by putting pressure on them to find particular verdicts and berating the jurors whose verdict he disapproved of.[52] Meymott addressed the Executive Council disputing the charges, but the Council resolved to remove him from office.

Joshua Frey Josephson

Joshua Josephson was a judge of the District Court of New South Wales in the late 19th century[53] who was subjected to a complaint about his pre-judicial conduct. He had been Solicitor-General during the short-lived Robertson Ministry of 1868-69. Judge Cary's resignation from the Bench on medical grounds created the vacancy that Josephson filled in August 1869. Indeed, Cary

---

50 At that time, District Court judges in New South Wales could be removed by the Executive Council, subject to the dictates of natural justice. It was not until the passing of the *Judicial Officers Act 1986* that they and magistrates in that State were given tenure equivalent to Supreme Court judges.

51 *Meymott v Piddington* (1877) Knox 306.

52 Holt, *A Court Rises*, p 77.

53 He held judicial office between 1869 and 1884: see generally Holt, *A Court Rises*, pp 87-92.

would die in Josephson's chambers the following year, but not before making allegations against his successor that the resignation had been procured by Josephson by a promise of public employment for Cary's son and a secret monetary payment. The matter was investigated by the Attorney-General WM Manning. The former allegation was withdrawn by Cary and formally dismissed. But the Attorney reported that:

> [Josephson had] succeeded in mitigating but not in removing the charge of having, by a secret payment of £240, induced or precipitated Mr Cary's resignation, in the expectation of becoming his immediate successor.

The Colonial Secretary, Cowper, wrote to Josephson in March 1870 that, although he was not chargeable with any intentional moral wrong or deliberate offence against public interests, yet "you cannot be acquitted of great imprudence and indiscretion, in having, while occupying the position of Solicitor-General, and being at the same time a member of Cabinet, become a party to the negotiations of the character above described". The matter was allowed to stand as a reprimand, and the judge was instructed to resume his duties on the Bench.

A more serious episode occurred in 1873 when a barrister named Belifante petitioned the Governor in Council to inquire into the legality of a number of Josephson's decisions. Belifante then applied to the Supreme Court for an order calling on the judge to show cause why criminal proceedings should not be commenced against him for misdemeanours in office. The barrister's allegations of habitual rudeness and bias towards him were denied by the judge, supported by 15 affidavits from jurymen, attorneys and others. The Court held that there was no evidence of malice or corruption on the part of the judge. But Stephen CJ remarked that Josephson had been "exceedingly wrong in some if not all the decisions mentioned". This prompted Belifante to present a second petition to the Governor in Council. The Attorney-General, Edward Butler, intervened to provide lukewarm support for the embattled judge. Lukewarm, because he endorsed the Court's view of Josephson's decisions, finding "a singular want of ordinary legal knowledge betrayed by him and a singular propensity to decide upon flippant and flimsy technicalities".

These assaults would have driven many from the Bench but Josephson continued in his official duties until 1884, doubtless labouring under a most distressing cloud.

William Henry Abbott Hirst

William Hirst was a police magistrate, then a Crown prosecutor, before his appointment as a District Court judge in Queensland. He was a Judge of the Northern District between 1869 and 1876 and of the Central District between

20 November 1876 and 5 January 1878 when his removal from office by the Governor, with the advice of the Executive Council, was gazetted.[54]

Hirst had fine-honed the practice of evading his financial obligations. He dishonoured cheques frequently. Many judgments were entered against him by default (although in his letter of defence addressed to the Governor he asserted that he had not been served or, if served, that he had been led to believe that judgment would not be entered on certain circumstances). On several occasions the debt recovery process issued out of the Court in the very District to which he had been appointed.

Controversial suspensions and dismissals

Alexander Campbell Onslow

Alexander Campbell Onslow was the Chief Justice of Western Australia between 1883 and 1901. Relations with Governor Broome soured after Onslow unwisely showed Attorney-General Hensman a letter in which Broome made critical comment about Hensman. The Governor had objected when Hensman appeared for a private party in a libel case.[55]

When the Governor requested the Chief Justice's advice on appeals for the remission of sentences handed down by the Supreme Court, Onslow returned the documents without comment in the belief that Colonial Office practice required him to do so. He held back some of the papers awaiting guidance from the Colonial Office despite Broome's request for their return.

When the Chief Justice wrote letters to the press disclosing parts of the contents of a confidential Colonial Office despatch Broome forbade the judge to exercise his office. That night a noisy mob burnt the Governor's effigy. *The West Australian* sided with the Governor, due no doubt to the antipathy that existed between its proprietor Winthrop Hackett and Onslow over passages of arms during recent libel trials. The Executive Council also supported the Governor in his decision to suspend the Chief Justice. However, the Colonial Office ordered that Onslow should resume his position, contenting itself with a reprimand for his disclosure of confidential information. He returned to the Bench on 14 May 1888, receiving a formal address of congratulation from leading members of the Bar.[56]

---

54 This summary is drawn from PV Loewenthal, "Judicial Inability or Misbehaviour" (1973) 8 *University of Queensland Law Journal* 151. See also Beanland, *A Court Apart*, pp 46-8.

55 On another occasion the Governor told Hensman that "as for your volunteered opinion, Mr Attorney on my policy, I don't care a snap of the fingers for it". One is reminded of the line in the *G I Jane* movie where the Master Sergeant told the recruit that "when I want your opinion I will give it to you".

56 This account of Onslow's suspension is taken from Bolton and Byrne, *May it Please Your Honour*, pp 78-83.

David Bevan

Bevan was the first permanent "Judge of the Northern Territory", appointed to the recently established Supreme Court of the Territory in 1912. His commission also required him to act as the legal adviser to the Administrator and to draft Ordinances. His closeness to the unpopular Administrator, Dr John Gilruth, carried the seeds of the trouble that followed although it must be said in his defence that Darwin was a very small town in the early 20th century. Relations between the administration and the Amalgamated Workers Association became increasingly bitter and the judge put himself in the crossfire. He did not help matters when, in 1915, he personally assisted in the unloading of a ship that was subject to an industrial strike. Led by Harold Nelson, the union would later attack Bevan for his lack of impartiality and his closeness to the administration. A number of strikes just after the close of the war led to ugly riots and criminal charges. In 1919 the Commonwealth government recalled the Administrator. A public meeting of enraged unionists called for Bevan and two other men in senior administrative positions (Carey and Evans) to leave town, threatening force if necessary. The three were forced to sail from Darwin (leaving their wives behind) in order to quell an incipient rebellion.

A Royal Commission was set up to inquire into the matter, under Ewing J, a judge of the Supreme Court of Tasmania. Historians consider that its report was hasty and in the words of Kriewaldt J[57] "a shoddy piece of work". There were findings against Bevan, the most serious of them being his silent support for a long-standing practice of locking up Aboriginal witnesses in Fannie Bay Gaol pending their being called to give evidence. On 30 September 1920, the Commonwealth terminated the appointments of Bevan and the two other (non-judicial) public servants. This was despite the absence of any recommendation to that effect by the Royal Commissioner let alone any charge being laid or discussion in Parliament. The three men brought actions for wrongful dismissal and for allowances until dismissal. The only case to go to trial, in the High Court, was *Carey v Commonwealth* where the plaintiff failed in the claim for wrongful dismissal but succeeded in recovering full allowances despite having left the Territory.[58] The Commonwealth then settled the claims by Evans and Bevan. Bevan was paid £2800 plus costs, a most substantial sum at the time, but he did not return to legal practice. Mildren J, whose history of the Supreme Court of the Northern Territory, engagingly titled *Big Boss Fella All Same Judge*, tells this story in much greater detail, concludes that:[59]

> Bevan no doubt was very unlucky. Remoteness, isolation, lack of accommodation, a bad decision to require him to act as legal adviser to Gilruth, wartime stringencies, Nelson's ambitions and sheer

---

57 A judge of the Northern Territory Supreme Court in the 1950s.

58 (1921) 30 CLR 132.

59 Page 63.

incompetence by others all played a part in his demise, as did his own inexperience.

Angelo Vasta

In 1988 three retired judges (Sir Harry Gibbs, Sir George Lush and the Hon Michael Helsham) were appointed by the Queensland government to inquire into matters concerning a Supreme Court Judge and a District Court judge. The Commission was authorised to range far and wide and it certainly did so, a matter of some controversy. It formed the opinion that several matters warranted Vasta J's removal from office.[60] These included the giving of false evidence, making and maintaining of allegations that the Chief Justice, Attorney-General and Mr Fitzgerald QC had conspired to injure him, and serious tax irregularities. The outcome was that the judge was removed from office under s 16 of the *Constitution Act 1867* (Qld). He was earlier permitted to address the Legislative Assembly from outside the Bar of the House.

60 *First Report of the Parliamentary Judges Commission of Inquiry*, 12 May 1989, para 12.

7 *Lawyers with Attitude*

Lawyers' beginnings in Australia

Between 1788 and 1815 there were no accredited lawyers in private practice in Australia. Convict lawyers would just have to do. Ellis Bent, who presided over the New South Wales Judge-Advocate's Court from 1810 to 1814, allowed three former English attorneys, the convicts Eager, Chartres and Crossley, to appear before him as a matter of necessity. But Ellis's more censorious brother, Jeffery, refused to countenance convict practitioners when he arrived as the judge of the first Supreme Court in 1814.[1] In consequence, his Court remained closed until 1815, when his intransigence persuaded the Home government to send qualified lawyers to the colony (and to sack the two Bent brothers).[2]

Two English attorneys, Moore and Garling, were originally permitted to function both as barristers and solicitors when they commenced practice in 1815. They became the first practitioners re-admitted and enrolled in New South Wales in 1824 under clause 10 of the Third Charter of Justice (1823) which contemplated a single class of lawyer in its reference to qualified persons admitted "to act as well in the character of barristers and advocates as of proctors, attornies and solicitors".[3]

The first man electing enrolment solely as a barrister was the unpleasant, incompetent Saxe Bannister who became the original Attorney-General for New South Wales. Shortly afterwards, two more English barristers arrived and were admitted on 10 September 1824. They were William Charles Wentworth and Robert Wardell. Immediately upon admission they coolly moved that "the gentlemen at present practising as solicitors and acting as barristers" be henceforth denied audience in the Supreme Court. The case was adjourned to notify the solicitors whose livelihood was affected. When they appeared, they so successfully advocated their own cause that the motion to divide the profession was dismissed. Forbes CJ held that clause 10 was intended to create a single

1 See *Admission of Convict Attornies* [1815] NSWKR 1.

2 See p 111.

3 There was a similar provision in the Charter for Van Diemen's Land. The two Charters expressly forbade those convicted of serious criminal offences from becoming legal practitioners.

body of lawyers who were entitled (though not obliged) to engage in advocacy as well as any other recognised branch of legal practice.

These proved to be the early shots in protracted and bitter engagements. Over the years the causes of fusion (or division) of the profession and of the administration of law and equity were at times intertwined.[4] In each instance, solicitors and lay people concerned about cost generated by division pressed for fusion, whereas the majority of barristers urged separation with arguments based on their specialised knowledge and skills. Economists would understand immediately what was going on. William Charles Wentworth grumbled in correspondence: "Though I have been degraded against my will to a level with the old practitioners in the court here – I will never quietly allow myself to be ousted of the scale of fees to which the higher branch of the profession, to which I really belong, entitles me".[5] As more English barristers arrived in the colony Wentworth enlisted them to the cause.

Forbes CJ was the only judge in town until he was joined in 1825 by John Stephen, and in 1828 by James Dowling. The worm began to turn early as Dowling pressed for things to be done as they were "at Home". It was probably Dowling J who drafted a rule providing for the division of the profession. Twelve "practitioners" opposed it. In 1829 the judges announced that it would be sent to London for Royal Assent. The draft then disappeared into limbo, in all probability because Forbes put it aside. Eventually, after protest from the barrister Wardell, it was sent to London in 1833. By this stage William Westbrooke Burton had arrived in New South Wales to join the Supreme Court.[6] He was an ultra-conservative, fervently believing that the more English customs introduced the better. As a judge he devoted much of his influence towards expunging Forbes' innovations. Royal Assent to the rule dividing the profession was proclaimed in Sydney in 1834.

Solicitors would bide their time, ultimately recognising that legislation trumping rules of court would be necessary to break the monopoly of the barristers and their opposition to the reform of the common law system of judicature and procedure. It would take time. New South Wales solicitors regained right of audience in superior courts in 1892. *Judicature Act* reforms in New South Wales in matters of pleading and the fusion of law and equity would have to wait until 1972.[7] Sadly, there were many who took pride in New South Wales as a legal Jurassic Park and perhaps one or two remain to this day.

The fusion of the profession remained highly controversial in the eastern States until the late 20th century. Victorian barristers would conspire to defeat

---

4 See further pp 174-6.
5 Forbes, *The Divided Legal Profession*, pp 38-9.
6 See further p 72.
7 As to the fusion of law and equity, see further, pp 174-8.

the will of Parliament in the 1890s.[8] As ever, Queensland produced some curious anomalies. Charles Mein was a solicitor and member of the Legislative Council there in the 1870s. He spoke against the Legal Practitioners Bills which made the elevation of solicitors to the Bench possible, even arguing that solicitors were not sufficiently well trained to serve as judges. Mein became Queensland's first solicitor to be appointed to the Supreme Court in 1885, but three years later would provide startling proof of his own parliamentary words.[9]

By contrast, the original judge of the Supreme Court of South Australia (Sir John Jeffcott) admitted the first lawyer there as a barrister, solicitor, attorney and proctor. Ever since, all lawyers in South Australia have been admitted in these compendious terms. In 1955 Christopher Legoe established himself as the founding member of that State's independent Bar, but the profession has remained formally fused. However, the Chief Justice requires applicants for silk to undertake that they will practise at the separate Bar so that they are accessible to all solicitors.

Women lawyers

I know of only one instance of women being permitted to practise law before the 20th century. There was a Lieutenant-Governor's Court with civil jurisdiction in Van Diemen's Land before the establishment of the Supreme Court there in 1824. In those lawless days, a handful of women were permitted to act as "agents" representing parties not all of whom were their (convict) husbands.[10] The standards of the common law were, in practice, difficult to enforce when the other "agents" were themselves convict males.[11] But with this exception, all other attempts by women to practise law were rebuffed on grounds that appear spurious to modern eyes. And, as women and their supporters pressed for change, extreme arguments (often of the slippery-slope variety) were rolled out against them.[12]

The arguments were trooped out in *Re Edith Haynes*[13] in 1904. Miss Haynes sought admission as a legal practitioner in Western Australia, but was

8 See pp 144-5.

9 It was discovered that he had contravened a provision of the *Supreme Court Act* that prohibited a serving judge from receiving any other salary. Mein had retained his commission in the Queensland Defence Force and was also a director of an insurance company. A Bill was rushed into Parliament to validate his appointment and judicial acts. See also p 71 as to the travails in the 1920s of Frank Tennison Brennan, the father of the future Chief Justice of the High Court.

10 Castles, *Lawless Harvests*, pp 69-70.

11 As to the situation in early New South Wales, see p 129.

12 A similar phenomenon has been experienced in the struggle for female ordination in the Anglican Church. One (male) priest, Father Ian Herring, said that it "would be analogous to consecrating a meat pie on the altar of God to ordain a woman".

13 (1904) 6 WALR 209. Miss Haynes was represented by her uncle, Haynes KC.

firmly rebuffed by the Full Court for a scattergun of unconvincing and circular reasons. According to Parker J: "The idea of a woman practising in the Supreme Court seems to me quite foreign to the legislation ... I am not prepared myself to create a precedent by allowing admission ... [I]f the Legislature desired that a woman should be capable of being admitted ... they should have said so in express language". Burnside J pointed out that no one had the right to be admitted. (So what?!) The applicant's reliance on statutes that spoke of "every person" or "any person" having the relevant right, the state of the common law at the time they were passed, did not assist the applicant either. His Honour ended with a flourish:[14]

> It appears to me that we must also bear in mind that throughout the civilised world, so far as we know, we have not been able to ascertain any instances ... where the right of women to be admitted to the Bar has ever been suggested. That being so, it is said here that it should exist, because the words in the Statute are 'every person'. That does not appear to me to be very forcible ... When the Legislature in its wisdom confers the right on women then we shall be pleased to admit them ...

It required legislation before women were allowed to enter the profession in the various States. The first was Grata Flos Greig who was admitted in Victoria in 1905 following the *Women's Disabilities Removal Act 1903* (Vic).

Ada Evans became Australia's first female law student, in 1898, when she enrolled at Sydney University during the absence overseas of the Dean, Professor Pitt Cobbett. Learning of this on his return, he summoned Ada to his office and (in Justice Mary Gaudron's unusually restrained words) "with a fine grasp of legal essentials, informed her that she did not have the physique for law and would find medicine more suitable".[15] She stuck to her guns and graduated in 1904. Thereafter she lobbied for almost two decades for legislative change, which only came to her jurisdiction in 1918. She was admitted to the Bar in 1921. Marie Byles became the State's first woman solicitor in 1924.

The law was changed in Queensland in 1905 and the first female solicitor, Agnes McWhinney, was admitted there in 1915. The *Daily Mail* reported that she was dressed for the occasion in a "white lingerie frock and a white chiffon hat, encircled with small French flowers".[16] In the 1890s, legislation to admit women to practise as lawyers was twice rejected by the Legislative Council of South Australia. In 1911 that barrier was lifted and the first woman to be admitted there was Mary Kitson, in 1917. Miss Kitson then applied to become a notary public only to be knocked back on the ground that this office was not

14 *Ibid* at 213, 214.

15 Hon Justice Mary Gaudron, "Speech for Women Lawyers Association of New South Wales 50th Anniversary Gala Dinner" 13 June 2002, <www.hcourt.gov.au/speeches/gaudron_wlasp.htm>.

16 McPherson, *Supreme Court of Queensland*, p 231.

expressly included in the language of the statute enabling women to become lawyers.[17]

It would not be until 1923 that the Western Australian Legislature opened the door to women lawyers and only in 1927 that it became possible for women to *study* law at the University of Western Australia – this, despite women getting the vote there in 1899. The irascible Northmore CJ greeted the first woman barrister appearing in his court with a snort: "What have we here?"

No woman was admitted to practise law in Tasmania until 1935.

Crown law officers

The executive arm of government is inevitably the principal litigant with its near monopoly of criminal prosecutions, its regulatory functions and its extensive dealings as property manager and employer of the "public service". From the earliest times, the Crown has needed the services of lawyers in the courts and legislatures.

Transported convicts with legal skills had to do the job in New South Wales until free men could be enticed to the colony and into government service. George Crossley was admitted in England as an attorney and solicitor in London in 1771. In 1796 he was charged with forging a will, thus defrauding the heir-at-law. According to an unsubstantiated story recounted by Therry J, Crossley's defence was that he placed a fly in the mouth of the dead testator before tracing the signature with the dead testator's hand, so that there could be evidence of life in the body. The prosecution, reliant on the evidence of an alleged accomplice, failed. A few months later Crossley and two other attorneys were called upon to answer charges of professional malpractice. Crossley produced an affidavit by himself to answer the charges, but the court did not find it credible. He was charged with perjury and convicted. After an unsuccessful appeal he was imprisoned for six months, ordered to be placed in the pillory and then to be transported to Australia for seven years.

Given his experience, acumen and availability, Crossley soon became Governor Macquarie's principal legal adviser. It was a slight improvement on using the Judge-Advocate for both initiating and hearing serious criminal charges, which was not a good look for avoiding bias. But having a convicted perjurer as de facto Attorney-General was not a good look for a Governor. Yet it was not until 1824 that the first Attorney-General and Solicitor-General were appointed, the former as one of the recommendations of the Bigge Report.[18]

17 *Re Kitson* [1920] SASR 230.

18 *Report of the Commissioner of Inquiry on the Judicial Establishments of New South Wales and Van Diemen's Land*, 1823, pp 34, 57. Bigge recommended an English barrister for New South Wales. The Vandemonians would be provided with "one of the stipendiary solicitors practising at Sydney". The Colonial Office nevertheless decided to

Saxe Bannister, the colony's first Attorney-General, is described by Dr Bennett as "an incompetent and unpleasant individual".[19] Dr Currey explained that:[20]

> A succession of defeats in court lessened confidence in [Bannister's] professional competence ... [Governor] Darling ... had scant respect for his judgment and resented his unsolicited advice. [Chief Justice] Forbes deplored his 'irascibility', 'indecorous conduct' in court, and tendency to megalomania. With Brisbane and Darling, he thought that the attorney-general was at times mentally unbalanced.

Law officers who get so far on the wrong side of both their principal client and the court before whom they urge that client's causes can always expect a hard time and a bad press.

Compared to Attorney-General Saxe Bannister, John Stephen SG was a saint. But comparisons are always odious and Stephen, our country's first Solicitor-General, only served in that job for a year before he secured appointment as a puisne Supreme Court judge. He would be the first of four from the Stephen clan to progress to the Supreme Court of New South Wales. John Stephen was by no means the last Solicitor-General who should have avoided judicial promotion. "Mr Stephen ... poor man", Governor Darling informed the Colonial Secretary in 1828, "is a tool in the hands of the Chief Justice, who works with him as best answers his immediate object". Stephen was admonished frequently by the Colonial Office for indiscretion. His own nephew, James Stephen, prepared a despatch for Governor Darling in 1831 in which the latter recorded that "if I have anything to reproach myself with, it is the forbearance I have shown in not reporting his unfitness for his office".

Stephen's death in December 1833 offered him a more dignified departure from the colony than Saxe Bannister, whose parting shot before sailing to England was at the leading barrister Wardell in a duel from which both men emerged uninjured.[21]

Like several of his early successors as Solicitor-General, John Stephen was appointed through lobbying and nepotism that would be scandalous today. The next appointee, James Holland, left behind in England Lord Bathurst's despatch nominating him for the office and so the Chief Justice refused to swear him in. This second law officer manqué was consoled by the fact that he was also a salaried Commissioner of the Courts of Request which were small debts courts. Several early incumbents also sat as magistrates or chairmen of Quarter Sessions concurrently with their position as second law officer. From

---

send them an English barrister as well, Joseph Tice Gellibrand. He proved to be quite unfit for the office (see p 137).

19 Bennett, *A History of the Supreme Court of New South Wales*, p 33.

20 "Bannister, Saxe (1790-1877)", *Australian Dictionary of Biography*.

21 In 1834 Wardell would be shot dead by an escaped convict. For other duels involving lawyers, see pp 41-2.

time to time they also "acted up" as temporary Supreme Court judges. And they invariably hoped that something good or bad would befall their Attorney-General so as to create a vacancy they expected to fill.

Colonial Governors who were unhappy with local advice could seek the views of the English law officers. One "courageous" local Crown Solicitor in the 1870s took this idea a step too far. George Leake[22] wanted to send one of Burt CJ's judgments to the Colonial Office in London for comment. When he found out about it, Burt told the Governor of Western Australia that such a proceeding was "erroneous and fraught with mischief". His decisions could only properly be reviewed by a Court of Appeal "as no opinion of Crown law officers can have any effect on his judgements except to dissatisfy the litigant".[23]

From very early times, there has been an officer called the Attorney-General exercising the role of principal advocate for the Crown in each jurisdiction.[24] This person was invariably a member of the Executive Council and the tradition of having an Attorney-General in cabinet has been preserved to this day although it has been abandoned in England. Indeed, in Victoria, the second law officer position was also political until 1951.

This closeness to politics could have its drawbacks. In 1893 Isaac Isaacs QC SG resigned his office and his seat in Parliament when the Attorney-General, Sir Bryan O'Loghlen, declined to prosecute Sir Matthew Davies, chairman of the Mercantile Bank of Australia, and others, on charges of conspiracy to issue false balance sheets. Relying on a forced reading of the relevant statute, Isaacs claimed that as Solicitor-General he had an independent right to institute proceedings in the circumstances and he announced in the press his intention to do so and to appear for the prosecution. The Attorney-General instructed his staff to ignore the instructions of the Solicitor-General. The Premier and cabinet upheld the Attorney-General and Isaacs was obliged to resign office.

Isaacs' intemperate conduct in the Davies matter was popular with the public and warmly endorsed in the press. The *Bulletin* noted that O'Loghlen had written to Isaacs saying, "I am ready to justify my exercise of the royal prerogative before the High Court of Parliament". "It would be possible", said that journal, "to justify worse things than that before the Victorian Legislature, which is only a *High* Court insofar as it smells a good deal". Isaacs' stance, which breached cabinet solidarity, not to mention overreaching the powers of the junior law officer, has justly been criticised by his biographer, Zelman Cowen[25] and others.[26] The biographer notes that one of the notable contributions to

22 See further, p 19.

23 Bolton and Byrne, *May it Please Your Honour*, p 62.

24 In South Australia, the officer was called the Advocate-General until responsible government.

25 Cowen, *Isaac Isaacs*, pp 35-6.

26 There is a detailed discussion of the matter in John Ll J Edwards, *The Attorney-General, Politics and the Public Interest*, Sweet & Maxwell, 1984, pp 373-9.

the press history of the case was a fine piece of writing in Gilbert and Sullivan style.[27] Three of the verses are reproduced here:

> They've discharged Sir Matthew Davies, and acquitted Mr Milledge;
> They have found them both not guilty of a criminal intent—
> Ruled that neither was concerned in a conspiracy to pillage—
> That the mercantile suspension was a simple accident,
> And this sudden termination
> Of a serious accusation
> Has resulted from the action – should you ask the reason why—
> Of a *nolle prosequi*.[28]
>
> Let us not despise the *nolle*; let us hesitate to brand it
> As a piece of stupid folly or miscalculated fun;
> It is really interesting when you come to understand it,
> It is simple and convincing when you know how it is done—
> 'Tis no conjuring illusion
> Based on natural confusion
> Of the quickness of the fingers and deception of the eye—
> *Presto*! *Nolle prosequi*!
>
> Let us rather view the *nolle* as a fine old legal fiction
> As a paradox most useful – though it seems a little odd—
> To express a mind convinced against all possible convictions,
> 'Tis an erat demonstrandum when denuded of its '*quod*'
> 'Tis an easy exposition
> Of a Euclid proposition
> When the QED is missing, the alternative reply
> Is a nolle prosequi.

Isaacs chose nevertheless to resign his seat in Parliament and stand for re-election where he was returned unopposed. In due course a private prosecution was launched, but the directors were acquitted by the jury.

Queensland as usual decided to take a different tack in dealing with unpalatable and inconvenient legal advice from its Attorney-General. For much of the 20th century it simply got by with a non-lawyer in that office. After the departure of TJ Ryan in 1919 the office was not held by a lawyer of any kind for nearly 70 years, barring the interval in 1929-32.[29] And between 1922 and 1989 the Solicitor-General occupied a public service position. 1989 saw the arrival of Geoff Davies QC who, like his successors, remained a member of the private Bar. Indeed, when Queensland followed other jurisdictions in legislating that its Solicitor-General should serve as "counsel for the Crown", it preserved a right of private practice. Sir Gerard Brennan suggested to the writer that

---

27 Cowen, *Isaac Isaacs*, p 37. The poem was published in the *Argus*, 20 May 1893.

28 A *nolle prosequi* (pronounced ˈnɒli ˈprɒsəkwi) is a formal decision by a law officer not to proceed with a prosecution. It does not establish the innocence of the accused and it is open for a fresh charge to be laid.

29 McPherson, *The Supreme Court of Queensland*, p 291.

this was, in part, a reaction to a long period of Crown law advice that some observers viewed as tainted by partiality towards the government in power. A Solicitor-General with one foot rooted in the private Bar would reinforce both the appearance and actuality of independence. When in 1990 Queensland pulled out of the *Incorporation Case* at short notice, Davies was briefed by the remaining States that were (successfully, as it turned out) challenging a Commonwealth law, thereby demonstrating that his right of private practice could produce unintended benefits for the public throughout Australia.[30]

This said, Attorneys- and Solicitors-General exercising a concurrent right of private practice caused many problems in the 19th century. Flare-ups often followed complaints by the law officers that they were overworked or needed extra resources. A serious episode of conflict of interest led to the dismissal of the first law officer for Van Diemen's Land in 1826. Lieutenant-Governor Arthur sacked Attorney-General Gellibrand for unprofessional conduct in drawing pleadings for a plaintiff and afterwards acting against him in court. The Lieutenant-Governor had previously tried to have him struck off, but Pedder CJ declined to interfere. Arthur was able to rely on his Solicitor-General, Alfred Stephen, to prepare the case for Gellibrand's dismissal. But Stephen would turn out to be mightily disappointed when he did not succeed to the senior office. The incoming Attorney-General would be Thomas McCleland, to be followed shortly by Algernon Montagu.[31] Stephen and Montagu would fight publicly for the next 13 years, initially as law officers who could agree on very little, later when Montagu went to the Bench and Stephen succeeded him as Attorney-General.

Samuel Griffith QC AG got a ticking off from the Queensland Full Court in 1875 for appearing privately in a divorce matter. This was seen to conflict with his duty of intervention against collusion in the role of Queens's Proctor. He accepted the rebuke "under protest".[32] While he was Attorney-General in Victoria, Isaac Isaacs QC once accepted a brief to appear against the Fitzroy municipality. Other future High Court justices, Barton QC AG and O'Connor, Minister of Justice, almost caused the downfall of their government when, in 1893, they were briefed to appear for a plaintiff against the Railway Commissioners. Barton tried to brazen it out by relying on the cab rank rule and the spurious argument that the Commissioners were not really a department of government. In the upshot, the two men resigned their ministries after a motion of censure was carried against them.

A century later, a better precedent would be set by Robert Ellicott QC. In 1977 he resigned as Attorney-General in the Fraser Ministry as a result of a dispute over instructions from the Prime Minister to terminate the prosecution

30 *New South Wales v Commonwealth* (1990) 169 CLR 482 at 483.

31 See generally pp 113-15.

32 McPherson, *Supreme Court of Queensland*, p 150.

and pay the defence legal costs in *Sankey v Whitlam*.[33] Ellicott was reappointed in the third Fraser Ministry in alternative portfolios. In 1981, disappointed at not being offered the chief justiceship resigned by Sir Garfield Barwick that went to Sir Harry Gibbs, he declined the High Court puisne justiceship that was then accepted by Gerard Brennan who would himself become Chief Justice in 1995.[34] Later that year, Ellicott resigned from politics to become a judge on the Federal Court of Australia. He left that office after two years and returned to a successful career at the Bar.

No Australian law officer has got into greater trouble than Thomas Ley MLA. In 1884 the New South Wales *Constitution Act* had been amended to remove the solicitor-generalship from those offices of profit under the Crown that could be held by members of the Legislative Assembly. This did not stop appointing as Solicitor-General someone from the Upper House, or a public servant, or making the office non-remunerative. The amendment also led to the second law officer being sometimes rebadged as "Minister for Justice". In 1922 the Crown Solicitor advised that, if made Solicitor-General, Ley would forfeit his Lower House seat and put a fragile government majority at risk. Ley had to settle for the Ministry of Justice. After his political career crashed in a flurry of litigation over fraud as a director of the ill-fated SOS Prickly Pear Poisons Ltd, Ley returned to his native England in 1928. In 1946 he arranged the murder of the man he wrongly suspected to be courting his aging mistress. On conviction, Lord Chief Justice Goddard pronounced sentence of death. But, to his extreme displeasure, the Home Secretary respited the sentence on the basis of medical evidence (first produced after the trial) that Ley was suffering from paranoia. Ley died of a stroke in Broadmoor Criminal Lunatic Asylum four months later. His biographer suggests that he had been responsible for two additional murders before he left Sydney.[35]

Leslie Katz was the Solicitor-General for New South Wales immediately after the author. He tells a story that illustrates one of the many uses of the office. One morning, someone from the Attorney-General's Department knocked meekly on his door and sought permission to place a pile of papers on the corner of his desk. Asked what they were about, the officer said that he would let him know later that day. Later in the day the officer knocked, entered and quietly removed the papers. Leslie later found out that a question had been asked in Parliament on a matter of urgency and that the House had been told:

33 This was a private prosecution launched against Prime Minister Whitlam and other ministers, including Lionel Murphy by then a justice of the High Court, for their participation in the "loans affair". It was alleged that the defendants had conspired to deceive the Governor-General in relation to a loan said to contravene the *Commonwealth-State Financial Agreement Act 1928* (Cth).

34 See Blackshield et al, *Oxford Companion to the High Court of Australia*, p 27. Ellicott is a distant cousin of Sir Garfield Barwick.

35 Dan Morgan, *The Minister for Murder*, Hutchinson of Australia, 1979.

"At this very time the file is on the desk of the Solicitor-General". The matter of urgency passed, as things have a habit of doing in politics, so the file could be returned unexamined.

Serjeants and silks

The office of Serjeant at Law was the highest degree to which a barrister in England might aspire.[36] The order of the coif, as the Serjeant's fraternity was called, did not however survive various reforms in England in the 19th century, although the last of the Serjeants, Lord Lindley, lived until 1921. One serjeant practised in Australia in the 1870s. He was William Campbell Sleigh who had short stints at the Bar in Sydney, Melbourne and Launceston. A paper of the day published a mock trading advertisement, concluding with the line: "Ask for the serjeant, and see that you get him". After serving in the Tasmanian Parliament, he returned to England.

New South Wales' and Australia's first Queen's Counsel was John Bayley Darvall who was appointed in 1853.[37] New South Wales' last was Peter Michael Jacobson,[38] the most junior of those appointed in 1992. The office was not then abolished, but (in an unusual abnegation of power by the executive) the government in that State announced that there would be no further appointments, effectively handing the matter over to the Bar Association with its replacement system of "Senior Counsel".

South Australia has had a formally fused legal profession from the outset and there was no independent Bar until 1955. It was therefore inevitable that, when the colony appointed its first Queen's Counsel in 1865, those who obtained silk were not exclusively from the ranks of barristers. The insufferable Boothby J protested loudly, declaring:[39]

> This union of the office of Queen's Counsel with that of practising Attorney has, I apprehend, never before been known of in any Court of Her Majesty where only the law and practice of the Superior Courts at Westminster are administered.

The first South Australian silk was Randolph Stow. When, in 1866, he announced his appearance for a prisoner charged with murder, Boothby inquired (in the presence of the Crown Solicitor) if he had a licence to appear against the Crown. "That is a matter entirely between myself and the Crown", replied Stow. Boothby J: "Oh, no. I must uphold the law, and cannot allow you to address the Court without a licence". Unwisely perhaps, the judge added: "There is no

36 See generally JM Bennett, "Of Silks and Serjeants" (1978) 52 *Australian Law Journal* 264.

37 The same Darvall who had served time in prison for contempt of court (see p 43).

38 Now Jacobson J of the Federal Court.

39 Quoted Emerson, *History of the Independent Bar of South Australia*, p 8.

power to appoint a Queen's Counsel in the Colony". Stow retorted: "Then I do not require a licence". When Stow stood his ground, the judge threatened to commit him into custody but appeared to have second thoughts due to his doubts whether there was a properly appointed tipstaff in the court. The proceedings were then adjourned. When they resumed a few days later, with another counsel appearing for the accused, Boothby quashed the information on the ground that there was no validly appointed Attorney-General in South Australia.

Paris Nesbit KC, whose career has been touched on elsewhere,[40] was once sitting at the back of a magistrate's court when he observed the beak giving a hard time to a man who had been charged with drunkenness. Nesbit decided to act for him but the magistrate thought it improper for any barrister to choose his client, still less a KC who should ordinarily confine his appearances to the superior courts. "Quite so", replied Nesbit, "but I hold letters patent from the King authorising me to assist in the administration of justice according to law".[41]

In 1910 Edward Mitchell, a Victorian silk, but not silk in New South Wales, appeared alone in the High Court in Sydney. The New South Wales Bar called the attention of the Victorian Bar to this gross intrusion but no action was taken.[42]

Some notable barristers have chosen not to seek appointment as senior counsel or were appointed to the Bench before achieving sufficient eminence at the Bar. These include Robert French, George Higinbotham, William Webb, Kenneth Whistler Street, Leo Cussen, Hayden Starke, Edward McTiernan, Cyril Walsh and Michael Kirby. Of Cussen, it was said that "it almost became a maxim that if a solicitor had a difficult case and did not consult Cussen, he was guilty of negligence". He had a distinguished career on the Supreme Court of Victoria between 1906 and 1933. Sir Owen Dixon considered it an extraordinary error by governments not to have appointed him Chief Justice of the High Court of Australia or the Victorian Supreme Court.

I know of five men who took silk *after* holding a permanent judicial office. In 1878 the Victorian government ran out of money and sacked all County Court judges, magistrates and many other public servants.[43] When offered re-engagement, Judge John Warrington Rogers declined in protest at the government's refusal to make the tenure of County Court judges the same as for Supreme Court judges. He returned to the Bar and was shortly afterwards

40 See p 60. Nesbit took silk in 1893.

41 Graham Loughlin, "Paris Nesbit QC Lawyer, Libertine and Lunatic" (1977) 3 *Journal of the Historical Society of South Australia* 49 at 52.

42 Dean, *A Multitude of Counsellors*, p 104. For other instances of restrictive trade practices by barristers and solicitors, see pp 143-5.

43 See p 109.

appointed one of Her Majesty's Counsel. Henry Wrenfordsley[44] became a Queen's Counsel in 1889, in between his two highly unsatisfactory terms as Chief Justice of Western Australia. Albert Piddington was made a King's Counsel shortly after he resigned his commission as a justice of the High Court in 1913.[45] He announced the appointment before the High Court on 9 May 1913. Barton ACJ (in the presence of Isaacs, Duffy and Rich JJ) "depart[ed] so far from the practice of the Court as to say that the Court welcomes your accession to the rank of King's Counsel with more feeling from the fact that you were recently one of its members, and resigned your commission as a Justice in this Court under circumstances which nobody who knows you can doubt evinced motives of the highest honour and the most delicate feeling".[46] Charles Dashwood took silk in 1906 after his term as a South Australian judge resident in the Northern Territory. Kevin O'Leary served as the second Chief Justice of the Northern Territory between 1985 and 1987 when forced to retire due to ill health. He was appointed Queen's Counsel shortly afterwards.

Appointment (or non-appointment) to silk has from time to time generated extreme controversy. Attorneys-General with little merit and a smaller practice have occasionally given themselves a silk gown. Even meritorious Attorneys have, at times, yielded to the temptation to reward a political mate or, by withholding silk, to punish an enemy. Otherwise suitable candidates have (for a time) been blocked because of their membership of the Communist Party, and (more recently) apparently because of membership of the Australian Labor Party, despite the overwhelming support of the profession.[47] For a range of reasons, governments and Chief Justices in some jurisdictions have now withdrawn from active roles in this source of patronage.

There is a touch of controversy about the propriety of a superior court judge resuming the appellation "QC" after retirement or resignation from the Bench. (The problem will not arise when our "SCs" start to retire or resign,

44 See generally p 123.

45 See p 85.

46 *Sydney Morning Herald* 10 May 1913, p 19.

47 In 1969, despite the recommendation of Bray CJ, Elliott Johnston who was a leading Adelaide barrister was not given silk. The government announced that cabinet had decided this because of Elliott's affiliation with the Communist Party of Australia: see generally WB Fisse and D St L Kelly, "Political Influence in the Appointment of Queen's Counsel" (1970) 44 *Australian Law Journal* 318. The matter was rectified the following year when the Dunstan government came to power. Herring CJ withheld silk from EA (Ted) Laurie for similar reasons: see p 100. In 1991, John Waters sought silk in the Northern Territory with the formal support of the Chief Justice, the Attorney-General, the Bar Association and the Law Society. The Country Liberal Party were in office and Waters had previously stood as an ALP candidate. Proceedings challenging the decision of the Executive Council were dismissed on the basis that the decision was not amenable to judicial review (*Waters v Acting Administrator of the Northern Territory* (1993) 46 FCR 462). Waters was later appointed silk under a new appointment regime: see Mildren, *Big Boss Fella All Same Judge*, pp 288-9.

because theirs is not a commission from the Crown.) On the "better view" (as lawyers say when they cannot deliver a knockout blow), the QC commission lies "dormant" during the judicial commission and it can be taken up again on resignation or retirement from the Bench. Outside Victoria, there are a good number of "Queen's Counsel" in demure retirement or practising at the Bar or as mediators, who formerly held senior judicial positions in State and federal courts, including the High Court. None of them, to my knowledge, has been dubbed afresh; indeed, most of them left the Bench after the "QC" system was terminated in their jurisdiction of practice.

According to the redoubtable JD Merralls QC of the Victorian Bar,[48] whilst a person appointed to an inferior court who is then a QC could be called "Judge X QC", a person appointed to a superior court such as the Supreme Court lost the QC appellation and could not regain it on retirement from the Bench. Merralls cites no case law on the specific matter but argues from principle, contending that the common law doctrine of merger of offices treated a person holding an office who was appointed to a higher one as having automatically lost the inferior office. At common law, appointment to an *incompatible* higher office does generally cause the inferior office to be vacated.[49] Merralls also cites the privately expressed view of Sir Owen Dixon and pointed to the English practice whereby retired members of the Supreme Court of Judicature (now the Senior Courts of England and Wales) do not refer to themselves as QC, as reference to the *English Who's Who* showed. Accordingly, the "growing legion of former superior court judges who profess to be Queen's Counsel are imposters ... The current Australian practice may be regarded as a symptom of the country's fondness for pseudo-titles".

Disclosing my interest in this controversy, a number of things can be said in reply:

(1) there continues to be a growing list of these QC imposters, some of them being recently retired members of the Federal Court of Australia and the High Court;

(2) Merralls' argument proceeds from the contestable starting point that judicial appointment in Australia still involves a prerogative act by the Crown as distinct from the exercise of a statutory power;

48 "Reversion is Impossible" (1994) 89 *Vic Bar News* 51. For the opposing view, much more fully developed, see Louise McCormack, "Effect on the Queen's Counsel Commission of a Judge's Commission" in Michael White and Aladin Rahemtula (eds), *Supreme Court History Program Yearbook 2008*, Supreme Court Library Queensland, p 25; The Hon James Thomas AM, *Judicial Ethics in Australia*, LexisNexis Butterworths, 2009, 3rd ed, pp 272-3.

49 See p 83 where I instance one of many situations when this doctrine was overlooked when a judge from one court was appointed to an acting position in a higher court to which an appeal lay. Some piecemeal legislative attention to this risk has been taken but only in very recent times.

(3) it is difficult to see why there is any incompatibility between being a silk and accepting any judicial appointment, given that none is seen in the case of the District Court judge who keeps the "QC" tag;
(4) the senior English judges do not need pseudo-titles given the invariable practice of giving out knighthoods on appointment;
(5) the Sydney Yellow Pages telephone directory outranks the *English Who's Who* in readership and it contains several references to post-judicial "QCs" in its lists of barristers and mediators;
(6) denizens of New South Wales do not like being lectured to by Victorians; and
(7) at least three official actions in New South Wales support the dormancy theory, namely (i) Darley CJ's accession to the chief justiceship in 1886 was gazetted "*vice* Mr J E Salomons, QC, resigned", (ii) the *New South Wales Law Almanac* lists as "QC" a number of barristers who were formerly judges of superior courts, and (iii) when steps were taken against the former Justice Marcus Einfeld following his gaoling for perjury and perverting the course of justice in 2009 they included the Governor revoking his earlier commission as Queen's Counsel.

John Somerville took silk on 28 November 1967, but did only one case as a QC before being appointed to the Victorian County Court Bench on 23 January 1968. He faced a ribbing because he was on the losing side in that solitary encounter.

The English practice of conferring silk on non-practising academics has generally not been followed in Australia. There have been isolated exceptions, the earliest being Dr Hearn, Dean of the Faculty of Law at Melbourne University.

Barristers and restrictive trade practices

The Bar is an extremely competitive environment. But the way in which it has conducted itself over the years has often sailed close to the wind as regards laws designed to prevent anti-competitive practices. We all have our blind spots but the Bar has been fortunate to have enjoyed the sympathy and support of the judges drawn exclusively from its ranks until recently.

I instance the Bar's opposition to solicitors practising as advocates that has now dissolved, and the unconstitutional blocking of entry by interstate practitioners that required a change of mind by the High Court in 1989 before it too ceased.[50] The "two counsel" and "two-thirds" rules,[51] and "ethical" restrictions on any advertising by lawyers or on direct access to barristers have gone kicking

50 *Street v Queensland Bar Association* (1989) 168 CLR 461, overruling *Henry v Boehm* (1973) 128 CLR 482.

51 Whereby a junior with a silk was expected to charge a fee that was two-thirds that of the leader. I know of one junior (later a judge) who boasted of having applied the

to similar graves, not before a number of practitioners of good will and later fame have suffered the indignity of disciplinary action for doing things that nowadays no one would question. Some observers would consider the system of senior counsel to be in a similar category given that it involves an artificial division of the Bar that can enhance the silk's charging power.

Until recently, restrictions on price competition were staunchly policed, with the back-up of court costing practices. In the 19th century David Buchanan was not popular with some of his brethren at the New South Wales Bar because he worked for less than union rates. Once, when taxed with charging a fee as low as £2.15.3 he explained: "Ah weel, Ah took evra penny the mon had".[52]

Across eastern Australia, but nowhere more vigorously than in Victoria, there were heated controversies about the fusion of the "two branches" of the profession in the late 19th century. Many private member Bills were introduced designed to allow solicitors to appear in court and barristers to receive instructions directly from the public. Freedom of choice and savings of cost were the benefits claimed. The apparent success of fusion in South Australia, New Zealand and the United States was trumpeted. The Bar did not speak with one voice, but it tended to oppose these measure with arguments based on tradition, independence, specialisation and competitive (dis)advantage compared with what was happening in other States. As happens when pocket books and established practices are threatened, things often got heated and personal. Judges intervened on both sides of the debate, but usually to support the barristers. By 1875 John Madden QC had emerged as the leader of the divisionist cause in Victoria and his skills in and out of Parliament kept the fusionist beast at bay for many years. By 1884 a fusionist Bill passed the Victorian Lower House, triggering the establishment of a Bar Association with rules forbidding members to do any kind of solicitors' work "in Melbourne or its suburbs". The Bill would not pass the Legislative Council on that occasion.

But eventually the *Legal Profession Practice Act 1891* (Vic) did pass through Parliament and receive assent. It converted all existing members of each "branch" into "barristers and solicitors" with rights of practice in every recognised legal field. Counsel were made liable for negligence to the same extent as solicitors and given an identical right to sue for their fees. The Bar's response, under Madden, was the "barristers' boycott". The members of the Bar Association proclaimed that they would not accept a brief from, or appear as counsel with, any lawyer who used the new rights of practice. The swift move was aimed particularly at hurting and cowing the larger firms of solicitors that could not do without barristers, at least overnight. "Amalgam" barristers were also threatened with shunning.

"four-thirds rule" when he was led by two silks representing separate interests in the Privy Council.

52 Blacket, *May it Please Your Honour*, p 30.

Had this been done by blue collar workers they would have been sued, if not charged with criminal conspiracy, in a flash. The Attorney-General was asked in Parliament "whether his attention had been drawn to the fact that a number of practising barristers had entered into a conspiracy for the purpose of defeating the Act, and if he was prepared to take some action in the matter".[53] The Melbourne *Age* branded Madden's followers as a "respectable body of conspirators against the law of their country" and condemned their "desperate and thoroughly despicable tactics". The more conservative *Argus* concurred:

> Public opinion declares that the principles of the Association are indistinguishable from those of trades unionism in its latest and most degrading form ... Voices that have sounded loud in condemnation of the Trades Hall sink to a softer key when the boycotting of a brother counsel is on the boards.

The Attorney-General deplored the conduct of his fellow barristers, and several leading barristers opted not to join the new Bar Association. A heated debate in February 1892 resulted in the Bar Association abolishing itself in response to the outraged public opposition. Matters then went underground, and evidence of any direct boycott appeared to dry up. No records of minutes or resolutions of the Victorian Bar seem to have been created or kept for the last decade of the 19th century. But only a handful of practising barristers were so bold as to declare themselves to be "amalgams" and they would come to feel the wrath of the judges who quietly discriminated against them in matters of costs and precedence. By 1901 the "Committee of Counsel" was bold enough to resolve that in future no counsel on the Roll of Barristers should appear or hold a brief with anyone not of counsel on the Roll. The Law Institute pondered its options but decided not to commence legal proceedings. Very few barristers joined the Law Institute and the stragglers eventually came on board with the Madden-led majority faction. The Committee of Counsel obtained statutory recognition; the risk of legal action passed; the Victorian Bar was well and truly established as a distinct (and eventually reputable) institution; John Madden became Chief Justice in 1893; and the rest, they say ...[54]

The High Court generally leaves it up to the State Supreme Courts to be the gatekeepers of professional rectitude. But even the High Court does its bit when required, as occurred with Richard Meagher whose saga is recounted in the next section. Hayne J was hearing an application for an injunction to prevent the deportation of a man who needed the assistance of an interpreter and who wished to be represented by a family friend named Mr De Alwis. The following discussion occurred:[55]

---

53 Dean, *A Multitude of Counsellors*, p 101.

54 The story is told in more detail and with differing emphases in Dean, *A Multitude of Counsellors*, and Forbes, *The Divided Legal Profession*.

55 *Gamage, In the matter of a proposed application* [2009] HCA Trans 309.

HIS HONOUR: ... Mr De Alwis, would you come to the microphone please? Mr De Alwis, Mr Gamage has asked that I give you leave to speak on his behalf. Are you a lawyer?

MR DE ALWIS: I was, your Honour. I was a lawyer admitted in Sri Lanka in 1973, August, then I came to Australia in July 1984 to do post-graduate studies at the Monash University, and I was helped by His Excellency, Justice ... to do international law and administration of criminal justice. Then I had certain personal difficulties, family problems, then we went to Sydney where I resumed my post-graduate studies.

HIS HONOUR: Mr De Alwis, my question was quite narrow. Are you a lawyer admitted to practice in the courts of Australia?

MR DE ALWIS: That is right, your Honour. I give a brief background to my experience and knowledge.

HIS HONOUR: Mr De Alwis, we will get on much quicker if you attend to my question and answer it.

MR DE ALWIS: I apologise, your Honour. I was admitted in Western Australia to the Supreme Court as a barrister and solicitor on 2 March 1995, and I did practise as an immigration lawyer, international law lawyer, human rights lawyer, and before that in Melbourne and Sydney and here too I worked as a migration agent; I was very successful. Then I appeared for a man called Mr Neville Taylor, and according to the advice I have from him, he refused to make a complaint against me when approached by the law complaints officer. His wife was approached by the law complaints officer, and a complaint was made that I misappropriated $10,000, which I vehemently denied and today also I deny. I denied it in the Federal Magistrates Court. I have denied it in the Federal Court when the matter was taken up regarding Mr Gamage. Unfortunately, from mid-2000 I was feeling very dizzy and began collapsing, and until 2002, the 21st night of August, 2002, no doctor, nobody advised me that I was bleeding profusely from my bowels due to stomach ulcers.

HIS HONOUR: Mr De Alwis, I do not wish to embarrass you by delaying about the state of your health. My question is very narrow. Are you a person entitled to practise as a barrister or solicitor in the Supreme Court of a State or in the Federal Courts?

MR DE ALWIS: No, your Honour. I was struck off the roll.

The solicitor who said too little and the barrister who said too much

Richard Denis Meagher was a rising Labor politician in New South Wales. He was also a solicitor with an advocate's practice in criminal law and he practised in partnership with a man named Crick who was also a Labor member of the Legislative Assembly.[56] During an election in 1895 the *Daily Telegraph* referred to Meagher as the gentleman "whose failure to oppose the singularly weak case against George Dean has put the country to the expense of a Royal Commission". As happened with Oscar Wilde that same year, Meagher's failure to turn the other cheek to this defamatory slight would lead to his downfall. In Meagher's case the saga would also leave a cloud over the reputation of his principal accuser, Sir Julian Salomons QC.[57]

Dean had been something of a popular public figure. He captained Sydney Harbour ferries and he was a lifesaver who received public recognition for bravery. In 1895 he was arrested and charged with the attempted killing by poison of his attractive young wife. Meagher seized the chance to make a name for himself by pitting himself as Dean's advocate against prosecuting counsel, the Attorney-General Mr Want QC. Meagher was in his 20s at the time.

There was evidence that several small doses of arsenic and strychnine had been ingested by the victim. It was common ground that she had undoubtedly been poisoned, the issue being who had administered the poison. There were only two hypotheses: Dean, or his wife and mother-in-law conspiring together to frame him. The principal witnesses for the prosecution were the victim and her mother and their credibility was strongly attacked. Dean's mother-in-law had something of a past that was used to blacken her before the jury and in the court of public opinion. Dean swore to his innocence and his counsel made much of the fact that, although every chemist in Sydney was called as a witness, none of them could point to any relevant sale of the poison. Dean was nevertheless found guilty and received the mandatory death sentence.

A firestorm erupted at the fate of this popular hero and it was fuelled by the efforts of Meagher and Crick inside and outside Parliament. The trial judge, Windeyer J, had acted roughly throughout the trial. He sat very long hours and his directions to the jury tended towards a conviction. When the jury seemed deadlocked, he had them brought in very late on Saturday evening and hinted to them that he would recommend mercy if a verdict of guilty were returned.[58]

---

56 William Patrick Crick "looked like a prize fighter, dressed like a tramp, talked like a bullocky, and to complete the pattern of popular virtues, owned champion racehorses": AW Martin and P Wardle, *Members of the Legislative Assembly of New South Wales 1856-1901*, ANU Press, 1959, p 48.

57 The story is told by Leslie Blackwell in *Death Cell at Darlinghurst*, Hutchinson, 1970. See also Carleton Kemp Allen, "R v Dean" (1941) 57 *Law Quarterly Review* 85; Jeremy Stoljar, *The Australian Book of Great Trials*, Pier 9, 2011, ch 5.

58 Such a recommendation was made and Dean's death sentence was commuted to penal servitude for life. In a press interview given two years later, after he had retired, Windeyer J explained this conduct on two bases. He believed that the jury were under the false impression that they would be discharged if they could not reach a verdict by midnight. And he had just learned that the foreman's 12-year-old son had died unexpectedly, being placed in the dilemma that he could not communicate this awful fact to him before the trial ended with the certainty that the jury would be locked up at midnight.

In the public agitation following the verdict and sentence, his conduct was attacked strongly and the vilification of the two women continued unabated. Crick and Meagher's endeavours in and out of Parliament resulted in a Royal Commission conducted by a Queen's Counsel and two medical practitioners. At that Commission Meagher's firm represented Dean and, through the senior counsel who was retained without being told that Dean was in truth guilty, the case was repeatedly advanced that Mrs Dean had administered the poison to herself and conspired with her mother to initiate a false charge supported by their perjured testimony. After sitting for 39 days, the Royal Commission reported by a majority (the two doctors) that Dean had been wrongly convicted. This led to his immediate pardon and release.

The *Daily Telegraph* had supported Dean in the campaign to secure his release. But it was politically opposed to Meagher, hence the defamatory reference to his lax conduct at the trial. Meagher sought the best possible advice about his prospects. He briefed Sir Julian Salomons QC. Salomons, who had previously accepted appointment as Chief Justice of New South Wales only to resign 16 days later,[59] and who was the leader of the common law Bar in Sydney. He had represented the Crown at the Royal Commission and was thus fully on top of the facts. Salomons was also a member of the Upper House of the colonial Parliament.

Meagher told Salomons something that caused Salomons to make a detailed record of the interview. It would precipitate the destruction of Meagher's legal career. And it would ensure that Salomons is remembered as much for his controversial handling of the dilemma in which Meagher placed him as for his earlier resignation from the office of Chief Justice of New South Wales. Salomons' record included the following:

> Meagher: Here is the paragraph. (Reads it.) Its suggestion is quite plain, that I bungled the defence of Dean.
>
> Salomons: Yes, I can see that that might be its effect – that Dean was innocent but you let him be convicted. He was an innocent man, and if you had got him off as you should have, the country would have been saved the expense of a Royal Commission. But I am troubled about the question of damages. If you were to succeed how would you be able to prove damage? It might be different if Dean were guilty.
>
> Meagher (smiling): But Dean was in fact guilty, and I absolutely know it.
>
> Salomons: From the first time I came into the matter as Counsel for the Crown on the Royal Commission, I never had the slightest doubt as to Dean's guilt. But what do you mean by saying that you know it absolutely?
>
> Meagher: After Dean had been convicted, and our firm Crick and Meagher, and the public outside were beginning to agitate for a

59 See pp 84-5.

> Royal Commission, I was determined to find out whether Dean was really guilty or not. I went to see Dean, who was then in the condemned cell at Darlinghurst, and I played a trick on him I told him that the police had found out where he had bought the poison ... Dean then, prompted as we went along by my questions, told me the whole story. He gave me the name of the chemist where he had obtained the poison. He said that he had used the two poisons, arsenic and strychnine, to make sure of getting rid of his wife ...

A few days later Sir Julian urged his client to tell the public that Dean's wife was wholly innocent and Dean wholly guilty. He reminded Meagher of his position as an officer of the Court. There was talk about raising money for the now destitute Mrs Dean and also for assisting Dean himself to leave the colony. But Meagher was already compromised by the stance he had taken in agitating for the Royal Commission and instructing his counsel as to how it should be conducted. He did not come back to Salomons. Instead he obtained the return of the brief and got on with his election campaign.

Salomons was perplexed. He consulted several members of the Bar, and the Chief Justice. He also informed the Attorney-General "in confidence". Rumours began to circulate that Dean had made a confession. A member of the Legislative Council asked questions of the Attorney in Parliament and his response, that whatever communications he had received on the matter were confidential, enflamed the public's curiosity. Meagher dug a deeper hole for himself by drafting for Dean a petition to Parliament complaining about the Attorney-General's ambiguous answer and demanding that Parliament appoint a Select Committee to inquire into the matter of his guilt or innocence.

This was the last straw for Sir Julian. He handed his record of the interview to the Attorney-General so that it could be laid on the table of the Legislative Council. Crick, who had meanwhile been assured by Meagher that he had only been pulling Salomon's leg, then viciously attacked Salomons in the Lower House. He referred to his past history of mental breakdown and made a sneering reference to his Jewish ancestry. Dean followed up his petition by presenting an affidavit swearing his denial of any confession and reasserting his innocence of the crime. He also spoke to the press. Meagher then rose in the Lower House and asserted his own belief in Dean's innocence, his denial of any confession by Dean, and his denial of having told Salomons of any confession.

The next evening, Salomons revealed all in the Upper House, giving chapter and verse of Meagher's admission to him. A few days later, a chemist named Smith came forward and informed the police that he had supplied arsenic to Dean at the critical time. He had not entered the transaction in his poison register, hence his silence. The Attorney immediately obtained warrants for the arrest of Dean, Crick and Meagher on a charge of conspiring to defeat the ends of justice. "That the Attorney General should order the arrest of two well-known Members of Parliament, practising solicitors, fellow members of the same legislature, within a day or two of the personal statement of one of them was something which had never happened before in the history of Australia."[60]

Crick and Meagher each made statements to the Legislative Assembly. Crick denied complicity in Meagher's deception and Meagher backed up his friend and partner. Meagher otherwise made a full confession and tendered his resignation. His legal and political careers were finished, or so it seemed. When it was announced at a Vice-Regal luncheon that Meagher and Dean had confessed, speeches were made congratulating Windeyer J on his vindication in the public eye. His Honour, a stern yet emotional man, broke down and sobbed. He retired from the Bench a year later. Dean was prosecuted for perjury both in his false affidavit and in his original trial. When convicted, he was sentenced to 14 years' imprisonment.[61]

Crick, Meagher and Dean were tried for conspiracy to pervert the course of justice. Meagher gave evidence that he had not told his partner about the gaol confession and Crick was then discharged by direction of the judge.[62] Meagher and Dean were convicted after a trial lasting 19 days. But a Full Court would later rule that the judge erred in admitting into evidence the report of the Royal Commission and the *Hansard* record of Salomons' speech to the Legislative Council. Verdicts of acquittal were entered because the law did not in those days allow for a fresh trial.[63]

Meagher, then aged only 29, was however struck off by the Supreme Court in separate proceedings.[64] One might have thought that that would have been the last heard of him. But his capacity for self-justification, a remarkable resilience, and the loyalty of his electors and political associates saw him returned to Parliament in 1898 only three years after his abject resignation. Meagher applied to the Court unsuccessfully for reinstatement as a solicitor in 1900,

---

60 Blackwell, *op cit*, p 92.

61 Allen, *op cit*, raises doubt about the lawfulness of the perjury charge stemming from the trial. It was unsuccessfully challenged on appeal on the ground that the statute which created the crime of committing perjury with intent to procure the conviction or acquittal of "any person" did not extend to the perjurer himself (*R v Dean* (1896) 17 NSWLR (L) 35). A recent decision by the High Court of Australia suggests that an acquittal obtained through the perjury of the accused cannot be controverted by laying a later charge of perjury (*R v Carroll* (2002) 213 CLR 635). Here, of course, Dean was convicted.

62 He continued with his parliamentary career and became Minister for Lands. His involvement in a land agent scandal saw him prosecuted for bribery. The jury twice disagreed and the prosecution was dropped. Crick was suspended from Parliament and afterwards resigned to escape expulsion. He was struck off the roll of solicitors in 1906 and died shortly afterwards.

63 *R v Dean and Meagher* (1896) 17 NSWLR (L) 132.

64 *In re Meagher* (1896) 17 NSWLR (L) 157. The Court found that his motivation had been self-glorification.

1902 and 1904.[65] He narrowly escaped implication in Crick's later misdoings in the Department of Lands. In 1909 the Supreme Court ordered his reinstatement as a solicitor.[66] The Law Institute appealed to the High Court of Australia. There Meagher was struck off because of his involvement in the intervening Crick land scandals and because it was found that the Court below had erred in failing to realise that Meagher had to show affirmatively his fitness to be trusted.[67] Griffith CJ declared that

> [T]he conduct now under consideration [the dodgy land deals] is to be regarded not as a first offence, if offence it be, committed by a person of previously blameless character; but as one committed by a person whose reputation is already grievously tainted, and who has been already convicted of an offence for which nothing short of absolute removal from the roll would have been an appropriate punishment.[68]

Was this at last the end for Meagher's ambition to be a solicitor as well as a highly successful politician? Would he accept the verdict of the High Court of Australia as to his unfitness to practise? Hardly! He embarked on a program of public meetings in which he continued to misstate his role in the Dean affair and to protest his innocence. He published a booklet with the front-page inscription:

> Vindication
>
> The Celebrated Dean Case
>
> Including Sensational Speech delivered by RD Meagher MLA in the Protestant Hall, Sydney (Hon WM Hughes, Federal Attorney General, in the Chair)

In 1912 a private member's Bill was introduced to place Meagher's name back on the roll of solicitors. Meagher was at that time the Deputy Speaker of the Legislative Assembly. Applications by the Bar Council and the Law Institute for leave to appear by counsel at the Bar of the House were denied. The Bill was carried in the Legislative Assembly by 37 votes to 28 but was defeated in the Legislative Council by 28 to 14. Two years later, Meagher had become the Speaker of the Lower House and the Chairman of the Labor Party. In 1916 he became Lord Mayor of Sydney. He served in these public offices with distinction. A further application to the Supreme Court in 1917 was also rejected.[69]

In 1919 Meagher went back to the Supreme Court, representing himself. Foolishly, he argued that the High Court's decision was wrong, rather than

---

65 His 1900 application was supported by a memorial signed by 103 members of Parliament.

66 *In re Meagher* (1909) 9 SR (NSW) 504.

67 *Incorporated Law Institute of New South Wales v Meagher* (1909) 9 CLR 655.

68 *Ibid* at 665-6.

69 *Ex parte Meagher* (1917) 17 SR (NSW) 305.

accepting its verdict and relying on his record of public service. He also recanted an apology earlier tendered, at the suggestion of the Court, to the family of the late Windeyer J, reverting to his claim that the miscarriage of the original trial justified his misconduct. Not surprisingly, the Supreme Court of New South Wales recognised that it had to bow to the High Court of Australia.[70] The application was rejected and the High Court confirmed the order in 1920. Meagher responded with a further pamphlet accusing the Chief Justice of New South Wales of being "a bigoted old gentleman, saturated with prejudice, racial and religious who is unfitted – and by his own act proved to be unfitted – for the judicial dignity".

Meagher was now 54. He had just lost a by-election for the Legislative Assembly. But readmission was about to be obtained as Parliament showed its capacity to trump the courts. Another private member's Bill was promoted over the howls of protest by the Sydney Bar, the Law Institute and the Society of Accountants. It passed, and so Meagher achieved reinstatement in his profession in the teeth of opposition from his legal peers and the courts of the land.[71] From this distance, the only thing that could be said for Meagher is that he did not fail to exhaust all alternative remedies.

Did Salomons do the right thing when, haltingly in private and then openly in Parliament, he divulged what he had been told in the course of a retainer to give legal advice? Sir Carleton Kemp Allen treated him sympathetically in an article in the *Law Quarterly Review* in 1941, suggesting that Dean's conduct in demanding a full statement in light of Attorney-General Want's evasive reply to the parliamentary question released Salomon from his professional obligation. Allen also states that Darley CJ gave Salomons a green light.

But I cannot agree, although I have the benefit of later rulings of law and I deeply sympathise with Salomons' dilemma. As the High Court would declare in *Tuckiar v The King*,[72] it is counsel's "paramount" duty to respect the client's privilege notwithstanding concern for the reputation of strangers. That Court would even later describe legal professional privilege as a field where the law has already struck the balance with a finite list of exceptions none of which includes the situation facing Meagher.[73]

A bemusing aspect of the saga was that Meagher himself had breached his own client's privilege when he told Salomons about the confession of guilt. There could hardly have been stronger circumstances mitigating Salomons' breach, but breach there was.

---

70 *Ex parte Meagher* (1919) 19 SR (NSW) 433. On other occasions, the Supreme Court and other courts lower in the judicial hierarchy have had to be reminded of this obligation of fidelity by the High Court, sometimes in firm tones.

71 *Legal Practitioners Amendment Act 1920* (NSW).

72 (1934) 52 CLR 335 at 346-7.

73 *Carter v Northmore Hale Davy & Leake* (1995) 183 CLR 121.

And, on the topic of breach, perhaps I should be craving the indulgence of the New South Wales Parliament for my own possible breach, in these pages, of Article 9 of the English Bill of Rights of 1688 which is still part of our law[74] and which states that:

> [T]he Freedom of Speech, and Debates or Proceedings in Parliament, ought not to be impeached or questioned in any Court or Place out of Parliament.

74 See *Egan v Willis* (1998) 195 CLR 424 at 444-5.

8 Layfolk in the Law

Legal insiders need constant reminding that the institution that gives them fascination and material reward exists to serve the whole community. Without the participation of layfolk as litigants, witnesses, jurors and support staff there would be no legal system anyway. Lawyers have no monopoly when it comes to interesting and amusing characters.

Vexing and vexatious litigants

Some self-represented litigants may achieve fame by their spectacular success or spectacular failure in a single leading case.

In 1884 Edmund Barton was the Speaker of the New South Wales Legislative Assembly.[1] He was faced with disruptive behaviour by Adolphus George Taylor, a Member of Parliament described by Barton's biographer as "an able and well-informed nuisance".[2] Barton, believing himself to have the powers of the Speaker of the House of Commons, suspended Taylor from the House for a week. When he twice attempted to take his seat during that period, he was removed by the sergeant-at-arms at Barton's command. Taylor sued the sergeant-at-arms and Barton, and was vindicated by the Supreme Court which held that the Speaker could suspend for no more than a single sitting.[3] Barton appealed to the Privy Council, retaining leading English counsel at government expense. Taylor represented himself, funding the journey to London for himself, his wife and his mother from the sale of a stamp collection. The Privy Council complimented Taylor for his advocacy and dismissed Barton's appeal, ruling that the colonial Parliament's *Standing Orders* were ultra vires.[4]

The doughty Sydney barrister Archibald Nugent Robinson/Robertson,[5] whose refusal to pay a second penny before exiting the wharf at Circular Quay

1 He became Prime Minister of Australia in the early years of federation and later became an original appointee to the High Court of Australia.

2 Geoffrey Bolton, *Edmund Barton*, Allen & Unwin, 2000, p 40.

3 *Taylor v Barton* (1884) 6 NSWLR (L) 1.

4 See *Barton v Taylor* (1886) 11 App Cas 197. Barton had a second loss in the Privy Council in 1890 in litigation involving the redemption of a mortgage: *Barton v Bank of New South Wales* (1890) 15 App Cas 379.

5 In the High Court reports the case is called *Balmain New Ferry Co Ltd v Robertson* (1906) 4 CLR 379 whereas in the Privy Council reports it is called *Robinson v Balmain*

after he missed his ferry home, has amused generations of law students and illuminated the law of false imprisonment. All this, despite his costly failures as a self-represented litigant in the High Court and (with English counsel) in the Privy Council. When Giancarlo Gambotto, representing himself, persuaded the High Court his minority shareholding could not be expropriated against his will,[6] he shocked most legal and commercial commentators, set off a new era of "greenmailing" and caused several leading lawyers to suffer a verdict for over $21 million in damages for professional negligence. This was because the High Court's ruling led the National Roads and Motorists Association to abandon an expensive program for demutualisation. The negligence verdict was later overturned by the New South Wales Court of Appeal that would rule that it was not negligent to fail to anticipate that the High Court might move the law's goalposts even if it had opened that possibility by granting special leave to appeal.[7]

Some litigants are extremely resourceful, some are just plain lucky. One of the latter was Mr Ross Mallam, a Northern Territory solicitor, who was suspended from practice for 12 months by Hogan DJ, a deputy Judge, for contempt of court for filing a false affidavit. He appealed to the High Court. There was an unrelated appeal by a man who had been convicted by Hogan DJ. The High Court, by majority, held that Hogan's appointment was invalid on the ground that there could be no Deputy Judge when the office of Judge was vacant.[8] Mallam's appeal was later struck out on the basis that, because Hogan's appointment was invalid, the order suspending him was a nullity and therefore there was nothing from which to appeal.[9]

Resourcefulness of the highest order was shown by a man named Seeley who was being tried at Newcastle Quarter Sessions before Judge Cross and a jury on a charge of break, enter and steal. Two detectives gave evidence that Seeley had confessed during an interview. Seeley made an unsworn statement from the dock in which he said:

New Ferry Co Ltd [1910] AC 295. A detailed account of the saga is provided by Mark Lunney, "Federation and beyond: what the history of Australian tort law can tell us" (2010) 33 *Australian Bar Review* 77 at 85-90.

6 *Gambotto v WCP Ltd* (1995) 182 CLR 432. The High Court held that an alteration to the articles of association passed by the 99.7% majority permitting the expropriation of his shares was invalid because, though passed for a proper purpose, it operated oppressively in relation to minority shareholders.

7 *Heydon v NRMA Ltd* (2000) 51 NSWLR 1. The trial judge, Giles J, had placed considerable weight on the fact that special leave to appeal had been granted and that, whenever it was, about 50% of appeals succeeded: see at 127.

8 *Presley v Geraghty* (1921) 29 CLR 154.

9 Mildren, *Big Boss Fella All Same Judge*, p 65. Owen Dixon represented the unsuccessful respondent in *Presley*. Perhaps this experience was the trigger for his later article showing that the invalidity of a judge's appointment did not invalidate his judicial acts unless his authority was directly challenged by proceedings in the nature of quo warranto: see his "De Facto Officers" in Woinarski (ed), *Jesting Pilate*.

> What Detectives X and Y said in their evidence was not true. It is the fact that they were interviewing me in the Newcastle Police Station and on that occasion what occurred was as follows. Some footsteps were heard outside the window of the room in which they were interviewing me and the local sergeant of police, Sergeant A, walked past the window.
>
> Detective X said to Detective Y, "Who is that?" Detective Y said: "That is the village idiot."
>
> Sergeant A then opened the door and said to Detectives X and Y: "What are you doing?"
>
> Detective X said: "We are in here putting a verbal on Seeley."
>
> Sergeant A said: "You had better watch out. Cross does not like verbals."
>
> Detective X said: "We don't care about Cross. We're only interested in the twelve idiots on the jury."

Seeley was acquitted.

Financial considerations lead some litigants to represent themselves. But for many it is an occupation of choice designed to permit them to inflict vexation freed of the costs and professional restraints of retaining lawyers to speak on their behalf. In McHugh J's words, "lack of legal knowledge is a misfortune, not a privilege".[10] But courts have traditionally cut a lot of slack towards the plight of the unrepresented, so much so that a represented party may sometimes have reason to fear that the scales are tipped too far in the opposite direction. Judges have not always heeded the warning of Bryson JA who said that "it is wrong and unjust to turn self-representation into a procedural advantage".[11]

Some self-represented litigants refuse to take no for an answer, launching repeated sallies at the same target even if blocked by the lack of evidence or legal grounds and the doctrines of res judicata, issue estoppel and abuse of process. Others pursue an ever-widening group of defendants accused of being parties to a conspiracy obstructing them in the pursuit of their rights. Lawyers and judges can get caught up in misguided but still vexing civil and criminal proceedings launched against them.[12] The plight of registry staff forced to deal with them is usually ignored.

Sadly, some vexatious litigants ("frequent filers") have been set off on their forensic careers by an initial miscarriage of justice. Others show or acquire symptoms of mental disturbance. Others see litigation as the means of making some political point again and again. Whatever the causes, these determined litigants often evince common traits such as verbosity, repetition, and the desire to fill every part of the page with verbiage typed in small fonts and severely underlined in a variety of colours.

---

10 *Gallo v Dawson* (1990) 64 ALJR 458 at 459.

11 *Uszok v Henley Properties (NSW) Pty Ltd* [2007] NSWCA 31 at [163].

12 See eg *Gallo v Dawson* (1992) 66 ALJR 859; *Rajski v Yeldham* (1989) 18 NSWLR 48.

Courts and parliaments have devised inadequate means of checking the onslaughts of the vexatious litigant. Like the poor, they will be with us till the end of time now that courts have shied away from insisting on legal representation.[13] There are many stories about vexatious litigants, many of them unpublished for fear of attracting defamation writs. In 2009 Simon Smith wrote an extremely sympathetic account of the personal stories of those who had to date been declared vexatious litigants, confining himself closely to tales of the dead or the facts set out in reports of decided cases.[14]

One of them was Edna Davis, a woman pushed over the edge by the machinations of Sir Isaac Isaacs, by this time an ex-Governor-General. Edna's 1938 marriage to his brother John (older than her by 44 years) lasted 11 months before she was turned out of the matrimonial home. The elderly John then secretly converted his sole ownership of that property into joint ownership with his brother. Sir Isaac then arranged for the electricity, gas, telephone and water of the house to be turned off and the furniture to be put into storage. When the woman pawned her wedding ring, a gift from her husband that had previously belonged to his mother, Sir Isaac convinced the pawnbroker that he (Isaac) had always remained its true owner. Edna sued, but Clyne J would accept her brother-in-law's testimony that he had only lent the ring to his brother in the first place. Not long before the trial, in May 1940, Isaacs wrote to his daughter about Prime Minister Chamberlain's appeasement of Hitler, going on to say:[15]

> There is another Hitler we are concerned with at the present moment. But the monster is in Female form and signs herself 'Edna' ... She keeps on bombarding Uncle Jack with protestations of love for him and denunciation of me ... for ill-will and persecution of a poor innocent and much injured woman.

Davis' later forays into litigation saw her spiralling out of control. Her action to recover the matrimonial furniture was dismissed with findings that she was utterly unworthy of credence. Further hopeless cases were launched, one of them against Sir Isaac Isaacs himself. Eventually a "Counter Attack" in the form of a "*Blitzkreig*" (Isaacs' words) came in the form of proceedings that saw her declared vexatious. The distinguished Victorian judge Sir John Barry wrote that:[16]

13 The High Court has in recent years required all applications for special leave to be in writing, reserving the right in the Court to dispose of them on the papers. This has proved to be a facially neutral way of handling "the problem" of the unrepresented litigant.

14 Smith, *Maverick Litigants*. There is an entry on "Vexatious litigants" in Blackshield et al, *Oxford Companion to the High Court of Australia*.

15 Smith, *Maverick Litigants*, p 144.

16 John Barry, "From Yackandandah to Yarralumla: the Enigma of Isaac Isaacs" (1967) 16 *Meanjin* 449.

> It was saddening to see a man of Isaacs' eminence in law and public life behaving with a venom and lack of reason that would have been deplorable even in a vexatious litigant.

Edna remarried and went on to better things, including a regular guest spot on the Don Lane show on late night television.

Joseph Slack frequently appeared for himself before Victorian courts in the 1860s, 1870s and 1880s. "A man of some means, he remained convinced that he was better able to present his case than any member of the bar despite accumulating evidence to the contrary."[17] Slack's deportment was combative and at times aggressive. He claimed the right, which the Court denied him, to conduct his cases from the Bar table. On one occasion he was imprisoned for contempt for flinging a heavy inkstand at the head of opposing counsel.

It was, however, the end of Slack's career that saw his most notable contribution to Australian legal history. While in Pentridge Gaol, a convicted burglar named Barnes heard that Slack kept valuable jewellery in his house. After his release in 1884 Barnes gained access to the house but was disturbed by Slack. He grabbed Slack around the neck and throttled him. He then cut Slack's throat with a razor, placed the razor in the victim's left hand, took the jewellery and some other goods and departed. The police accepted the theory of suicide and there was no autopsy.

Barnes returned to his nefarious career and found himself back in prison. While there he learnt that the police had discovered a case containing some of Slack's clothing at his (Barnes') house. Although no suspicion of complicity in Slack's murder had yet been aroused, Barnes began behaving strangely and was placed under observation. A warder heard him muttering what a shame it was for him to have killed poor old Slack. This at once brought police inquiries with the result that a full confession to the murder was obtained. Slack's body was exhumed and it revealed that his death was the result of throttling and could not have been suicide. Furthermore, he was a right-handed man and could not have cut his throat in the way it had been cut. At his trial Barnes contended that the confession was untrue and the product of a disordered mind. He was convicted and hanged.

Judges often pray for deliverance from particular litigants in person, but never hopefully by such means.

Leonard Lindon, aka Citizen Limbo, graced a number of courts in the 1980s. He was a legal practitioner admitted in South Australia who was charged with trespassing at the Joint Space Research Facility at Alice Springs, commonly known as Pine Gap. Having obtained a retrial after an initial conviction he launched a wide-ranging defence, asserting that Pine Gap was a nuclear target

---

17 Dean, *A Multitude of Counsellors*, p 121. Other information about Slack is provided by Forde, *The Story of the Bar of Victoria*, pp 245-7.

and that the courts had an ancient legal duty to prevent imminent extinction of the human race, irrespective of the laws of the Territory or the Commonwealth. He issued subpoenas for the attendance of all manner of worthies, including President Bush and Premier Gorbachev. He also sought to interrogate all potential judges as to matters that might in his view lead to their disqualification. At various stages in the litigation he sought orders that he be paid legal fees for acting for himself and that the prosecutor be required to accept his reverse charge telephone calls.[18]

Mr Limbo sought leave to intervene in the High Court constitutional proceedings of *Polyukhovich v Commonwealth*.[19] After addressing the Court, the following dialogue ensued:[20]

> Mason CJ: Thank you, Mr Limbo.
> Mr Limbo: Sir, could I be addressed as "Citizen" rather than "Mister" to be non-gender specific about it?
> Mason CJ: Well, Mr Limbo, I am addressing you in the normal manner.

Handling the self-represented is often trying and vexatious for the judge. The restraints of professional discipline are absent and the litigant may have no will, insight or capacity to understand what is relevant. Threats to invoke the contempt power are usually just that, although I record with wry approval Montagu J's intimation that he would fine a self-represented accused who persisted in asking irrelevant questions £5 "for each question he put unconnected with the case". He was ultimately fined £10 and imprisoned pending payment for irrelevance in his final address to the jury.[21]

Gallop J (ACT Supreme Court) had the following kindly encounter with a thirsty and hungry litigant in person:

> Sheriff's Officer to Litigant in person seated at the bar table: "What's in that flask you are sipping from?"
> Litigant: "Just some spirits."
> (The matter is dutifully reported to the Associate.)
> Litigant: "Your Honour I'm fairly nervous. Is it OK if I sip from this flask (holding it up)?"
> His Honour: "I've never had anyone ask if they could consume alcohol in Court – it is alcohol, is it?"
> Litigant: "Yes."
> His Honour: "I wouldn't want to impede your presentation of your case if it will overcome your nerves. Do whatever you like."
> Litigant: "Well, I won't sip it then. Is it OK if I eat a banana then?"

---

18 See Mildren, *Big Boss Fella All Same Judge*, pp 279-80; *Limbo v Little* (1989) 45 A Crim R 61.

19 (1991) 172 CLR 501.

20 High Court of Australia, Transcript, 3 September 1990.

21 BA Keon-Cohen, "Mad Judge Montagu: A Misnomer?" (1975) 2 *Monash University Law Review* 50 at 60.

> His Honour: "Look, just sit down will you, and don't talk nonsense. This is a serious business here and there are others wanting to get their cases on. I won't let you make a farce of the proceedings."
> Litigant: "Can I get an adjournment to get some legal advice?"
> His Honour: "Well, that's the most sensible thing you've said so far."

Yeldham J was confronted by Dr Rajski, a self-represented litigant who made many appearances in the Supreme Court of New South Wales during the 1980 and 1990s. In my hearing, Rajski objected to the judge hearing a matter because "the last time I was before your Honour you called me a pest". "I still think you are a pest, but I am not going to disqualify myself" was the judicial retort. Yeldham became one of the many lawyers who were later sued by Rajski.

Although he never sat as a trial judge, Meagher JA was generally sympathetic to the plight of those faced with an irritating witness or party. In *Galea v Galea*[22] he agreed with Kirby P's reasons, including his lengthy consideration of arguments that the trial judge, Powell J, had enlivened a reasonable apprehension of bias or otherwise misconducted himself by his interventions and hostile remarks during the appellant's evidence. But, as usual, there was nothing tentative about Meagher JA's approach.[23] He found it hard to take the appellant's submissions seriously. After referring to the leading High Court decisions, he continued:

> [The principle laid down by the High Court] has led to appellants, in cases otherwise devoid of merits, seizing on any acerbic utterance made by the trial judge and urging that utterance as a ground for appeal on the basis of bias. This is a tendency which is not justified by these authorities and must be resisted. Where, as in the present case, a judge is confronted by a witness who is both deceitful and evasive, there is no principle that he is not at liberty to express his measured displeasure at being trifled with. There is no principle that he must endure the ordeal with ladylike serenity ... In my view, if a reasonable disinterested bystander had heard the passage at arms complained of in the present case he would not have reasonably apprehended that the trial judge was prejudiced, he would only have noted that an exceptionally irritating witness had eventually succeeded in irritating the judge.

Witnesses

In 1823 a magistrate in Hobart Town ordered a witness to be taken from the court and given 100 lashes, in order to get more satisfactory information from him.[24] In his history of juries in New South Wales Ian Barker QC records another incident that same year when a similarly recalcitrant witness was flogged for his

22 (1990) 19 NSWLR 263.

23 See *ibid* at 283-4.

24 James Fenton, *A History of Tasmania*, Walch Brothers and Birchall, 1884, p 61.

contempt. Barker adds that "such a process in the courts of New South Wales in 2003 would, I think, wonderfully concentrate the mind of witnesses, although it would probably become more difficult to serve subpoenas".[25]

Witnesses who tell too much tend to be as much a menace (to their own cause) as those who refuse to testify. This is usually because, in Handley JA's words, "from time to time a party with a good cause is unable to resist the temptation to improve it".[26] But there have been notable situations where witnesses gave entirely unexpected answers. Thus:

- The credibility of an Irish witness was challenged under cross-examination. Hickman Molesworth (later Judge Molesworth) asked him if he had once been put upon his trial for sheep-stealing. "I was!" said the witness with alacrity: "and I was ably defended by Counsellor Molesworth, and honourably acquitted by a jury of my fellow-countrymen".[27]
- Robert Stitt QC had the following exchanges with a female witness:
  - Stitt: I would like to put a couple of propositions to you.
  - Witness: You would? My luck has changed at last.
  - His Honour: I think you had better wait until you hear what the proposition is.
- At the next adjournment Stitt QC happened to be in the same lift as the witness and the sparring continued:
  - Witness: Still interested in that proposition?
  - Stitt: You have to realise, whatever I get, my junior gets two-thirds.[28]
- The late Peter Hely QC once asked a witness: Q. "Do you prefer to be referred to as Miss O'Keefe, Mrs O'Keefe or Ms?" She answered: "You can call me Julie. I don't mind that". "In other circumstances I would be happy", he replied.[29]
- An accused who, having told the magistrate that he had not had a drink for two years, was asked "Was that on medical advice?" replied: "No, on yours".[30]
- Kirkham DCJ presided at the trial of a young man charged with a serious robbery with wounding at a Bowling Club. Two offenders, one armed with a double barrel shotgun and the other a knife, menaced the victims with their weapons. The male victim was stabbed twice. The other victim was asked in chief:

25 Barker, *Sorely Tried*, p 48.
26 *Harrison v Schipp* [2002] NSWCA 78 at [98].
27 Hewitt, *Judges*, p 31.
28 As to the two-thirds rule, see p 143.
29 *ASC v Crane* (NSW Supreme Court, Coram Levine J, 30 August 1994).
30 *Order in the Court*, p 46.

> Did you notice anything about the demeanour of the two men?
> To which she innocently answered: "The one with the knife was the meaner of the two."[31]

A plaintiff in the 19th century claimed damages for injuries suffered when he was crushed by a fall of earth. A doctor came from 30 miles away and found him so badly hurt that he stated that there was no chance of recovery. The doctor said that, as he could not come so long a distance again, it would be as well he should leave a certificate as to the cause of his death. He did so. The man recovered and produced in court the certificate of the cause of his own death.[32]

A witness who made an affirmation before giving oral evidence, but who had sworn his affidavits on oath, reminded Katz J of the American scholar Wigmore's story of the man who said he wished to affirm, rather than swear an oath, before giving evidence. Wigmore's judge said that he recalled the witness having given evidence before him on an earlier occasion, at which time the witness had sworn an oath. Why, the judge asked, was he not prepared to do so now? The witness's explanation: "Your Honour, I was more sure of my facts that time".[33] Another witness, called for the prosecution, was reminded by counsel for the prisoner, "now, sir, recollect you are on your oath". The witness coolly replied, "No, I am not to you", thereby showing his true allegiance.[34]

Under cross-examination by the redoubtable Purves QC, a witness made an interjection audible to the barrister but not to the trial judge, Sir Thomas a'Beckett (Supreme Court Victoria 1886-1917). Purves protested, exclaiming: "Your Honour, the witness mumbled something to the effect that I was a rude, bullying barrister". A'Beckett J said: "Is it true, witness? Did you mumble something to that effect to Mr Purves?" The witness admitted that he had done so, and added that he was justified in expressing that view. "Well", said a'Beckett, "you mustn't mumble, you really must not mumble".[35]

Some witnesses have had their testimonies rejected in memorable terms. Murphy J once observed that:[36]

> The record shows that Richard Seary, drug addict, informer and mentally disturbed fantasizer, must be one of the most unreliable persons ever presented as the principal prosecution witness on a charge of serious crime.

Judge Villeneuve-Smith delivered himself of the following in December 1984:[37]

> Ananias, Casanova, and Baron Munchausen have long enjoyed historical recognition in the academy of illustrious liars. But had

31 *R v Visser* (NSW District Court, 1993).
32 Forde, *The Story of the Bar of Victoria*, p 140.
33 *Blacker v National Australia Bank Ltd* [2000] FCA 681 at [126].
34 Forde, *The Story of the Bar of Victoria*, p 139.
35 Dean, *A Multitude of Counsellors*, p 139.
36 *Alister v The Queen* (1984) 154 CLR 404 at 525.
37 *Order in the Court*, p 86.

> that mendaciously talented trio been present to hear the sweep and scope of the carefully structured and unblushingly articulated perjury presented on the hearing of this appeal, they would, without demur, have relinquished the accolade hitherto bestowed upon them, and conceded at once their status to be no more than mere artless narrators of simple fables for the amusement of young children.

Priestley JA described a witness as having "an Achilles heel which reached up to his knee".[38]

Jurors

The administration of the law involves much more than the doings of judges and lawyers. Serious crimes are prosecuted before judge and jury. And, until recently, juries were used extensively in civil actions such as motor vehicle and industrial injuries claims, not to mention defamation cases (the only area where they survive). Jurors do not have to give reasons for their verdicts, thus attracting Lord Denning's remark that a general verdict was "as inscrutable as the Sphinx".[39] This prompted Samuels AP to observe:[40]

> The Sphinx, of course, was a mythological monster, and the name is usually translated 'strangler' or 'throttler'; although it is said that it 'more probably means "tightbinder", the demon of death': ... Whichever translation is to be preferred, it hardly seems an appropriate emblem for a tribunal designed for the wise and rational determination of civil disputes.

In 1854 a Victorian Crown Prosecutor, George Mackay, was reported by a newspaper to have been drunk during a trial. He sued for libel. The paper called several witnesses to establish the truth of the allegation, including the trial judge.[41] One of the witnesses was the foreman of the juries before whom the relevant series of trials took place. He testified that Mackay was drunk, adding that "in consequence of the slovenly manner in which the cases were conducted the jury were obliged to return verdicts contrary to the evidence". Mackay nevertheless represented himself so well in the libel case that the jury awarded him damages of £800.

The pre-eminent Victorian silk, James Liddell Purves, discovered to his horror that one of the jurymen he was addressing in a civil case was his landlord, to whom a considerable sum was owing for rent. Throughout the trial Purves could see the disdainful and unsympathetic eye of that man cast upon him. At the conclusion of his address this juryman observed: "It's no good, Mr

38 *Attorney-General v Radio 2UE Sydney & Jones* (unrep, NSW Court of Appeal, 28 August 1992), p 4.

39 *Ward v James* [1966] 1 QB 273 at 301.

40 *Morgan v John Fairfax & Sons Ltd* (1990) 20 NSWLR 511 at 521-2, citations omitted.

41 See Dean, *A Multitude of Counsellors*, p 32.

Purves, we are not listening to you". Purves promptly retorted: "None of my observations, Sir, are directed at you. Had you been paying proper attention you would have noticed that I said: 'Gentlemen of the jury'."[42]

Human nature being what it is, jurors sometimes disregard their instructions to attend only to the evidence, listen to submissions, follow directions and render a just verdict. Often departures go undetected, and there are restrictions on the receipt of evidence that would disclose the content of jury deliberations. Jurors have nevertheless been known to conduct their own researches to supplement the paucity of the evidence or what is to them the uncomfortable requirement of deciding a case according to a particular onus or standard of proof. Windeyer J once observed that:[43]

> Lawyers are accustomed to the concept of a civil action as a matter to be decided on the evidence produced by the parties, one of them bearing the burden of proof. They do not always appreciate that laymen may well feel, not only that such proceedings are not well designed to get at the real truth, but that they ought to be.

Australian law offers very old and very new examples of trials that miscarried because jurors conducted their own experiment or inspection of a place that may well have altered since the events in question. In 1835 the Full Court of the NSW Supreme Court ordered a new trial in a building case where some of the jury, accompanied by the plaintiff, went to the premises during an overnight adjournment. The matter came to the attention of the judge who found that no improper communication had occurred. The whole jury later returned to the site under proper supervision. Their verdict in the plaintiff's favour was set aside and a new trial ordered.[44]

It was only the failure to make timely objection that prevented new trials being ordered in two civil cases where the jury conducted an unauthorised view. In a 1902 libel case based on a newspaper report about the decency of an actress's dress on stage, the lawyers for both sides made a private arrangement for the jurors to attend a performance and see for themselves. Unsurprisingly, some jurors wanted their wives to be present but this proposal was rejected. The jurors decided, however, that it would be safer to avoid the wrath of their wives than that of the barristers, so they took them along nonetheless, discussing their observations with them. The Full Court brushed off a complaint with the observation that the Court could not say that the jury had reached an unreasonable conclusion when they found that fair comment had been established.[45] In 1928 a jury had to decide whether adultery had occurred in a watchmakers'

42 *Ibid*, p 149.

43 *Jones v Dunkel* (1959) 101 CLR 298 at 317-18.

44 *Chadley v Wyatt (No 1)* (1835) NSW Sel Cas (Dowling) 669.

45 *Menzies-Stuart v McLeod* (1902) 18 WN 82 (discussed by Fricke, *Libels, Lampoons and Litigants: famous Australian libel cases,* Hutchinson of Australia, pp 124-5).

shop in Angel Place, Sydney. The petitioner had testified that he stood outside the shop at six in the evening and had seen all. When the judge asked the jurors if they wished to see the premises for themselves some admitted that they had already done so. No complaint was raised until the appeal, too late.

In 2004 jurors went on an unauthorised and unsupervised view of a park where a very serious sexual assault had occurred and where the complainant's capacity to identify the accused at night was the principal issue. The matter only came to attention after verdict and, miscarriage having been found, a new trial was ordered.[46] Jurors searching the internet are a major problem for modern trial management.[47]

Jurors are not the only persons known to have ignored the rules. A High Court associate once told John Bryson[48] about an appeal heard in Hobart over a collision at a railway level crossing. There was a lot of evidence either way about the view which a motorist would have when approaching the crossing. After dinner at a club, some of the justices went down to have a look for themselves. As they paced up and down the track a train approached which caused them to jump out of the way with agility usually reserved for more cognitive processes. The following day the Railways got a rough hearing.

A juror in a trial before Lowe J asked to be excused because his wife was about to conceive. Counsel helpfully corrected this by stating that she was about to be confined. Lowe ruled that "in either case the presence of the husband is highly desirable".[49] This contrasts with the attitude of the County Court judge who was Victorian in both senses of the word, Edward Hamilton. A proposed juryman sought excusal on the ground that his wife was expecting a baby very shortly. "Well, they won't want *you*", roared the Judge. "Application refused."[50]

46 *R v Skaf* (2004) 60 NSWLR 86.

47 See eg *R v K* (2003) 144 A Crim R 468.

48 Later a judge of the New South Wales Court of Appeal.

49 JR Poynter, "Lowe, Sir Charles John (1880-1969)", *Australian Dictionary of Biography*, National Centre of Biography, Australian National University, <http://adb.anu.edu.au/biography/lowe-sir-charles-john-10865/text19285>.

50 Hewitt, *Judges*, p 37, citing Jacobs, *A Lawyer Tells*.

9 Legal and Judicial Academics

Citing and writing law books

"Sir William Owen from the Bench said, 'You have a great pile of books on the table [*Mr Salomons*]. Do you intend to cite from all of them?' 'No, not if your Honours know the law', was counsel's reply; and then he added very deliberately, 'but I expect I shall have to cite most of them. Yes, I think my argument must last the whole day'."[1] Once, with Foster J on the Bench, another judge informed Salomons that the view he was putting to the Court was supported by a passage "in my brother Foster's *District Court Practice*". Most ungraciously counsel retorted that "it might be very good law for all that!'."[2] Return of service in the opposite direction occurred when Sir James Martin was told by counsel: "I should like to inform the Court that I assisted in the preparation of the edition of *Benjamin on Sales*, from which your honour is quoting". "It may be a good book for all that, Mr Butterworth" flashed back from the Chief Justice.[3]

Mr Paris Nesbit KC[4] caused a flutter when arguing an appeal in the High Court. He made some statements regarding the law of trusts. "That sounds rather startling", said Sir Samuel Griffith: "what is your authority for that proposition?" "I should have thought", Nesbitt replied, "that it was unnecessary to require authority for something so obvious". Turning to his instructing solicitor, he said, "Get me a textbook on the law of trusts from the Supreme Court library". As the solicitor was approaching the door leading out of the court, Nesbit called out, in the hearing of everyone, "Any elementary book will do!"[5] Sir Owen Dixon told of an occasion when counsel appearing before Sir Thomas a'Beckett quoted from a well-known book on patent law. A'Beckett asked if it was a reputable book. Counsel asked why not. "Oh", answered a'Beckett, "I thought that the last passage you read must be wrong. It sounded like common sense".[6]

---

1 Blacket, *May it Please Your Honour*, p 34. This and the following anecdote concerning Julian Salomons support Dr Bennett's description of him as "a man whose regard for decorum was suspect" (p 84 above).

2 Piddington, *Worshipful Masters*, p 204.

3 Blacket, *May It Please Your Honour*, 1927.

4 As to his brushes with madness, see p 60.

5 Jacobs, *A Lawyer Tells*, p 153.

6 Dean, *A Multitude of Counsellors*, p 139.

A different attribution occurred when Goldsmith Collins was well advanced in his sorry career as a vexatious litigant.[7] Early in life he had played Australian Rules football for Fitzroy when it won the premiership. But a tussle with the local council over a fence built without a permit spiralled out of control. By the 1950s Collins had been declared vexatious by both the High Court and the Supreme Court of Victoria and he had spent time in prison for contempt. Collins was later barred from the Victorian Supreme Court Library, a dispute that he took to court with allegations of a fraudulent conspiracy against its judicial chairman, Sir Charles Lowe. This action was stayed as vexatious or an abuse of process[8] and Collins perforce shifted his major research efforts to the Public Library of Victoria. There, in the legal book section, he befriended another "frequent filer", Constance May Bienvenu.[9] He told her that he had an expert knowledge of constitutional law, having purchased the books of former High Court Chief Justice and Fitzroy supporter, Sir John Latham. He offered to help Bienvenu draw up legal documents.[10]

All academic lawyers learn as they teach. "Explaining legal doctrines, orally or in writing, to neophytes in the law is an excellent way of increasing the understanding not only of those who are taught, but of those who teach."[11] Some very distinguished legal academics have progressed to the Bench, including Peter Nygh, Paul Finn, Ronald Sackville and Dyson Heydon (the first two without intervening stints of practice at the Bar). Some judges have continued their academic roles, as writers and teachers, while remaining on the Bench. When, on the New South Wales Court of Appeal Heydon JA once referred to "the restitution industry (academic division)",[12] one suspects that he was being polite to an immediate judicial colleague who was a member of the "judicial division" of that industry which he and others saw to be attempting a hostile takeover of traditional "Equity".

The work of judges is more constrained than that of academics. Sir Victor Windeyer once distinguished the roles of judge and academic as follows:

> A judge is a working hand part of the crew of a vessel, the courts, for which each case is a separate voyage. He has not the time to be a cartographer of lands discovered. That is the task which is undertaken by academic writers.

---

7 See generally Smith, *Maverick Litigants*, ch 7.

8 *Collins v Supreme Court Library Committee* [1953] VLR 161,

9 See Smith, *Maverick Litigants*, ch 8.

10 Latham himself was mistaken as a vexatious litigant by a young academic lawyer at the Melbourne University law library. "He was extremely pleasant and helpful to everybody, and so we assumed that he was a new member of the class of vexatious litigants" (Mary Hiscock, as reported by John Waugh, *First Principles. The Melbourne Law School 1857-2007*, Miegunyah Press, 2007, pp 195-6).

11 Heydon J in *Australian Crime Commission v Stoddart* [2011] HCA 47 at [86].

12 *Brambles Holdings Ltd v Bathurst City Council* (2001) 53 NSWLR 153 at 183 [93].

Some academics have had a huge influence on the development of the law, because of a leading treatise or a perceptive article. Others have published on the eve of a vast shift in the law, an event capable of rendering their work suitable only for remaindering. Professor Michael Coper falls into both categories. His monograph, *Freedom of Interstate Trade under the Australian Constitution*,[13] hit the bookshops not long before the High Court in *Cole v Whitfield*[14] ripped up the entire law on the subject. Coper had at least the comfort of appearing as junior counsel for one of the successful parties that, in large part, argued in favour of his thesis. (Incidentally, his two leaders would, like him, be a professor of law at the University of New South Wales at various stages of their non-judicial careers.) The outcome in *Cole* would help project Coper into a tenured quasi-judicial position as a member of the Inter-State Commission which was revived in 1983. This "Second Coming of the Fourth Arm"[15] of the Constitution would, however, be short-lived. The legislation constituting the Commission was repealed in 1989, although serving commissioners kept their tenured emoluments until their seven-year terms ran out.

The number of textbooks on law by Australian lawyers grows exponentially. Some address very small pockets. Regrettably it is no longer possible to acquire Alfred Lutwyche's *Inquiry into the Principles of Pleading the General Issue* (1838) or John Fletcher Hargrave's *Treatise on the Thelluson Act* (1842). But Clifford Pannam's *The Horse and the Law* is now in its third (2004) edition. Another boutique title, David Fraser's *Cricket and the Law "The man in white is always right"*,[16] discusses the "neglected areas of intersection of cricket and the law" and much else besides.[17] The book starts: "Australian legal scholarship is boring" and goes on to explore the links between law and popular culture.

No legal author has been more prolific than Dr John Bennett who has written monographs on the history of the Supreme Court, the Bar, and the Solicitors in New South Wales, as well as biographies of no less than 13 Chief Justices at last count and much besides.

Index jokes

Writers have been known to embed in-jokes into indexes and lawyers are no exception.

13 Butterworths, 1983.

14 (1988) 165 CLR 360.

15 Michael Coper, "The Second Coming of the Fourth Arm: The Role and Functions of the Inter-State Commission" (1989) 63 *Australian Law Journal* 731.

16 The Institute of Criminology Monograph Series, No 4, Sydney 1993.

17 See further p 230.

Regina Graycar's and Jenny Morgan's important work, *The Hidden Gender of Law*,[18] contains an index reference "Feminist Methodologies humourlessness, 1-449" (ie the entire spread of the book).

Professor Mark Aronson has been a giver and receiver in this genre. The work he co-authored with Bruce Dyer and Matthew Groves, *Judicial Review of Administrative Action*,[19] contains in its index such tantalising entries as "Laws J, nude [3.90]" and "exhibitionism, Laws J [3.90]" (with reference to his Lordship's statement that the principles of judicial review "have nothing to do with the intention of Parliament, save as a fig-leaf to cover their true origins. We do not need the fig-leaf any more"). There are also entries such as "control freak, Ms Gillick", "corruption, made easier", "devil, positivism", "fairies", "happy days", "judicial proboscis, fallible", "judiciary's fans, lefties", "men, are like that", "merits, in drag", "mistakes, and mistakes", "Viagra" and "Yes Minister" that will tempt the reader. Mark Aronson's festschrift[20] (produced by his many admirers) contains an entry: "Aronson, Mark Prince Charming".

Prime Minister Bob Hawke is not alone in leafing through the index of books to check what is said about him. But, for him, there is a helpful entry in the index to David Marr's *Barwick:*[21]

> Hawke, RJ, no mention of.

Prefaces

Textbook writers invariably pen a preface by way of explanation and dedication. "Thank yous" and disclaimers of error tend to follow conventional lines. But not always. And sometimes publishers have to be attentive in their "legalling" skills because prefaces can be used to attack the living rather than the dead.

Some prefaces adopt feigned and rueful tentativeness. When issuing the first edition of *The Standard Contract for Sale of Land in New South Wales*,[22] Dr Peter Butt recorded:

> Looking back on the time and effort taken to write this book, I am reminded of the saying of the preacher of old: 'Of making many books there is no end; and much study is a weariness of the flesh.' The dual modern phenomena of case law explosion and statutory satiety, coupled with the ever present publisher's deadline, have given the lie to Trollope's aphorism that 'Three hours a day will produce as much as a man ought to write'. I empathise with the opening words from a review of one of the first Australian law texts (Barton's *Manual of the*

18 Second edition, Federation Press, 2002.

19 Fourth edition, Lawbook Co, 2009.

20 Linda Pearson, Carol Harlow and Michael Taggart (eds), *Administrative Law in a Changing State*, Hart Publishing, 2008.

21 George Allen & Unwin, 1980.

22 Law Book Co, 1985.

> *Practice of the County Court in the Colony of Victoria*), to be found in (1856) 1 *Victorian Law Times* 8: 'Of all the men who devote their time and talents to literary pursuits, there is no one whose labour is so wearisome and generally so ill paid as the author or compiler of legal works.' My only hope is that my readers do not empathise with the opening words of a review of a more recent English law text (which, for obvious reasons, will remain nameless): 'It is difficult to see the occasion, or a use, for this book' ((1973) 47 ALJ 56).

Other prefaces contain ineffective disclaimers of liability. Lawyers of all people should know of the law's aversion to exemption clauses first disclosed after a contract of purchase is formed, or expressed in vague or contradictory terms. Little weight could therefore be placed on Dr Warren Pengilley's statement, hidden inside a longer paragraph, saying that "whatever has to be done in order to avoid liability for negligent advice, I wish to be taken as having done it".[23]

Extreme caution can only explain the preface penned by Les Nethercott and Geoff Shaw to CCH's *Australian Taxation Study Manual*.[24] The learned authors were obviously not content with the **Important Disclaimer** by the publisher opposite the title page which warned that "No person should rely on the contents of this publication without first obtaining advice from a qualified professional person" before continuing with a detailed exclusion of liability. In the preface, they added their own disclaimer:

> The authors of this book expressly exclude themselves from any contractual, tortious or other form of liability to any person for any loss or damage sustained or for any consequence which may be thought to arise either directly or indirectly from reliance on statements made in this book. Persons using this book should rely upon their own enquiries or their taxation adviser in making any decisions relating to their own interests.

The last sentence really opened the flank of liability because, by the use of "or", it seems to be saying that users of the book might safely decide to choose themselves as a tax adviser. Surely that would be a dangerous inducement to the tax-ignorant readers being courted by the publishers?

Other writers accept that legal liability might ensue and they concentrate on its apportionment. Thus, Chisholm and Nettheim in their *Understanding Law* (1974) state:

> We collaborated closely in writing this book, and, as lawyers say, we accept 'joint and several responsibility for it'. In other words, I wrote the good bits, and he wrote the rest.

The risk was implicitly shared by the joint authors of *The Honest Politicians Guide to Crime Control* who wrote:[25]

---

23 Warren Pengilley, *Trade Associations, Fairness and Competition*, Law Book Co, 1981.

24 Tenth edition, CCH Australia Ltd, 2000.

25 Norval Morris and Gordon Hawkins. The book was published by University of Chicago Press in 1970.

> Contrary to long-standing tradition, we accept responsibility for any virtues in this book.

Roger Douglas and Melinda Jones, the authors of *Administrative Law Commentary and Materials* (2nd ed),[26] helpfully admit that (in contrast to the first edition):

> [W]e have each worked on 'each other's' area. As a result, responsibility is even more diffused and the authors have even less excuse for refusing to accept joint responsibility for any errors which appear (while reserving the right to take joint credit where credit is due).

Later on the preface subdivides as the authors turn to offer personal thanks. Melinda Jones thanked her children by name, observing that her youngest daughter "learnt more about administrative law in the first year of her life than about sandpits and parks". Roger Douglas thanked his wife, apologising that he was unavailable when housework was to be done and implicitly promising to lift his game in between editions. Perhaps the final stages of preparation were more than usually stressful for his marriage because he noted that his wife spent them in the Antarctic. (She fled to Namibia and Uzbekistan during the preparation of the third and fourth editions.) The family pets are then singled out for thanks and apologies, coupled with a reminder that they lack standing to seek a review of the RSPCA's failure to attend to their complaints. (It was an administrative law book after all.)

Peter Clyne was a clever practitioner with a profound lack of wisdom and a pathological reluctance to pay any taxes. In 1960 he was struck off for professional misconduct that showed him not to be a fit and proper person to practise as a barrister.[27] Four prosecutions had, on his advice, been launched as a means of intimidating a solicitor into ceasing to act for a woman in civil proceedings pending between her and Clyne's client. In opening those proceedings, Clyne attacked the solicitor's professional character in extravagant terms, alleging fraud, perjury and blackmail. He knew that he had no evidence to substantiate such allegations. At the end of his opening, Clyne intimated that, if the accused were to cease to act for his client, the criminal proceedings would have achieved their object and could be discontinued.

Having lost his career as a barrister, Clyne turned to advocacy as an "agent" in the residential tenancy field where his tricks and stratagems saw the eviction of many protected tenants. Faced with a threat of his disbarment being extended to such advocacy in the Courts of Petty Sessions he devised a fresh means of continuing his tenancy practice there. He would take a concurrent lease from his landlord client and then, purporting to act in his own right as a litigant in person, set about hounding the unwanted tenant in and out of

26 The Federation Press, 1996. The work is now in its sixth edition.

27 *Clyne v New South Wales Bar Association* (1960) 104 CLR 186.

court. He offered his debatable wisdom to the profession in a *Practical Guide to Tenancy Law*,[28] a work containing such devilish stratagems as:

- A landlord is entitled to have his rent paid where and when he likes, *within reason*. The bit about 'within reason' shuts out the Ayers Rock scheme, also the otherwise tempting idea of making your tenants pay the rent, personally, unaccompanied and at midnight, on top of some convenient high cliff. On the other hand ...
- If your client is the landlord and wants the place for his aged mother, mum must be brought into court. Preferably at the end of a stick on one side and a seeing-eye dog on the other. Your client will try to talk you out of this, mainly because he knows the old lady is likely to blurt out that she owns five other properties ... As a last resort, white-haired, dignified widows are often available for hire at the nearest theatrical agency.

Clyne's Introduction to this amoral work concludes with the following revelation:

> My heart is on the side of the landlord. No attempt is made to conceal this. For me to try and appear objective and impartial would be sheer hypocrisy. But twenty years of fighting tenants has brought me up against many gambits and techniques which tenants have either used against me, or which I thought they should or might have used, and breathed a sigh of relief and gratitude when they didn't. I have included these, and made a genuine effort to look at each situation from the tenant's point of view.
>
> One of my hobbies is playing chess against myself, so this was not difficult. When I play against myself, tenants will be glad to hear that *black* usually wins! My psychiatrists are still busy, trying to work out what this might mean.

Forewords

Two adulatory forewords from the inimitable pen of the late Mr Justice RP Meagher should be preserved. When Roddy lavished praise on a hero, friend or former tipstaff, he piled it on with a trowel. His foreword to the reprinted second edition of *Asburner's Principles of Equity*[29] offered the following portrait of the original author, disclosing several of the judge's own passions and how he would himself like to be remembered:[30]

> Dr Walter Asburner ... was Assistant Reader in Equity to the Council for Legal Education from 1898 to 1903. In that year, at the age of 39,

28 Rydge Publications, 1970.

29 Second edition by Denis Browne, Butterworth & Co (Publishers) Ltd, 1933, reprinted 1983.

30 See Keith Mason, "Roddy as I Saw Him" (2011) 35 *Australian Bar Review* 34.

> he retired permanently to Fiesole, 'to eat peaches and drink Bourbon whiskey' ...
>
> In 1926 he was recalled from retirement to succeed to the Chair of Jurisprudence at Oxford, formerly held by Maine, Pollock and Vinogradoff. For the next three years, he voyaged to England three times a year to fulfil his professional duties, whatever they were, for no one knew ...
>
> [Asburner's] lectures were said to be full of dry wit, immense learning, great charm, illuminating *apercus*, and mordant reflections on mankind. Nobody attended them, except inadvertently.
>
> In private, he was known as a great scholar, devoted to all forms of literature, a *bon vivant* whose appreciation of wine and food equalled his devotion to the classics, a brilliant conversationalist, and much beloved by his fellow dons. He was very happy. He never married.
>
> His *Principles of Equity* was a work of the utmost importance ...

Meagher also wrote an adulatory foreword to the second edition of Anforth and Thawley's *Residential Tenancies Law and Practice New South Wales*:[31]

> It is only two years since the first edition of this *lepidum novum libellum* was published. Yet, in that time, it has sold out. Its readers are clamouring for more.
>
> And so they should.
>
> In that time, the legislation has been amended at least once, Parliament has passed the *Residential Tribunal Act*, thousands of cases on residential tenancies have been decided; and, despite the Tribunal almost never delivering reasons for judgment, and despite a statutory injunction restraining appeals to the Supreme Court, a weak body of precedent is already germinating.

Meagher's foreword to the 1990 reprint of Pollock and Wright's *An Essay on Possession in the Common Law* took pains to ensure that his readers were in no doubt as to which particular member of the Pollock family (Sir Frederick Pollock) was the co-author of the book in question. It was definitely not "Sir Ernest Pollock, later Viscount Hanworth MR, who had the honour to be, apart from Eve J, the stupidest and least distinguished English judge of the 20th century. Scrutton LJ, it will be remembered, was appointed to the Court of Appeal 'to keep poor Ernest on the rails'." Roddy then warmed to his authors, praising them for their mastery of languages and the classics, noting still that Frederick Pollock was "a failure at the bar, and when appointed to the Corpus Chair of Jurisprudence at Oxford, he was a failure as a lecturer".

The *Essay* itself finally received attention and praise as a "masterpiece of legal analysis" before the foreword ended on a sombre note:

> More recently, it has perhaps received what is currently called negative deference. This is partly because it has been out of print. It is also because it does not mention semiotics, hermeneutics or structuralism.

31 LBC Information Services, 1998.

> It has no social relevance whatsoever. The President of the New South Wales Court of Appeal never refers to it; it does not live in any 'progressive' lawyers library; women barristers have been known to deny its existence. It is pure scholarship. It has unqualified excellence.

The worm could well and truly turn, as with Meagher's review of Simon Gardiner's *Introduction to the Law of Trusts* extracted below. That review must, however, be placed in its context. The topic of Equity in Australia has produced crusading apologists whose hectoring of each other and of selected heretics is a genre all of its own. The progression of some of these pugnacious greats onto the Bench expanded the theatres of war rather than dampened their fiery passion for the cause.

The Equity wars

Equity is a branch of the law that makes virtue of necessity by proudly abjuring any quest for rational definition beyond that of "not common law". Its historical claim is connection with the English Court of Chancery that was abolished in 1875, although other English Courts (notably the Court of Exchequer) also applied "equitable" principles for centuries. The Court of Chancery itself applied large slabs of "common law", justifying this by selective use of the maxim that "Equity follows the law". Other branches of the law that once had a specialist Court, like admiralty, probate and ecclesiastical law, have never displayed a similar desire for eternal taxonomical separation triggered only by a tenuous connection with a long-abolished English Court.

Much of what masquerades under the topic of Equity is now statutory or, as the Equity apologists will be the first to point out, was invented by Courts other than the Court of Chancery "without jurisdiction" well after 1875. The English Court of Appeal under Lord Denning MR comes under particular fire. Equity is usually mentioned in opposition to common law, with "common law" being stripped of the capital letter that "Equity" retains, as a reminder that it pulls rank in the handful of occasions when the rules conflict. But to further confuse the uninitiated, "common law" can also be used for the entire system of non-statutory law (Equity included) that was the birthright of our earliest white settlers and which the High Court regards as a seamless whole when it speaks of "the common law of Australia". There are fierce debates in academe over whether "Equity" should be taught as a separate subject, although anyone who dreamed of doing the same for "common law" would be ushered quickly into a padded cell.

Mention of the substantive "fusion" of law and equity is equivalent to crying fire in a crowded theatre if raised in certain parts of New South Wales. The folks in England and the United States (who achieved their Judicature reforms in the 19th century) scarcely know what is being talked about. Proposals to "fuse" the administration of law and equity, to avoid certain discrepant distinctions between rules of each system have been around for centuries.[32] But they have always encountered fierce opposition from those trained in the arcana of Equity, many of whom believe as a matter of faith that their topic is conceptually distinct from other branches of the law requiring the maintenance of a high fence around its invisible boundaries.

The law and practice of the Court of Chancery arrived as part of the birthright of Australian settlers along with every other part of English law capable of application on these shores. Chancery jurisdiction was later poured in an undifferentiated mass into the fledgling Supreme Courts along with the jurisdiction of other English Courts that are now abolished, as the Court of Chancery was in 1875. "It was as if the Colony had been granted a judicature system, a blessing neither understood nor appreciated at the time."[33]

Bold republicans like the first Chief Justice of New South Wales, Francis Forbes, saw no need for specialist procedures, pleadings or judges. This was hardly surprising since there were then only two judges in town. "Forbes, not being a chancery man, was probably well content that the court was absorbed in its other work."[34] He was not alone. Shortly after arriving in New South Wales in 1844 to become one of the four judges on the Supreme Court, Dickinson J wrote:[35]

> I endeavoured to get up Equity. Having never read any Equity before, I found myself dreadfully at fault whenever any Equity cases came before the Court.

(The tradition of New South Wales judges being "found ... dreadfully at fault" when deciding "Equity cases" has continued into the 21st century.)

Late in the 19th century, every Australian jurisdiction except for New South Wales would adopt the *Judicature Act* measures that fused the administration of law and equity and removed all barriers to appropriate substantive fusion as well. But in New South Wales the barristers mounted a long and effective rearguard campaign against this obvious reform. New South Wales declined to adopt the English *Judicature Acts* of 1873-75 until 1972.[36] Professor Forbes, the historian of the divided legal profession in Australia, has observed that "it

---

32 Geoffrey Robertson records in his biography of the courageous regicide John Cooke, *The Tyrannicide Brief*, Chatto & Windus, 2005, pp 254-5, 262-3, that Cooke declined Oliver Cromwell's offer of high judicial appointment in Munster until law was fused with equity. Two years later he was hanged, drawn and quartered for the related crime of killing a king.

33 Bennett, *History of the Supreme Court of New South Wales*, p 32.

34 *Ibid*, p 94.

35 JM Bennett and JK McLaughlin, "Sir John Dickinson. Almost a Chief Justice (1970) 56 *Journal of the Royal Australian Historical Society* 315 at 317.

36 Prompting Sir Kenneth Jacobs' description of the *Supreme Court Act 1970* (NSW) as the "Great Leap Forward to 1875".

would be interesting to have a monograph comparing professional opposition to Torrens Title, the Judicature Acts, and fusion [of the two branches of the profession]".[37] He points out that:[38]

> In 1824 Forbes [CJ] had virtually given New South Wales a Judicature Act system fifty years before England received that benefit, and 150 years before Bench and Bar finally allowed it to prevail in Sydney. 'As a judge, much of Burton's influence went towards expunging Forbes' innovations.'[39] So effectively did he and others pursue that end that New South Wales was a museum of early nineteenth century procedure until 1970. Rationalisation of procedure called forth much the same reactions as fusion of the profession.

Throughout the 19th century judges and politicians in New South Wales squabbled over creating a separate court for equitable matters, as in England, or accepting the possibilities inherent in having been blessed with a fused administration from the outset.[40] According to the historian of the Supreme Court, the rot set in with the arrival of Willis J, who was a knowledgeable Chancery lawyer. At first arrangements were made by the other judges to allow Willis to do all of the Equity cases, "almost a conspiracy to defeat the clear intentions of an Imperial statute",[41] in Dr Bennett's words. Later, when Willis pressed his nomination as "Chief Baron" controlling a separate Equity Court, Governor Gipps demurred. The fallback would be legislation which was passed in 1840 that contemplated the appointment of a "Primary Judge in Equity". But Dowling CJ (who could not abide Willis)[42] promptly arranged for Willis to be sent off to Port Phillip as Resident Judge there where he was free to look after all manner of litigation arising down south. These antipodean separatist adventures took place at the very time when the English were reading *Bleak House* and debating the abolition of the Court of Chancery as well as the fusion of the administration of law and equity which arrived in England in 1875.

Before Australian courts caught up with the English developments there were some strange contortions as judges within a single colonial Supreme Court endeavoured to administer justice as closely as possible to the perceived English model. A litigant before Lutwyche J sitting in Equity failed because his only remedy was before Lutwyche J sitting at common law.[43] Or the judge, now sitting in Equity, might restrain a party to a dispute from prosecuting his claim before the judge himself sitting at common law.[44]

37 Forbes, *The Divided Legal Profession*, p 179.
38 *Ibid*, pp 40-1.
39 Bennett, *A History of the Supreme Court of New South Wales*, p 35. Further as to Burton, see p 72.
40 See Bennett, *A History of the Supreme Court of New South Wales*, pp 59-62.
41 *Ibid*, p 279.
42 See p 116.
43 *Purser v Halloran* (1862) 1 QSCR 85.
44 See Macpherson, *Supreme Court of Queensland*, p 160, for instances.

On another occasion, a judge issued "equitable" orders in an assumption of non-existent appellate jurisdiction. In 1882 Manning J issued an injunction restraining certain proceedings pending an appeal to the Privy Council from a decision of the Full Court of the Supreme Court of New South Wales. The matter involved no grounds of Equity that might conceivably have attracted the remedy of a common injunction. A Full Court was convened and Martin CJ gave his judicial brother a ticking off in the following terms:[45]

> This was a very singular state of things ...
>
> The superior authority assumed by the Primary Judge to control the action of the Court cannot be submitted to for one moment, because, if it were allowed in this instance, we do not know where it would stop.[46] We should find it applied in cases which altogether depend upon the common law principles, and which ought to be disposed of in a common law Court. His Honour is no more than a member of the Court. When sitting in equity in a suit disclosing equitable grounds, he would have the power exercised by him in this instance. But, where no such case was before him, he had no such power, still less had he a right to express an opinion condemnatory of the course taken by the Court in any case. I regret that His Honour has not only arrogated this position to himself, but that he should have gone out of his way to endeavour in an elaborate manner to throw discredit upon the judgment of the Court in a case triable only at common law.

In the 19th century some piecemeal reforms were adopted. But the basic problem of trying to combine discordant "jurisdictions" within a single Supreme Court remained. Small wonder that an Irish woman sought direction to the "Iniquity Court", showing a Victorian barrister a piece of paper headed "In Equity".[47]

For a time in the early 20th century it looked as if the High Court under Sir Samuel Griffith would seize the opportunity of moulding judge-made law into a coherent whole that asked itself "why not?" rather than "why?" whenever presented with the opportunity for the substantive fusion of legal and equitable doctrines and remedies.[48] In *Turner v New South Wales Mont de Piete Deposit and Investment Co Ltd*[49] the Bench would criticise the procedural anachronisms which the unreformed New South Wales system encouraged. Griffith CJ rued that: "The defendants' case rests upon some supposed ancient technicalities of the law, which are said still to linger in New South Wales, after they have been abolished in, I believe, all the rest of His Majesty's Dominions".[50] The "ancient

---

45 *Brown v Patterson* (1883) 4 NSWLR Eq 1 at 10, 11-12. It seems that the law reporter got the last laugh, by reporting the decision in the Equity side of the NSWLR.

46 An example of "floodgates" reasoning.

47 Forde, *The Story of the Bar of Victoria*, p 291.

48 See *McLaughlin v Fosbery* (1904) 1 CLR 546; *Maiden v Maiden* (1908) 7 CLR 727.

49 (1910) 10 CLR 539.

50 *Ibid* at 543.

technicalities" of Equity practice, procedure and remedies continue to delight senior judges who have been educated at Sydney Law School, especially the learned judicial authors of a famous textbook discussed below.

Australian Equity barristers are sometimes accused of whispering. But the volume is turned up when they take to print. As textwriters and judges, some have launched personal attacks on those identified as heretics. But the most vigorous attacks involve spats between the writers themselves, when some decidedly unacademic tones have been adopted. The study of so-called heresies throughout history shows that those who move from within a fold, departing in good faith and by small degrees are seen as the biggest threats; and that the response of the guardians of a faith system is to seek out external enemies for the purpose of deterring further defections and binding ever closer the remaining core of true believers. Thus it has been with the "Equity wars".

A good starting point is the first edition of Meagher, Gummow and Lehane's *Equity Doctrines and Remedies* (1975) (*MGL*). In the preface, the learned authors said that they had "little doubt but that we can rely on the charity of our friends to draw to our attention any mistakes we might have made; if not the malice of others will supplement the deficiency". But in case the malice of others might be slow in coming, the authors larded their work with malice aplenty directed at English and New Zealand heretics, most notably Lord Denning, Lord Diplock and Sir Robin Cooke. Abiding concerns were the "fusionist fallacies" committed by those jurists, with the concurrence of the senior judiciary in England and New Zealand. "Fusion" is a non-venial sin involving applying "equitable" notions to solving "common law" problems and vice versa, notwithstanding that the practice has been around for centuries. Evidence of this fallacy gets detected in the highest of places, for example in the landmark negligence case of *Hedley Byrne & Co Ltd v Heller & Partners Ltd*, a case that has been approved and applied by the highest courts in every land.[51]

In the second edition (1983) of *MGL*, the preface adopted fluvial metaphors, but not for conveying any soothing effects. The authors described a decision of Lord Diplock in the House of Lords[52] as representing "the low water-mark of modern English jurisprudence", comforting themselves that 19th century English lawyers migrating to Australia would still be of good heart despite a tide of new material lapping against virtually every topic. The preface to the third edition (1992) conceded that this rosy confidence was "somewhat over optimistic", although the problems now seemed to include the homegrown variety with the reference to "equitable doctrines ... crimped by vigorous, but somewhat incoherent, invocations of 'unconscionability' as the equitable grundnorm".

51 [1964] AC 465. See *MGL*, 4th ed, 2002, p 58.

52 *United Scientific Holdings Ltd v Burnley Borough Council* [1978] AC 904 at 924.

The fourth edition (2002) recorded the recent death of the irenic John Lehane, the inability of Gummow J to participate and the arrival of two co-authors JD Heydon and MJ Leeming, to supplement the endeavours of the founder, RP Meagher. On this occasion the chosen metaphors became decidedly martial. The "attacks" of Lords Denning and Diplock had been repelled and there had been "the reconquest of areas of law temporarily under their sway". Lord Cooke (as he had become) remained singled out for his "misguided endeavours", with the reminder "that one man could, in a few years, cause such destruction expose[d] the fragility of contemporary legal systems and the need for vigilant exposure and rooting out of error". A much-respected Australian judge was derided as "the poor man's Robin Cooke".[53] The new challenge at the ramparts of the keep was identified as coming from "proselytising members of the restitution industry (academic division)", a group with which the author has been at least a fellow-traveller. Fortunately, that enemy did not present a united front because, adopting an observation from one of my judgments, the authors gleefully noted that disagreement about the very structure of the law of restitution and its interrelationships with other branches of the law seemed to be a badge of membership.[54]

As indicated below, the textbook crusaders opened a second front, in the High Court itself, whence Gummow and Heydon JJ had repaired as guardians of Equity orthodoxy, New South Wales style.

Mr Justice Meagher penned a brutish review of Simon Gardiner's *Introduction to the Law of Trusts* in the following terms:[55]

> This book, by an author who has been a Fellow of Lincoln College, Oxford, since 1978, is one of the Clarendon Law Series, a series which produced masterpieces such as HLA Hart, The Concept of the Law and Barry Nicholas' Introduction to Roman Law. Alas, it is not of like quality ... No one should yield to the temptation to buy this book, and the author, the publisher and the editors of the Clarendon Law Series, ought all to be ashamed of themselves and of each other.

With return of service to the Antipodes, the Regius Professor of Civil Law at Oxford University, Peter Birks, launched a stinging review of the fourth edition of *MGL*[56] in the prestigious *Law Quarterly Review*.[57] Birks' opening remarks set the scene:

> This book will be 30 years old next year. It has become authoritative and in a sense indispensable. It arouses very mixed feelings. As an

53 Page 839.

54 *Brambles Holdings Ltd v Bathurst City Council* (2001) 53 NSWLR 153 at 155.

55 (1991) 8 *Australian Bar Review* 183.

56 Edited by RP Meagher, JD Heydon and MJ Leeming, 2002.

57 (2004) 120 *Law Quarterly Review* 344. See also the milder tones of Andrew Burrows (another Oxford don) in "We Do This At Common Law But That In Equity" (2002) 22 *Oxford Journal of Legal Studies* 1.

> immense repository of accumulated knowledge it invites admiration, even wonder. That tribute can be paid with unfeigned respect. Yet the awe resembles that which in a museum of natural history might be offered to a life-sized but lifeless mammoth. The learning belongs to the past, to an age in which law books were content to collect the utterance of authority but felt no responsibility to make sense of it to the contemporary world ... This is law as a mystery for lawyers, and the days for that have gone.

As he wound up, Birks turned to the preface in *MGL*:

> Warned that I would not like it, I should have resisted the temptation to read it. It leaves a nasty taste. Try as one will to read it as good-humoured, that interpretation does not stick. The nasty taste seeps through the book. Page by page there lingers the vestige of a suspicion that the argument may be led by an angry fundamentalism, and that disagreement will engender contempt. The civility of legal argument has been one of the glories of the common law tradition. It is more than ornament. In minimising animosity it offers an assurance that opposed positions will be weighed only on their rational merits.

Service was returned against Birks by Gummow J and Heydon J after they went onto the High Court.[58] Latterly, with the arrival of Bell J on the High Court, there has come a more nuanced and sustained attempt to address Birks' allegation that "Equity" lacks the necessary "exacting taxonomic mentality". In *Bofinger v Kingsway Group Ltd*,[59] the Court acknowledged that the unjust enrichment concept is here to stay as a useful legal concept, so long as it recognises its place. At the beginning of the 21st century, the Court appears to be attempting to draw a unique Australian line, indicating that "Equity" and unjust enrichment are commensurate yet mutually exclusive concepts, adhering to the mantra that statements such as "orthodox equitable principles" tell the reader something of utility.

Despite battle being raged in the name of a distinctively "Australian Equity", the noisy judicial participants were all from New South Wales, the jurisdiction which alone had resisted *Judicature Act* reforms for a century. You do not have to be a legal archaeologist to detect the influence of two generations of barrister teachers from Sydney Law School.

The Sydney Diocese is also proudly combative in its role as the puritan outpost of the worldwide Anglican Church. Small wonder that Spigelman CJ could ask why it has come to pass that "Sydney has become a world centre, indeed one of the bastions, of both evangelical Anglican theology and evangelical Equity scholarship. Is there a connection?"[60]

58 *Roxborough v Rothmans of Pall Mall Australia Ltd* (2001) 208 CLR 516 at 544; *Farah Constructions Pty Ltd v Say-Dee Pty Ltd* (2007) 230 CLR 89 at 158 (digs at Birks).

59 (2009) 239 CLR 269 at 299-302.

60 Speech on the retirement of the Honourable Justice Mason AC Sydney, 30 May 2008, in Tim D Castle (ed), *Speeches of a Chief Justice: James Spigelman 1998-2008*, CS2N Publishing, 2008.

In the meantime, another fierce protagonist entered the Equity lists, from Melbourne, Sydney's traditional rival in many matters. Dr Ian Spry QC is from Melbourne. The first edition of his textbook, *The Principles of Equitable Remedies*, was published in 1971. It did not emulate the hectoring tones of *MGL* but he did start to get stuck into Gummow J as later editions came out.

Dr Spry's bitterly contested matrimonial proceedings came to the High Court in 2008[61] where his efforts to restructure a discretionary trust in such a way that his wife ceased to be one of the objects of a power of appointment were found to be ineffective for avoiding the Family Court's jurisdiction to rearrange the "property" of married persons. Spry countered with a series of letters written personally to "Mr French" and "Mr Hayne" accusing those justices of the High Court and named colleagues of a string of serious departures from judicial propriety. For example, the letter to French CJ reminded him of criticisms of "the somewhat eccentric views of Justice Gummow" in the sixth edition of Spry's own textbook and asserted that:

> During the recent hearings of my appeals Justice Gummow persistently leered triumphantly at me.

Dr Spry wound up by stating that:

> I was an associate to Sir Owen Dixon, who as well as being probably Australia's greatest judge was a model of ethical propriety. He would have been highly dismayed both by the reasoning of the court in these matters and by the justices' allowing personal considerations to affect their decisions.

The letter to "Mr Hayne" raised Melbournian matters going back a long way with which this Sydneysider has no interest or means of testing.

Dr Spry then wrote a new preface to the eighth edition of his textbook (November, 2009) in which he ruminated about the evils of judges in final courts of appeal who placed themselves "above the law". He noted "a tendency for some Australian judges to prefer their own personal views to legal precepts and precedents". Ramming the point home, he continued:

> Reflection shows how perilous it is to give way to this tendency, which allows unelected and in that sense irresponsible judges to out-legislate the legislatures. Unfortunately appointments to the High Court of Australia have also been influenced by political and sectional pressures from various sources. The standing of the High Court first suffered substantially through the appointment of Justice Murphy, formerly Senator Lionel Murphy. It was alleged that Justice Murphy had associations with criminals, but he died before proceedings could be completed for removing him from the court. In the

61 *Kennon v Spry* (2008) 238 CLR 366. The majority of the Court who found in favour of Mrs Spry were French CJ, Gummow J, Hayne J and Kiefel J.

> decades following his death[62] the quality of the court's equity analysis has diminished markedly. Justice Gummow has been referred to in an earlier edition of this book for the eccentricity of his judgments. Indeed at the present time, in matters of equity as in other matters, the quality of the decisions from the New South Wales Court of Appeal can be recognised as superior to the High Court's. The disparity between the two courts is clearly evident, and these matters should be taken into account when it is being decided what weight should be accorded to recent Australian equity decisions.
>
> It may be hoped, although perhaps not expected, that future appointments to the High Court of Australia will eventually restore the High Court's reputation in the area of equity.

The idea that the Court of Appeal in New South Wales might know more than the High Court in matters of Equity is unlikely to be shared by the High Court itself, but I am hardly a disinterested observer.

Law teachers

During the hearing of the *State Banking Case*[63] in 1947, counsel observed that Dixon J had not sat in the *Uniform Tax Case*.[64] Starke J (who had found himself in the minority in the earlier case) interjected: "No, worse luck". In 1949, students at the University of Melbourne were set a constitutional law exam question by the renowned Professor Geoffrey Sawyer in which they were invited to comment on the implications of Starke's remark. Latham CJ, who was one of the majority in each case, was so enraged that he protested by letter to the Chancellor, Sir Charles Lowe,[65] asserting that his Court was being held up to ridicule and contempt. The Chancellor took the matter up with the Dean of the Law Faculty, Professor Paton, telling him that the exam question was "quite indefensible". Paton's rather grovelling response to Latham reflects attitudes of deference towards the courts and academic freedom that seem strange to modern observers.[66] Latham would have been well advised to keep his silence. Starke's remark was remarkably inoffensive by his own standards,[67] or generally.

Professor Tarlo threatened to sue Queensland Trustees for defamation when his paper given at the 1968 Queensland Law Symposium was not published along with the other papers. He considered that this conveyed a defamatory innuendo and he called for the distribution of the published papers

62 In 1986.

63 *Melbourne Corporation v Commonwealth* (1947) 74 CLR 31.

64 *South Australia v Commonwealth* (1941) 65 CLR 373.

65 See p 87.

66 PWY, "Offending the Chief Justice of Australia" (2001) 75 *Australian Law Journal* 719.

67 See pp 53-4.

to be stopped or he would seek an injunction. The Law Society defended the existing publication on the ground that the paper was not presented in a form suitable for publication and that the nature of the publication did not lend itself to publication. The professor was appeased when Queensland Trustees agreed to print and publish his lecture separately.[68]

When he was a legal academic teaching constitutional law, Zelman Cowen was faced with a student who had repeatedly failed his subject. Generously he offered the student a viva. Cowen told a colleague that there would be only one question: "Does the Australian Constitution contain a section 90?" "But what if the student says 'No'?" was the reply. "Then I will reason him around to the other view."

Professor Tony Blackshield taught a generation of students living in Sydney and authored many books and articles on constitutional law. His versatility and verve are illustrated by the song he composed about the 1920 *Engineers' Case*.[69] Sir Isaac Isaacs was the principal author of that decision and it is possible to see Blackshield impersonating Isaacs and singing the song on Youtube. The song goes to the tune of "When You Are Old and Gray" by Tom Lehrer:

> Australian arbitration
> Had lagged behind for years
> With no affiliation
> For public engineers.
> Because they were employed by States
> Their logs of claims lay dead;
>   Isaacs resented it
>   So he un-precedented it
>   And this is what he said:
>
> The implied immunity of instrumentalities
> Gives no opportunity for social realities.
>
> The doctrine is risible; the Crown's indivisible;
> The States are subordinate; they can't be coordinate.
>
> When power is plenary, that gives the machinery
> To fill up the scenery with federal greenery.
>
> The problem's constructional; the answer's deductional;
> The text is instructional; the States are effluxional.
>
> This new interpretation
> Should fill us all with hope:
> The powers of the nation
> Are limitless in scope.
> Good legalistic arguments
> Should keep the States in line
>   And if that's not enough

---

68 Gregory, *The Queensland Law Society Inc*, p 166.

69 Reproduced from Michael Coper and George Williams (eds), *How Many Cheers for Engineers?* Federation Press, 1997.

We can always get tough
With section 109!

In *Pirrie v McFarlane*
It all worked out OK
But then Sir Owen Dixon
Resolved to have his say.
I'the Melbourne Corporation Case
He threw the States a crumb;
    But in Cigamatic
    He produced a dramatic
    Disequilibrium:

The Commonwealth's prominence and total predominance
Is quite categorical, and simply historical:

'Parthenogenetical' is not too poetical;
It's just theoretical and epexegetical.

The federal polity was novel in quality;
Its powers inhere in it; States can't interfere in it.

They can't impose Acts on it, or levy a tax on it;
They can't be derogative of its royal prerogative.

So, in our federation,
The rules today are these:
There *is no legislation*
Unless the Court should please.

The Constitution's overlaid
With what the Court begot
    But if you're perplexed,
    Just go back to the text,
    And overrule the lot!

Courts are often called upon to construe wills in situations that the testator never envisaged and they have devised a number of technical rules of interpretation. Nevertheless, Bryson J once reminded himself that "it is, after all, testators who are telling the Courts what dispositions they wish to make, and the process of construction of wills is not a process of legal education administered by Courts to testators".[70]

70 *Perpetual Trustee Co Ltd v Attorney General (Estate late Richard Harris)* (unreported, NSW Supreme Court, 27 March 1987), p 8.

Part 3

Law and the Wider World

10 *Literature and the Law*

Statutes vary in style across time and place. Enactments may adopt a fussy or fuzzy mode of expression. Clarity and "plain English" may be constant aspirations but those who draft Bills do not always achieve these goals and they never seek literary recognition. No compliment was intended when Sir Samuel Griffith was satirically praised as having rendered the poetry of Dante into the language of a parliamentary enactment.[1]

By contrast, there have been judgments of real literary merit, whether or not planned as such. But some attempts at embellishment have fallen well short of their author's intentions, just as some judges have (like Griffith) failed miserably when seeking literary fame outside the law.

Judicial reasoning can be elevated by references to literature or the classics. The judge may be motivated by conceit or the desire to relieve boredom, but the law is usually none the poorer for that. A classical allusion may also be the honest way to explain the motivation for a particular idea. Only the gullible believe that legal reasoning is always driven by inexorable logic. Classical allusions can also make factual narratives memorable or at least readable.

Judgments as literature

From time to time a judgment will be expressed in sublime or striking terms, ranking as literature in its own right.

The 1888 judgment of Darley CJ in *Ex parte Woo Tin*[2] is a very fine piece of sustained judicial rhetoric. The Chief Justice was delivering the strongest of warnings to Sir Henry Parkes whose government had thrice defied the Supreme Court in refusing to obey orders by way of habeas corpus to release wrongfully excluded Chinese immigrants.

The Queensland-born Lord Atkin's dissent in *Liversidge v Anderson*[3] was an abrasive tour de force. Described by one commentator as a result of "an explosion in Atkin's mind",[4] the response of wounded colleagues in the

1 Piddington, *Worshipful Masters*, p 239.
2 (1888) 9 NSWLR (L) 493.
3 [1942] AC 206.
4 RFV Heuston, "Liversidge v Anderson in Retrospect" (1970) 86 *Law Quarterly Review* 33 at 37.

House of Lords led Justice Kirby to suggest that "perhaps their Lordships put Atkin's lack of manners down to his Australian origins".[5] *Liversidge* involved the Home Secretary's wartime power to order the detention of any person whom the Minister "has reasonable cause to believe ... to be of hostile origin or associations". Was the test objective or subjective? Atkin's objective test would be later vindicated[6] but he was a lonely voice in wartime Britain and his language mightily affronted his brethren:[7]

> I view with apprehension the attitude of judges who on a mere question of construction when face to face with claims involving the liberty of the subject show themselves more executive minded than the executive.
>
> In this country, amid the clash of arms, the laws are not silent. They may be changed, but they speak the same language in war as in peace. It has always been one of the pillars of freedom, one of the principles of liberty for which on recent authority we are now fighting, that the judges are no respecters of persons and stand between the subject and any attempted encroachments on his liberty by the executive, alert to see that any coercive action is justified in law. In this case I have listened to arguments which might have been addressed acceptably to the Court of King's Bench in the time of Charles I.
>
> I protest, even if I do it alone, against a strained construction put on words with the effect of giving an uncontrolled power of imprisonment to the minister. To recapitulate: The words only have one meaning ...
>
> I know of only one authority which might justify the suggested method of construction: 'When I use a word,' Humpty Dumpty said in a rather scornful tone, 'it means just what I choose it to mean, neither more nor less.' 'The question is,' said Alice, 'whether you can make words mean so many different things.' 'The question is,' said Humpty Dumpty, 'which is to be the master – that's all'.[8]

Rich J was renowned for his pithy prose.[9] Once, when observing that the nature of goodwill depended on the type of business concerned, he penned a zoological taxonomy of customers:[10]

> The cat prefers the old home to the person who keeps it, and stays in the old home although the person who has kept the home leaves, and so it represents the customer who goes to the old shop whoever keeps it, and provides the local goodwill. The faithful dog is attached

---

5 Justice Kirby, "Literature in Australian Judicial Reasoning" (2001) 75 *Australian Law Journal* 602 at 603.

6 *Nakkuda Ali v Jayaratne* [1951] AC 66; *R v Inland Revenue Commissioners; Ex parte Rossminster* [1980] AC 952 at 1025.

7 [1942] AC 206 at 244-5.

8 *Through the Looking Glass* c vi.

9 See also *O'Dea v Commercial Bank of Australia Ltd* (1933) 50 CLR 200 at 213 and *James v Cowan* (1930) 43 CLR 386 at 422.

10 *Federal Commissioner of Taxation v Williamson* (1943) 67 CLR 561 at 564.

> to the person rather than to the place; he will follow the outgoing owner if he does not go too far. The rat has no attachments, and is purely casual. The rabbit is attracted by mere propinquity. He comes because he happens to live close by, and it would be more trouble to go elsewhere.

Evatt J's reasoning in *Chester v Waverley Corporation*[11] also deserves mention, both for its impact as and use of literature. He dissented, but his views would later be approved by the House of Lords[12] and the High Court itself.[13] In *Chester*, the High Court dismissed a claim for nervous shock by Mrs Janet Chester whose child drowned through the negligence of the local council. The council had dug a trench in the street and left it exposed, where it filled with water. The plaintiff went looking for her child after he had been missing for a time, became distressed on failing to find him, and suffered severe nervous shock when the boy's body was removed from the ditch some time later. The majority in the High Court "rejected her claim, apparently dismissing any notion of something distinctive about the relationship between a woman and her child".[14]

Evatt's lengthy dissent is a masterpiece of sustained rhetoric and contains extensive references to William Blake's poetry and Tom Collins' novel *Such is Life*. Here is an extract:[15]

> The plaintiff was a woman of Polish extraction, and found special difficulty in narrating the precise nature of her feelings, her fears, her hopes and her sufferings. But it is quite easy, I think, to perceive the order of events. It is abundantly clear that until the recovery of the body she did not know that her child had been drowned in the trench. Like most mothers placed in a similar situation, she was tortured between the fear that he had been drowned and the hope that either he was not in the trench at all, or that, if he was, a quick recovery of his body and the immediate application of artificial respiration might still save him from death. In this agonized and distracted state of mind and body she remained for about half an hour, when the police arrived and the child's body was discovered and removed.
>
> During this crucial period the plaintiff's condition of mind and nerve can be completely understood only by parents who have been placed in a similar agony of hope and fear with hope gradually decreasing. In the present case the half hour of waiting was the culmination of a long and almost frantic searching which had already reduced her to a state of nerve exhaustion. Even after the finding of the body, an attempt at artificial respiration was made and abandoned only after expert lifesavers had worked on the child's body for some time.

11 (1939) 62 CLR 1.

12 *McLoughlin O'Brian* [1983] 1 AC 410.

13 *Jaensch v Coffey* (1984) 155 CLR 549; *Tame v New South Wales* (2002) 211 CLR 317.

14 Regina Graycar and Jenny Morgan, "Women" in Blackshield et al, *The Oxford Companion to the High Court of Australia*, p 720.

15 (1939) 62 CLR at 17-18.

> William Blake's imaginative genius has well portrayed suffering and anxiety of this kind:—
>
> Tired and woe-begone
> Hoarse with making moan …
> Rising from unrest
> The trembling woman prest
> With feet of weary woe:
> She could no further go.
>
> The Australian novelist, Tom Collins, in Such is Life,[16] has also described the agony of fearfulness caused by the search for a lost child:—
>
> > Longest night I ever passed, though it was one of the shortest in the year. Eyes burning for want of sleep, and couldn't bear to lie down for a minute. Wandering about for miles; listening; hearing something in the scrub, and finding it was only one of the other chaps, or some sheep. Thunder and lightning, on and off, all night; even two or three drops of rain, towards morning. Once I heard the howl of a dingo, and I thought of the little girl; lying worn-out, half-asleep and half-fainting—far more helpless than a sheep.
>
> At a later point, in the same novel:—
>
> > There was a pause, broken by Stevenson, in a voice which brought constraint on us all. Bad enough to lose a youngster for a day or two, and find him alive and well; worse, beyond comparison, when he's found dead; but the most fearful thing of all is for a youngster to be lost in the bush, and never found, alive or dead.
>
> Not only its poets and novelists, but, at any rate in recent years, those engaged in the administration of the common law of England have recognized that shock of the most grievous character can be sustained in circumstances analogous to those of the present case.

Judge Leonard Stretton[17] sat as a royal commissioner to inquire into the Victorian bush fires of 1939. His report was recognised for its literary quality as well as the analysis of carefully assembled information. An excerpt reads: "The soft carpet of the forest floor was gone; the bone-dry litter crackled underfoot; dry heat and hot dry winds worked upon a land already dry, to suck from it the last, least drop of moisture".[18]

Another Victorian judge (Cummins J) opened a dramatic contempt decision with a rural landscape in the style of Lord Denning:[19]

> The hills of south of Yarragon are green and shaded. The hourglass of the Latrobe Valley is there at its most slender, nestling between the grandeur of the Great Dividing Range to the north and the finely delineated Strzelecki Ranges to the south. Nine kilometres south of

16 The same work contains the unforgettable description of a character as "educated for the law, his innate honesty shrank from the practice of his profession".

17 Victorian County Court 1937-64.

18 Hewitt, *Judges*, p 61.

19 *Anissa Pty Ltd v Parsons* [1999] VSC 430.

> the Princes Highway, off Yarragon South Road, in pastoral serenity stood fifty trees. They had the ill fortune to stand on the property of the defendant – landowner, disaffected son and solicitor of this honourable Court. The defendant, Mr Simon Parsons, owned the property, off Yarragon South Road ... Contiguous to his property immediately to the west was a property ... occupied by his parents. There had been a falling out between parents and son. It appeared to be irreconcilable. The parents decided to move away. The western property was in the name of Anissa Pty Ltd, a family company one share of which was held by the defendant's father, one by his mother, and two by him. It was resolved by the Company on 4 November 1998 that it be wound up. The western property was to be sold. A public auction was fixed for Friday, 23 April 1999 at 2.00 pm on site. A handful of suited professionals attended to effect the sale – a solicitor, a liquidator, an accountant. The defendant was not present. But his alter ego was – a bulldozer.

In the *Corbishley Case* Holmes JA vividly depicted a magistrate's abuse of his discretion to grant bail:[20]

> The picture is one which shows how the poor, sick and friendless are still oppressed by the machinery of justice in ways which need a Fielding or a Dickens to describe in words and a Hogarth to portray pictorially.

Judicial borrowings from literature and Scripture

The law reports are shot through with literary allusions and quotations from famous works. This form of "top-down reasoning" is widely practised, often by those who decry the technique in principle. It shows that law and lawyers are happily connected with wider currents of learning and discourse.[21] It also shows that judges can at times get carried away.

Homeric and other classical allusions

Classical allusions appear frequently in reasons for judgment.[22]

Homer seems to be at the top of the list. In an essay on *English as She is Taught*, Mark Twain cited a schoolboy blooper that states:

> Homer's writings are Homer's Essays Virgil the Aeneid and Paradise Lost some people say that these poems were not written by Homer but by another man of the same name.

Since there is uncertainty about whether Homer really existed, to be categorical about his doppelganger is fraught with danger. But this scarcely excuses the

20 *Ex parte Corbishley; Re Locke* [1967] 2 NSWR 547 at 549.

21 See generally Justin T Gleeson and Ruth CA Higgins (eds), *Constituting Law: Legal Argument and Social Values*, Federation Press, 2011.

22 See generally Elwyn Elms, "On the Use of Classical Allusions in Judgment Writing" (2008) 31 *University of New South Wales Law Journal* 56.

false attribution of qualities that have no sources at all in classical literature. One can accept that (if he existed) Homer was blind. But there is no authority other than the New South Wales Industrial Commission for the view that he was also deaf and therefore an example of someone with profound learning difficulties who achieved the heights of success.[23]

Several Australian decisions pick up the notion of Homer having "nodded", which is a suggestion recorded by the Roman poet Horace in his *Ars Poetica*. Judges reach for this allusion when gently letting down a colleague who has written infelicitously or departing from a distinguished forebear whose unorthodox views they choose not to confront directly in the particular instance.[24] Thompson DP of the South Australian Workers Compensation Appeal Tribunal seems himself to have nodded in making a similar point, because (if his reasons are correctly recorded) he followed a quotation from a transcript with the following comment:[25]

> If the transcript is accurate, it indicates that *Homer Noded*.

The circumstances of the bard's death have also attracted attention. One tradition records (with several variants) that Homer died from chagrin due to his inability to solve the "riddle of the lice".[26] Brooking JA recorded this event as a prelude to expounding the complexities of s 568(1) of the *Crimes Act 1958* (Vic).[27] Homeric allusions are also dotted throughout the caselaw, for example in references to the Trojan horse and to being between Scylla and Charybdis. Bryson J was dealing with how certain documents of title found their way into the custody of a firm of solicitors. He remarked that "their odyssey is conjectural, but they reached its Ithaca at the solicitors' office ... by 15 September".[28]

When attempting to defend the constitutionality of the *Communist Party Dissolution Act*, Sir Garfield Barwick argued that it was "a preventative Act, it is not a punitive act in any sense". He went on to say:[29]

---

23 *Police Association of New South Wales on behalf of Adam Tregonning and New South Wales Police Service* [2000] NSWIRComm 14 at [146]-[147].

24 See eg *Coleman v Power* (2004) 220 CLR 1 at 90 [234] (Kirby J); *World Best Holdings Ltd v Sarkar* [2010] NSWCA 24 at [41] (Handley AJA).

25 *Workcover Corporation (Le Cornu Furniture) v Ortlepp* [1996] SAWCAT 151, emphasis in original.

26 One version of this riddle involves boys who fished without success who spent their time searching for lice. The riddle told to the bard was: "We have what we did not find; what we did find we left behind". See generally Leslie Katz, "Homer in Australian Reasons for Judgment or Decision": <http://papers.ssrn.com/abstract=1322208> and Daniel B Levine, "Poetic justice: Homer's Death in the Ancient Biographical Tradition" (2002) 98 *Classical Journal* 141.

27 *R v Gallagher* [1998] 2 VR 671 at 672.

28 *Shawyer v Amberday Pty Ltd (in liq)* (2001) 10 BPR 18,869 at 18,879.

29 Quoted by Jeremy Stoljar in his chapter on the *Communist Party Case* in Stoljar, *The Australian Book of Great Trials*, p 123. See also Priestley JA's description of a witness having "an Achilles' heel which reached up to his knee" (p 163).

> It of course proceeds on the broad theory that you do not have to wait until the contents of the Trojan horse have been spilled into your city, it acts on the theory that you can burn the horse before the doors open.

Other ancients have spoken to and through modern judges, sometimes in rather forced analogies. For example, Kirby J invoked the account of Icarus in Ovid's *Metamorphoses* when making a strained point about the dangers of flight in a case relating to deep vein thrombosis.[30] On the other hand, that judge's use of Virgil's account of the futile endeavours to pile Ossa on Pelion was most effective in an earlier case.[31] He used it to paint a dramatic picture of the futility of reasoning that piled one legal fiction on another.

Alluding to Cicero, Burchett J observed that the Commissioner of Taxation was not given a particular power "so that he may bring to the collection of the Commonwealth's revenues the rapacity of a Verres who takes what he can, but because wide discretions, fairly exercised, have been found necessary. There must be ... fairness".[32] The same judge elsewhere remarked: "Counsel for the applicants described the schedule as a bed of Procrustes, to which the Commissioner demanded that they conform. For the Commissioner, it was contended that, unlike Procrustes' victims, they were at liberty to remake their bed".[33]

Aesops' fables have also been popular, with many concepts that have passed into general currency like "dog in the manger", "wolf in sheep's clothing", "lion's share" and "swan-song". Judges often use these notions with uncharacteristic failure to acknowledge the source. One exception was McGarvie J who observed that the criminal law "must not earn Aesop's reproach that: 'The law will catch small flies but wasps will break through': *The Judge and the Poor Man*".[34]

Until quite recently *Water Conservation & Irrigation Commission (NSW) v Browning*[35] was often cited for its discussion of the scope of administrative review when there is a broadly expressed statutory discretion. The facts of the case are often skipped over, which is hardly surprising given the embarrassing conclusion reached by the embarrassed but faint-hearted justices of the High Court. At issue was the Commission's refusal to approve the transfer of an

30 *Povey v Qantas Airways Ltd* (2005) 223 CLR 189 at 219 [88].

31 *Grincellis v House* (2000) 210 CLR 321 at 331 [24]-[28].

32 *Edelstein v Wilcox* (1988) 83 ALR 99 at 112, referring to s 218 of the *Income Tax Assessment Act 1936* (Cth).

33 *ONE.TEL Ltd v Deputy Commissioner of Taxation (Cth)* (2000) 101 FCR 548 at 561-2. For other classical allusions by this judge, who was once described by Callinan J as rolling out "literary allusions like a rather gaudy carpet", see Elms, *op cit*, pp 74-5.

34 *R v Rumpf* [1988] VR 466 at 478. See also *Toohey v Gunter* (1928) 41 CLR 181 at 203 (Higgins J); *National Employers' Mutual General Association Ltd v Waind (No 2)* [1978] 1 NSWLR 466 at 474 (Moffitt P).

35 (1947) 74 CLR 492.

irrigation holding in the Riverina area. The proposed transferee was Antonio Carbone a man of Italian birth who had been naturalised as an Australian citizen in 1934. The granting or refusal of consent lay "entirely in the discretion of the Commission" according to the statute. The Full Court of the Supreme Court of New South Wales found that the discretion miscarried because the Commission had regard to its opinion that Italians were not, as a general rule, good farmers under irrigation methods and that a considerable aggregation of Italians in the area was undesirable. The year was 1946 and the policy was coloured with concern about friction between Italians and returned soldiers. It may confidently be stated that a modern court would have endorsed the view of Jordan CJ when he concluded that the Commission had taken account of matters that were none of its business as an irrigation authority. Nevertheless, the High Court allowed the appeal because it accepted some slender evidence that the Commission considered "the individual" circumstances of the case. Rich J nevertheless protested:[36]

> This case is rather embarrassed by the nature of the answers given by or on behalf of the Commission. Some of the answers appear to be erroneous or irrelevant, as the Supreme Court has suggested; for instance, the statement that Italians as a general rule are not good farmers under irrigation. One remembers that during the centuries BC the Romans were farmers and that in the Augustan period Virgil in the Georgics wrote a treatise or sort of handbook on agriculture and husbandry.

Psalms and other Biblical citations

Since there is Biblical authority that the Devil himself can quote Scripture,[37] it is hardly surprising that judges have seen the Bible as a source of ideas and literary quotations. Yet in this field above all, the citations are often strained and the analogies forced.

Young J once suggested that "the words of Psalm 15" would tend to give the flavour of a person who, as a stockbroker, had to satisfy statutory requirements of honesty and fairness as a stockbroker. These remarks were adopted in a later case by a judge who reproduced the translated text, describing Young J's reference as "Delphic".[38] (I would respectfully point out that the description "Delphic" in the context of the monotheistic religion of ancient Israel involves a degree of religious confusion.)

The author was assisted by the Psalms in reasoning to a conclusion that a mosque was a "church, chapel or other place of public worship" for planning

---

36 *Ibid* at 497.

37 *Matthew* 4: 5.

38 *Farley v Australian Securities Commission* (1998) 16 ACLC 1502 at 1523 [149] (McMahon DP).

purposes. The Bankstown City Council had argued otherwise, raising noise concerns at the mosque on Fridays. Given, however, that the Council conceded that any form of Christian liturgy was within the scope of an earlier planning consent in favour of a "church or office", the noise argument was met with the observation that:[39]

> [This concession] entails recognition that a very wide range of religious observances (and by implication environmental or amenity impacts) would be embraced. Some of these would be guaranteed to take literally the biblical injunction to 'make a joyful noise unto the Lord': Psalm 100 v1; see also Psalms 66, 150.

As a young man I incurred a judge's wrath for citing Scripture directly in support of a submission. I was acting for a charity that ran an art union. There was a dispute over the ownership of the first prize. My client did not care who ended up with the Mercedes Benz but was wasting good money maintaining the car while the husband, wife and family company fought over the ownership of the winning ticket. I had little to do but inform the Court of the facts as the charity knew them and leave it to the three defendants to make what they could of those facts. So, to brighten up an otherwise dull brief I gave as my one authority the account of King Solomon offering to cut the baby with a sword in order to discover the true mother.[40] Holland J was most annoyed.

Both Kearney J of the Northern Territory Supreme Court and Deane J of the High Court have cited Psalm 146: 3[41] about not putting trust in "Princes" (King James version) or "men in power" (Jerusalem Bible). Given that these citations occurred in solemn judicial rulings, one must view them as examples of the ubiquitous liar paradox that is itself noted in Scripture[42] and can be traced to ancient times.[43]

Kirby J surely stretched the bounds of rhetoric when he invoked Psalm 91 to support propositions about "the common fear of injury to the foot"[44] and universal recognition of the dangers of flight.[45] Sir Laurence Street, Chief Justice

39 *House of Peace Pty Ltd v Bankstown City Council* (2000) 48 NSWLR 498 at 510 [52].

40 1 *Kings* 3: 16-28.

41 See *Northern Territory v Skywest Airlines Pty Ltd* (1987) 90 FLR 270 at 295 (Kearney J citing the King James version) and *A v Hayden* (1984) 156 CLR 532 at 592 (Deane J citing the Jerusalem version).

42 *Titus* 1: 12, in which the idea is sourced back to the sixth century BC writer Epimenides.

43 See generally RS Lancy and FKH Maher, "Some Legal Oddities? Some Thoughts about Paradoxes and the Law" (1986) 6 *Otago Law Review* 260.

44 *Johnson v American Home Assurance Company* (1988) 192 CLR 266 at 268 [5]. The case involved an injury and sickness insurance policy insuring against "permanent total loss of use of one limb". In a speech on "Appellate Reasons" (2007) 30 *Australian Bar Review* 3 at 13 Kirby J rued that this citation was "under-appreciated".

45 *Povey v Qantas Airways Ltd* (2005) 223 CLR 189 at 219 [88]. See also his contrasting of God and the Water Board by reference to *Revelation* 21: 6 in *Water Board v Glambedakis* (1992) 28 NSWLR 694 at 695.

of New South Wales, also reached a tad too far when, in deciding whether or not the game of blackjack was unlawful, he observed that:[46]

> The gaming laws reflect no innate moral philosophy. One finds frequent uncritical reference in both the Old and New Testaments to the casting of lots as a means of determining the acquisition of property (eg Numbers 26, v 55-56; Psalm 22, v 18). The casting of lots by the Roman soldiers at Golgotha (Matthew 27, v 35) is recounted not as a moral affront, but rather as a demonstration of insensitivity and heartlessness – a subtle reminder of the lament 'they know not what they do'.

Before leaving the Psalms as a point of judicial reference, one cannot overlook McKenna C's invocation of the "Non-Unionists Psalm" parodying Psalm 23 when holding that he had power to make a "members only" industrial award. It goes:[47]

> The dues paying member is my shepherd
> I shall not want
> He provideth me with rest days and vacations,
> So that I may lie down in green pastures
> Beside the still waters.
> He restoreth my back pay,
> He guideth my welfare without cost to me.
> I stray in the paths of the non-righteous,
> For my money's sake.
> Yea though I alibi and pay no dues
> From generation to generation I fear no evil, for he protects.
> The working conditions which he provides,
> They comfort me.
> He anointeth my head with the oil of workers' compensation,
> Sick pay, annual leave and long service leave,
> And the 38 hour week.
> And my cup runneth over with ingratitude.
> Surely his goodness and loving kindness
> Shall follow me all the days of my life
> Without cost to me.
> I shall dwell in his house forever
> And allow him to pay the bill.

In *CES v Superclinics (Australia) Pty Ltd*[48] Meagher JA boldly proclaimed that "every child is a cause of happiness to its parents. Every parent looks on his child as David did on Absalom, or Oedipus on Antigone. In *St John's Gospel* (16.21) it is said: 'A woman when she is in travail hath sorrow, because her hour has come: but as soon as she is delivered of the child, she remembereth no

46 *Tahapi Pty Ltd v Avery* (1986) 6 NSWLR 138 at 141.

47 *Re Hospital Employees HREA Members (State) Award* (1997) 75 IR 7 at 29-30. According to a footnote in the judgment the origin of this poem is obscure.

48 (1995) 38 NSWLR 47 at 86-7. Meagher JA was in dissent.

more the anguish, for joy that a man is born into the world'." These sentiments may well reflect the happiness of Meagher's relationship with his child, but in a related case the majority of the High Court drew a line at this type of reasoning. Interestingly, it was Kirby J of all people who chided his usually black-letter brethren with presenting their "personal religious beliefs or 'moral' assessments concealed in an inarticulate premise, dressed up, and described as, legal principle or legal policy".[49]

The New South Wales Court of Appeal was confronted with the novel legal point whether a child who was born profoundly disabled could sue the doctor whose negligence in testing her pregnant mother for rubella had led her to carry the child to full term. In reaching opposing conclusions, the Jewish Chief Justice cited from the New Testament[50] and the Christian President of the Court of Appeal cited from the Old Testament.[51]

Gaudron and McHugh JJ alluded to Christ's admonition that "no man can serve two masters" when they observed that "duty and self-interest, like God and Mammon, make inconsistent calls on the faithful".[52] Another reference to the Gospels occurred when the New South Wales Industrial Commission was exercising its jurisdiction to set aside industrial contracts that are unfair or unconscionable. Sheldon J said that

> [N]othing in the evidence suggests that this contract was registered and, if it had been, it would have afforded Davies no more than public evidence of his own folly ... With all this, and the expenditure he was incurring, Davies was entitled to look for a contract which really gave him bread. What he received, in my opinion, was a stone".[53]

Fullagar J alluded to the Gospels when, in a tax case, he observed: "If the appellant is right, more than two generations have been straining at gnats of informality while swallowing the camel of invalidity".[54]

Shakespeare

Many Shakespearean allusions and references are to be found in the law reports.[55] Some have gone beyond embellishing judicial reasoning on points of law.

---

49 *Cattanach v Melchior* (2003) 215 CLR 1 at 53 [137]. See also at 58 [151].

50 *Harriton v Stephens* (2004) 59 NSWLR 694 at 700 [17] (*Matthew* 19: 19). The High Court upheld the conclusions and central reasoning of Spigelman CJ and Ipp JA: *Harriton v Stephens* (2006) 226 CLR 52.

51 (2004) 59 NSWLR 694 at 721 [155] (*Job* 3: 3).

52 *Breen v Williams* (1996) 186 CLR 71 at 108, citing *Matthew* 6: 24.

53 *Davies v General Transport Development Pty Ltd* [1967] AR 371 at 382.

54 *James v Deputy Commissioner of Taxation* (1958) 32 ALJR 339 at 345.

55 In addition to those discussed below, see also Isaacs J's invocation of *The Taming of the Shrew* in *Wright v Cedzich* (1930) 43 CLR 493 and Legoe J's invocation of *A Midsummer Night's Dream* in *In Estate of Slavinsky* (1989) 53 SASR 221.

Sir James Cockle, the first Chief Justice of Queensland, was a brilliant mathematician who was elected a Fellow of the Royal Society. He held a guarded approach to expert evidence. According to Dr Bennett,[56] this accorded with his opinion that "professional men were not the best witnesses – they were perhaps the least reliable, as their evidence was frequently founded on opinions rather than facts – and they were naturally desirous to establish the soundness of their opinions". Cockle's close scrutiny of medical evidence sometimes took the expert witness by surprise. For example, in *R v Fanning*, a trial for murder, a doctor gave evidence as to the victim having been strangled. Not content with that testimony, Cockle recalled him and asked him to elaborate on his opinion, not by reference to medical texts, but to Shakespeare's *Henry the Sixth* where the Earl of Warwick described the body of the slain Humphrey, Duke of Gloucester:[57]

> But see, his face is black and full of blood;
> His eye-balls further out than when he liv'd;
> Staring full ghastly like a strangled man;
> His hair uprear'd, his nostrils stretched with struggling;
> His hands abroad display'd, as one that grasp'd
> And tugged for life, and was by strength subdued.

The doctor agreed that the description was medically accurate, save that it would not necessarily follow that the hair of every victim of strangling would stand on end.[58]

In his famous dissent about the unequal status of women in *Wright v Cedzich*, Isaacs J drew upon *The Taming of the Shrew*[59] and Macbeth. On the latter score he lamented that:[60]

> [L]ike Banquo's ghost, the shadows of 'dominion,' '*potestas*,' 'possession' and 'servant' still stalk about as if they were living realities.

Shakespeare's *Henry IV* was invoked in a New South Wales case deciding that a royal commissioner lacked compulsive powers, absent statutory authority. Ferguson J ruled that:[61]

> The appointment [of a Royal Commissioner] constitutes him the trusted agent of the Crown for the purposes of the inquiry; but it gives him no powers as against his fellow subjects that he did not possess before. Like Glendower he 'can call spirits from the vasty deep' and they are unlikely to come when he does call.

---

56 JM Bennett, *Sir James Cockle*, Federation Press, 2003, p 98.

57 For an earlier forensic use of this passage, see Bolton and Byrne, *May it Please Your Honour*, p 29, referring to a jury address in Western Australia in 1855.

58 Bennett, *op cit*, citing *Courier*, 19 April 1864.

59 *Wright v Cedzich* (1930) 43 CLR 493 at 501.

60 (1930) 43 CLR 493 at 513.

61 *Ex parte Walker* (1924) 24 SR (NSW) 604 at 615. Cf Shakespeare, *Henry IV*, III, i, 53.

Wilcox J drew on *Measure for Measure*:[62]

> But the reasonable exercise of great powers – granted for easily justifiable reasons – to enter premises and to destroy private property thereon should not need to depend upon the personal sense of fairness of the officer involved.
>
> 'O, it is excellent to have a giant's strength;
> But it is tyrannous
> To use it like a giant.'

The Merchant of Venice was cited when Higgins J observed:[63]

> These words cannot be treated as idle and inoperative. They do not mean that express words used are not to have their full implications, but there is to be no implication beyond the express words used. The 'pound of flesh' for which Shylock bargained would probably in our Courts be treated as implying the blood which the flesh carries, but it would not be treated under such a clause as implying something which appears to be a probable inference.

Dante

Dante was a great favourite with Australian lawyers in the 19th century.

Judge Henry Cary, a New South Wales District Court judge between 1859 and 1869, devoted much of his spare time compiling a concordance to the Italian of Dante, with an English translation of each word. This would have been a gargantuan task before the age of the word-processor. Most of the concordance was ready for the press, but Cary was unable to finish the job when ill health prompted him to abandon the project and (urged on by the man who would succeed him) to resign from the Bench.[64]

Sir Samuel Griffith's interest in Dante manifested itself in his translations of the *Inferno* and the *Divina Commedia*. Their production and publication, during the period of his chief justiceship of the High Court, would have been an immense effort. Yet they were panned universally for their stodgy translation. Griffith's reasons for persevering say much about his desire for fame as a man of letters above all of the honours he deservedly attained. Clifford Pannam's assessment can serve as a reminder to all lawyers (including this writer) who venture abroad:[65]

> [T]he poetical excursions of Sir Samuel Griffith will only be remembered for the insights that they afford into his character rather than as successful reflections in English of the poetry of Dante. If we are

62 *Hanson v Commonwealth Director of Quarantine* (1984) 57 ALR 365 at 387. *Measure for Measure* II, ii, 107.

63 *Marcus Clark (Victoria) Ltd v Brown* (1928) 40 CLR 540 at 554.

64 Holt, *A Court Rises*, p 38. As to Cary's resignation, see pp 124-5.

65 Clifford L Pannam, "Dante and the Chief Justice" (1959) 33 *Australian Law Journal* 290 at 294.

> surprised that the character revealed is that of a man who had his share of human failings, it is probably only because we persist in regarding appointment to judicial office as some form of dehumanising process.

Brooking J once commenced reasons for judgment as follows:[66]

> When Dante reached the gate of hell the first thing he saw was an inscription which ended with the words, "All hope abandon, ye who enter here." Dante read the notice with care and, turning to Virgil, his guide, exclaimed, "Master, these words import hard meaning."
>
> When Anne Moore arrived at the gate of Wobbies World, an amusement park in Nunawading, and passed through the turnstile, she must have come within inches of a sign which, while not as alarming as the one Dante encountered, was not in encouraging terms—
>
> > "PERSONAL INJURY OR PROPERTY LOSS OR DAMAGE IS YOUR RESPONSIBILITY.
> >
> > Your entry is your acceptance of these conditions."
>
> Unlike the inscription over the gate of hell, the characters of which were "in colour dim", the sign at the amusement park was in bright red lettering, and, instead of being "over a portal's lofty arch', it was at eye level, just to the right of the turnstile facing those who were about to click their way into Wobbies World. More cheerful, at first sight, was the much larger notice displayed on the wall above the ticket window. "Welcome to Wobbies World," it began, and continued,
>
> > [Then followed a very detailed disclaimer of liability which the defendant was held to have invoked unsuccessfully in answer to the injured plaintiff's claim for damages] "

Lewis Carroll

Lewis Carroll has been a popular point of reference on several fronts,[67] despite Sir Samuel Griffith's assertion that his work is not usually cited in Courts of Justice (made as it was being cited by Griffith himself).[68]

Often Carroll is cited for observations about Parliament's capacity to give a word any meaning it chooses and for denigrating irrational positions taken up by public figures or litigants.[69] Lord Atkin's invocation of Humpty Dumpty which has already been set out[70] is one among many.[71] Dr Gerber once observed that "in the state of the 'evidence', the taxpayer cannot succeed in the

---

66 *Macleay Pty Ltd (trading as Wobbies World) v Moore* (1992) Aust Torts Rep ¶81-151 at 61,149.

67 See generally Ken Barlow SC, "Alice, Humpty Dumpty and the Law" (2011) 85 *Australian Law Journal* 365.

68 *Bridge v Bowen* (1916) 21 CLR 582 at 599.

69 See eg *Franklin Mint Pty Ltd v Commissioner of Taxation (Cth)* [1993] ATC 4,062 at 4,073.

70 See p 188.

71 See also eg *Smoker v Pharmacy Restructuring Authority* (1994) 53 FCR 287 at 289.

absence of any explanation of events and transactions which, left unexplained, make no sense even to Alice in Wonderland".[72]

In his dissent in *South Australia v O'Shea*[73] Deane J cited another extract from *Alice in Wonderland* in response to a submission that a sexual offender was not entitled to a further hearing before Cabinet when seeking release from indefinite incarceration:

> To echo the rhetoric of Lord Atkin in *Liversidge v Anderson*, I know of only one authority which supports such an approach ... 'No, no!' said the Queen. 'Sentence first – verdict afterwards'.[74]

Carroll's famous Cheshire cat has faded in and out of many judgments.[75]

Charles Dickens

There are numerous references to *Bleak House*[76] in judicial tirades about the law's delays.

Passages from that work have also been cited to emphasise the evils of undue technicality in the law. Thus, Kirby J spoke[77] of the need to "leave an approach of excessive technicality in pleadings to the legal history of the 19th century where it properly belongs",[78] citing the following passage from *Bleak House:*

> [I]t's being ground to bits in a slow mill; it's being roasted at a slow fire; it's being stung to death by single bees; it's being drowned by drops; it's going mad by grains.

In like vein, Hunt J once asserted that, if a particular point was correct, defamation pleadings had become:[79]

> as complicated as a quadrille. I am reminded somewhat of Charles Dickens' description of lawyers as 'tripping one another upon precedents, groping knee-deep in technicalities [and making] mountains of costly nonsense'.

Bleak House also contains Mr Guppy's "without prejudice" proposal of marriage. Young J observed that Dickens was satirising the great growth of

---

72 *Case Y35* (1991) 91 ATC 343 at 348 (Cth AAT).

73 (1987) 163 CLR 378 at 419.

74 *Alice in Wonderland,* ch xii.

75 See eg *Jennings v Credit Corp of Australia Pty Ltd* (2000) 48 NSWLR 709 at 717-18.

76 The vexed question whether Dickens' fictional *Jarndyce v Jarndyce* was entirely apocryphal (cf McColl JA in *Lemoto v Able Technical Pty Ltd* (2005) 63 NSWLR 300 at 322 [95]) is discussed by Leslie Katz in an unpublished paper, "Bleak House in Australian Reasons for Judgment" (available for download at <http://papers.ssrn.com/abstract=1315862>).

77 *Director of Public Prosecutions (SA) v B* (1998) 194 CLR 566 at 608 [69].

78 Cf the approach of Gummow J in *Scott v Davis* (2000) 204 CLR 333 at 390-2.

79 *Burrows v Knightley* (1987) 10 NSWLR 651 at 654.

the significance of the words "without prejudice" that occurred between 1820 and 1850.[80] Kearney ACJ dealt with a similar matter, pointing out that:[81]

> It is as sensible and effective to use 'without prejudice' in relation to the particulars of a Statement of Claim, as it was for the lawyer's clerk in Dickens' Bleak House to make a 'without prejudice' proposal of marriage.

Other borrowings

Other writers whose ideas or words have been drawn upon by judges seeking to explain or enliven some point include Verne,[82] Eliot[83] and Chesterton.[84] The Victorian Full Court had the brothers Grimm in mind when their Honours observed that "the plaintiff, like the witch in Hansel and Gretel, may want a receiver to cage the defendant and fatten him up so he will make better eating, or at least to prevent him from wasting away".[85]

A future Chief Justice of Australia once invoked Coleridge when observing:[86]

> It was in the summer of 1797 while under the influence of a powerful anodyne that the poet Coleridge dreamed the well-known verses that begin:
>
> 'In Xanadu did Kubla Khan
> A stately pleasure-dome decree.'
>
> A less splendid vision, but equally powerful inspiration, led to the construction in 1985 of Perth's own pleasure-dome, the Burswood resort Complex.

The views of Conan Doyle's Sherlock Holmes[87] about probability have, however, been consistently rejected as a guide to probability reasoning.[88] So too was the

---

80 *Lukies v Ripley (No 2)* (1994) 35 NSWLR 283 at 286.

81 *Jumitogad Pty Ltd v Garraway* (unrep, NT Supreme Court, 9 October 1998).

82 Windeyer J in *Prowse v McIntyre* (1961) 111 CLR 264 at 279 (observing that since time is a local phenomenon "some interesting situations can be imagined ... with results even more striking than the experience of Phileas Fogg". He instanced the situation of twins who had been born at Greenwich on the same day, when the younger (in Sydney) rang the elder (in London) to wish him happy birthday just after midnight).

83 Glass JA in *Lohar Corporation Pty Ltd v Dibu Pty Ltd* (1976) 1 BPR 9177 at 9186 ("There is no universal rule that conveyancing performance is to be 'measured out in coffee spoons'").

84 Fullagar J in *Harris v Wagner* (1959) 103 CLR 452 at 461 ("This case [about border-hopping in order to attract the protection of s 92 of the Constitution] reminds one of Chesterton and 'the night we went to Bannockburn by way of Brighton Pier'").

85 Kaye, Murphy and Brooking JJ in *Bond Brewing Holdings Ltd v National Australia Bank Ltd* [1991] 1 VR 386 at 553.

86 French J in *Famel Pty Ltd v Burswood Management Ltd* (1989) 15 ACLR 572 at 573.

87 See generally Hon Leslie Katz, "Sherlock Holmes in Australian Judgments" *Bar News*, Summer 2009-2010, p 40.

88 *Paton v National Mutual Life Association of Australia Ltd* [2000] FCA 684 at [66] (Cooper J); *Guest v Nominal Defendant* [2006] NSWCA 77 at [109] (Ipp JA); *Chen v Zhang* [2009] NSWCA 202 at [49] (Sackville AJA).

foresight of this detective as a guide to a reasonable driver's response to a sudden dilemma. In *Lee Transport Co Ltd v Watson*, Rich J offered a mixed literary metaphor as well as a double entendre stemming from the name of the respondent driver. He was explaining why no negligence was found when that driver hit an unlit vehicle that had broken down in the road rather than swerve into the path of an oncoming vehicle:[89]

> It was a case of Scylla and Charybdis. Mr Ligertwood's argument appeared to suggest that in these unexpected and difficult circumstances Dr Watson should have possessed and exercised the prescience of Sherlock Holmes.

The joint reasons of the five (male) justices in *Zhu v Treasurer of New South Wales* open with a parody of Jane Austen's *Pride and Prejudice*:[90]

> It is a truth almost universally acknowledged – a truth unpatriotic to question – that the period from 15 September 2000 to 1 October 2000, when the Olympic Games were held in Sydney, was one of the happiest in the history of that city. The evidence in this case, however, reveals that the preparations for that event had a darker side.

Many other literary allusions or citations could be added.

89 *Lee Transport Co Ltd v Watson* (1940) 64 CLR 1 at 5.
90 (2004) 218 CLR 530 at 535 [1].

11 *Law and the Artist*

A two-way street with blurred signage

Outstanding lawyers have been accomplished contributors to the arts, creatively and financially. And artistic men and women have brought many disputes to law, thereby indirectly filling their patrons' pockets.

As we shall see, judges faced with disputes as far-ranging as contract, copyright, defamation, design, tax and trust law have been forced to touch the intangible and grapple with the undefinable as they try to explain essentially impressionistic judgments. Putting legal ideas into words has sometimes proved as hard for the judge as for the artist grappling with translating a concrete vision into chosen form and medium.

There have been several cases in which artists sued for unpaid fees when their works were rejected by those commissioning them, presenting the judge with the problem of judging their quality or adequacy.[1]

In resolving disputes over copyright and design, courts have faced difficulty putting into words their reasons for finding claims of infringement proved or disproved. In *Re Wolanski's Registered Design*[2] Kitto J had to decide whether a registered design of a "neck-tie support" had been previously published. Functionality was not an issue because the proprietor of such a registered design only gets a monopoly over the particular appearance. Required to decide whether "the identical conception of shape" was previously disclosed, his Honour pointed out that the question was essentially one on which the eye must be the judge. The matter before him was no "exception to the rule that the eye, like the heart according to Pascal, has its reasons that reason does not know".[3]

In *Commissioner of Taxation v Murray*[4] the Federal Court ruled that the test for deciding whether something was a "work of art" for the purposes of a sales tax exemption was primarily an objective one, although the artist's intention had some influence. In case of doubt, judges were to trust their own

1 *Parr v West* [1814] NSWKR 3 was an early case.

2 (1953) 88 CLR 278.

3 *Ibid* at 281.

4 (1990) 21 FCR 436.

subjective impressions as to whether a work was "utilitarian and artistically pleasing". Sheppard J observed:[5]

> I think that the intention of the creator must be all important. I think this is established by the circumstance that, whether one is considering the matter in the context of copyright law or revenue law, the article will either be an artistic work or a work of art from the moment it comes into existence. It will not become a work of art at a later point of time if it is not a work of art from the moment it comes into existence. At that time many works of art will not have been seen by anyone except their creator. In any event, one would not attribute to an article the quality of a work of art if its creator did not intend that it should have that quality. Nevertheless I do not think that objective considerations are without substantial importance and significance. It is by making a judgment of the thing itself, of what it purports to be, that one usually determines whether it is a work of art or not. This is a matter, notwithstanding the wide range of objects which are displayed in the art galleries of the world, which occasionally vexes the minds of distinguished connoisseurs of art. But it is the way in which one is struck by a particular object which will very often determine whether or not an object is properly regarded as a work of art. In borderline cases it may be appropriate to inquire of the creator what his or her intention was.

The Archibald Prize

Jules Francois Archibald was the proprietor and editor of the *Bulletin*, a magazine that made significant contributions to the law and lawyers through publication of defamatory pieces over the years. But Archibald's greatest such contribution was his bequest for an annual prize for "the best portrait preferentially of some man or woman distinguished in Art Letters Science or Politics painted by an artist resident in Australasia". No less than four Supreme Court cases have been generated to date.

The most famous was in 1944 when the Prize was awarded to William Dobell whose painting of the artist Joshua Smith[6] satisfied the judges but raised a storm of protest. Two unsuccessful entrants launched relator proceedings,[7] contending that the painting was not a portrait but a caricature in which the subject's features were distorted and exaggerated. The *cause celebre* saw Barwick KC leading the case for the informants, Kitto KC leading for the Trustees of the Art Gallery and Dwyer KC for Dobell himself.[8]

---

5 *Ibid* at 442.

6 Smith would himself win the Archibald Prize the following year.

7 These are proceedings promoted by private individuals in the name of the Attorney-General to enforce a public right (in this case the proper administration of a charitable gift).

8 See Mr Justice John H Phillips, "Barwick v Kitto" (1997) 71 *Australian Law Journal* 832.

The trial judge (Roper J) would conclude that any such distortion or exaggeration did not prevent the particular painting from being a portrait if the panel of judges so concluded.[9] Somewhat inconsistently, he added that it was a portrait in any event. He ruled that "portrait" in the gift referred to an ordinary English word meaning "a pictorial representation of a person, painted by an artist. This definition connotes that some degree of likeness is essential and for the purpose of achieving it the inclusion of the face of the subject is desirable and perhaps also essential".

Roper J recognised that the picture in question was characterised by some startling exaggeration and distortion clearly intended by the artist. It bore, nevertheless "a strong degree of likeness to the subject". The judge and counsel were able to see for themselves because Smith, the sitter, came to Court. Smith's parents had pleaded with Dobell to withdraw the portrait from exhibition and Smith himself refused to speak to the artist, joining in the general condemnation of the work. The experience in court must have confirmed all of his fears. Barwick's first witness was a Melbourne art critic who had stirred the controversy with a letter to the *Mirror* describing the picture as "qualifying for a freak exhibit in circuses" and who described the painting as a "pictorial defamation of character",[10] explaining:[11]

> A portrait allows of your consideration, your scrutiny. You do not feel as if it was your bounden duty to ring for the ambulance, as you do when you see that sort of thing ... [The subject of the painting looked like] an elf-person, a person sick in body and brain.

The acting director of the National Gallery, John Young, denounced the painting as a "biological absurdity":[12]

> No being could live like that. I remember seeing in a text book of psychiatry some pictures of some poor sub-human creatures who were never humans and who had been allowed to live and maintain one posture, not even a fixed idea, but a fixed posture, and they developed very strange proportions, but they are sub-human.

In his opinion, "no man could be as sick as [Smith was depicted] and produce the beautiful things that Joshua Smith produces".[13] In similar vein, the informants called a general practitioner who swore that the picture represented "the body of a man who had died in the position and has remained in that position for a period of some months and had dried up".[14] Dobell's counsel put

9 *Attorney-General v Trustees of the National Art Gallery of New South Wales* (1944) 62 WN (NSW) 212. A transcript of the trial is in the library of the New South Wales Bar Association.

10 Transcript, p 14.

11 Transcript, p 7.

12 Transcript, p 77.

13 Transcript, p 77.

14 Transcript, p 94.

a single question in cross-examination, "Do you know anything about art?", and, getting a negative answer, sat down. Dobell gave evidence defending his approach to portraiture and explaining how aspects of his personal knowledge of Joshua Smith were represented in the painting. In retrospect, the case was hopeless.

The stoush was grist for the mill for the experienced barristers and it made Dobell's name. But it "broke him physically",[15] also scarring Smith for life. Smith's parents had wanted to buy the portrait after the controversy but Dobell refused to sell it to them, fearing that they were intent on destroying it. Instead, he sold it to Sir Edward Hayward. In 1958 the work was burnt in a fire at Hayward's Adelaide home. The top half of the painting was destroyed, thus obliterating the portion that had enabled the judge to declare it a portrait. Hayward had the painting restored by a conservator, with the result that it could no longer be considered an original work by the artist.

The Dobell trial was re-enacted in the Banco Court in 1999 as part of the 175th anniversary of the Supreme Court. The inimitable Mr Justice Meagher presided and arrived at a similar conclusion to Roper J, expressing it in his own words:[16]

> In 1921 the late J F Archibald established an annual art prize. It was to be a prize for portraiture. It has operated until this day. Before Mr Dobell won the prize, one can say three things of the winning entries:
>
> (a) they were usually of admirals or generals,
> (b) they looked like each other, and
> (c) they looked like boiled codfish.
>
> Now Mr Dobell has produced a work which does not look like any of the others, and he has won the prize. The two plaintiffs, who might be considered representatives of the boiled cods, object to Mr Dobell's painting. They say his painting is not a "portrait". They say the Trustees of the Art Gallery acted in breach of trust in awarding him the prize. Why, *on se demande*? The case has not been made any easier to judge by the plaintiffs' refusal to propound any definition of the word "portrait". Instead their witnesses have chattered about likeness, caricatures, fantasies, exaggerations and comics, drowning both definition and meaning.
>
> A portrait need not end up a "pretty" picture. If one were painting portraits of the other judges of this Court one would hardly expect the results to look like Adonis or Marilyn Monroe.
>
> One does expect a certain degree of representation. But here one has it. The portrait looks like the sitter. If in the portrait the arms seem sadly thin that is not due to pictorial exaggeration, it is simply because Mr Smith does not eat enough fresh cream.

15 Marr, *Barwick*, p 42.

16 See (1999) 73 *Australian Law Journal* 710.

> And representation is not enough. One must show something of the sitter's character. Here one has the poetry, the diffidence and the integrity of Mr Smith.
>
> In addition, one's needs must always indulge one's own point of view: so a Van Dyke always looks like a Van Dyke, a Dobell like a Dobell. All Rembrandt portraits look like portraits of Margaret Olley. All Goya's sitters – mostly members of the Spanish Royal Family – look as if they had cleft palates.
>
> And, finally, there is the necessity for a portrait to be a work of art. This little fact escaped Mr Barwick, though not the trustees.
>
> The case will be dismissed with costs.

As indicated, the Dobell case was but the first of four. In 1983, in *Bloomfield v Art Gallery of New South Wales Trust*,[17] Helsham CJ in Eq decided that a portrait painted from a photograph, rather than from life, fell outside the terms of the trust. The decision was criticised by the editor of the *Australian Law Journal*[18] on the basis that "If a live sitting were the primary criterion, there would be difficulty in accepting as portraits the self-portraits of Rembrandt and Rubens [which] must have been painted on the basis of images in a mirror: is there any distinction of significance between a photographic image and a mirror image?"

In 1985, Powell J rejected a challenge to the validity of the trust, ruling that it was a bequest for the advancement of education and therefore a valid charitable trust.[19] And in 2006 Hamilton J upheld the Trustee's decision to award the Prize to Craig Ruddy for his portrait of the Aboriginal actor David Gulpilil, rejecting the unsuccessful entrant's argument that the portrait had not been "painted" because the principal medium was charcoal.[20]

Several defamation cases have been launched in connection with the Prize. One of them involved an Art Gallery employee who complained about a piece suggesting that her influence in assisting the Trustees justified the assertion that she was a "hanging judge".

The naked lady

A painting of a different genre caused a major blue within the New South Wales Bar Association between the late 1970s and the mid 1990s.

In 1975, the same Roderick Pitt Meagher who later "judged" the retrial of the Dobell Case presented the Association with "an untitled Renoiresque

17 Unreported, NSW Supreme Court, 23 September 1983. The case involved a "portrait" by John Bloomfield of Tim Burstall.

18 JG Starke, "Literary and Artistic Competitions" (1984) 58 *Australian Law Journal* 52.

19 *Perpetual Trustee Co Ltd v Groth* (1985) 2 NSWLR 278.

20 *Johansen v Art Gallery of NSW Trust* [2006] NSWSC 577. As well as charcoal, the artist used acrylic paint, aquarelle pencils, chalk pastels and other materials. Hamilton J concluded that the portrait could not be excluded from the category of a work which had been "painted". Unlike Roper J, he held back from also expressing his own finding of fact on the issue.

lady" by Geoffrey Proud.[21] The cost appears to have been a little over $1000. Roddy was a generous donor especially since he had adopted a method of gathering funds for worthy gifts that became known as the "Meagher touch". A small group of his friends would be notified that they had become joint venturers and asked to contribute their share of something already acquired. The Proud donors, who were profusely thanked by the then President, the Hon TEF Hughes QC, included Mr Justice Hope and a group of senior barristers including Lockhart QC, McHugh QC, Simos QC, O'Keefe QC, Reddy QC, Cripps QC, Morris, Poulos and Hely.

The portrait was initially hung in the Bar Association Board Room but at some stage it moved into the Common Room. There it occupied a prominent spot for several years, attracting much attention, a lot of it of the admiring sort in those days of male insensitivity. Over the next 20 years motions to have the painting removed from the Common Room were put and lost before an increasingly divided Bar Council. But by the early 1990s the worm was turning and there were calls by and on behalf of female barristers for the painting to be removed from its prominent spot – just for starters.

It was a picture of a woman sitting naked, legs apart, with her right hand near her dark panties. The hand was resting, according to the more nervous supporters of the gift. Giving the sitter the benefit of the doubt, Clive Evatt,[22] later described her as "unaware of section 576 of the Crimes Act, the section dealing with indecent exposure". But the opponents were quite certain that she was masturbating or, as AW Street put it in his passionate memorandum calling for the painting's removal, in "an apolaustic act of hedonism, at least capable of provoking a prurient or lascivious response to the observer". In 1993 Street spoke on behalf of what was still a minority of troubled barristers when he pointed out that:[23]

> In simple terms, it is capable of conveying an approach to women as 'a sex object' and does not add to the dignity or decorum of the Bar Common Room.
>
> 'Controversy' is not to be found as an object within clause 4 of the Memorandum of Association. In the present case this controversy must be resolved according to the object in clause 4(b) 'to uphold the honour and dignity and promote the interests of the bar of New South Wales'.

Articles appeared in the Sydney press. As often, the Bar divided for a mix of reasons. Female barristers, who were on the whole opposed to the painting, had represented a small percentage of the practising barristers in 1975, but their numbers and ire were steadily rising. To many, the painting symbolised the sexist

21 Proud would win the Archibald Prize in 1990 for his portrait of the feminist author Dorothy Hewitt.

22 Clive Evatt, "The Artful Bar" *Bar News*, Summer 1988.

23 Memorandum to Bar Council, 13 July 1993.

and clubbish ethos of the Bar of those days. The redoubtable Janet Coombs donated a painting of a nude male, but it was rejected by the Association on aesthetic grounds, the work being said to be not competent enough. This threw more oil on the flames. At one stage, the painting was moved to a less prominent spot in the Common Room. However, the immediate outcome of the 1993 push was that the painting was moved back into a position of prominence by (majority) decree of the Bar Council.

Ruth McColl, later President of the Bar and later still a Judge of the Court of Appeal, explained what was afoot:[24]

> The view expressed by members that the painting is inappropriate for the Common Room in 1994 does no more than reflect the reality that the Bar is a very different institution from that of 1974. Both then and now the bar was numerically dominated by men. However, attitudes to women at the Bar have undergone a sea change in the last two decades. That change is appropriate bearing in mind that the Association is but a microcosm of a society whose attitudes to women in the workplace have been changing over the same period. Part of the process of change is the increasing recognition that matters which were appropriate in a male dominated world are no longer appropriate.

Such attitudes were bound to draw fire from males of the older school. Anyone familiar with the late Roddy Meagher knew him to be a complex personality with a devilish sense of humour and a passion for art.[25] He was also a stirrer of the first order whose claims to be "just teasing" could never be taken entirely at face value. According to Babette Smith, who was the Chief Executive of the Bar Association between 1993 and 1997, Roddy "knew what he was doing" when he arranged the purchase and gift at a time when the women's movement had got a hold on Australian society.[26]

The controversy raged on in 1993-94. In an attempt to defuse it, the incoming President, Murray Tobias QC, decided to consign the painting to the Robin Gibson Art Gallery by way of extended loan. But this only reignited the controversy. Meagher (by now a Judge of Appeal) fired off a letter to Smith ("Dear Madam") asserting that "Tobias QC, beset with strident harridans, had no authority to make whatever arrangements he did" concerning the painting. Issues of censorship, free speech, discrimination against women, political correctness, the role of the Bar Council vis-à-vis the Bar membership as a whole, and much else besides swirled around. This was an issue *par excellence* where societal attitudes were changing, although this in itself only stiffened the resolve of the defenders of the status quo.

24 Memorandum to Bar Council, 16 February 1994.

25 There are several tributes to him in (2011) 35 *Australian Bar Review* 1.

26 Radio interview with Sally Loane on 2BL, 5 June 2000. Smith described her job as the first female chief executive of the Bar as being with a group of people "marooned on an island in a sea of social change and bewildered by it".

Tobias wrote to the original donors soliciting their support before the showdown at the Bar Council meeting of 17 February 1994. But most of them proved reluctant to move, seeing the matter had become one of "censorship". Some (like Morris QC) expressed their views firmly. He urged the Council to hold its line and to concentrate on more vital issues, adding: "Should the Association have any spare time, they should then turn their minds to putting trousers on dogs". The ever irenic Theodore Simos QC[27] confessed to having no present recollection of being a donor in the first place:

> [B]ut, upon the assumption that I was, it is my view that, upon acceptance by the Association, the painting became the property of the Association to deal with as the Council of the Association deemed fit in the interests of the members of the Association.

Nevertheless, many letters of support for Tobias flooded in, especially from female barristers who repeatedly affirmed that the painting made them feel unwelcome in the Common Room.

On 8 February 1994 Mr Justice Meagher resigned from the Bar Association. A month later he withdrew the resignation on the basis that "the decision to remove Geoffrey Proud's work from the Bar has been reversed" as it had been, although the location of the painting when it would return was placed in the hands of a sub-committee. Eventually Babette Smith offered to hang the picture in her office. This was only slightly less public than the Common Room but it proved to be the circuit-breaker.

In October 1995 an unsigned memorandum was delivered to the Bar Council. It purported to be from "probably the best known woman in the New South Wales Bar Association but no-one knows my name. Geoffrey Proud didn't give me one. He didn't give me many clothes either". Claiming natural justice, the model begged for her views to be taken into account. She pointed out how much things had changed since the heady days of 1974. "As I condensed from Proud's palette, Laurence Street became Chief Justice, Murray Gleeson was still a junior and the Bar was ruled by Tom Hughes. Oh, what a golden age ... I am rather glad I was painted with but a wisp of lingerie. After all – who would want to spend eternity in a pair of 1970's flared jeans?" The model found that her little trip to the Robin Gibson Gallery had given her a taste for the outside world:

> Besides, I feel sorry for just about everyone around me. Being Babette Smith's resident mural has its drawbacks. Her male visitors don't seem to know which way to look. Murray Tobias was punished for just trying to show me a good time.
>
> Worst of all though, I feel a bit funny about my donors, Meagher, McHugh, O'Keefe, Cripps, Morris, Poulos and Hely (to name but a few). With the exception of Poulos, they are starting to lose their

27 Later Simos J. Theo was the author's pupil master.

> enchanting Adonis-like figures. I've kept mine. That's my dilemma. I'd like to look elsewhere but I don't want to offend them.
>
> If I stay, I know I'll offend half the Bar. If I go, I know I'll hurt my donors. In situations like this I look to my old pin up girl, Mae West. She had a saying, "When I'm faced with a choice of two evils, I always choose the one I haven't tried before." Do you mind if I go? Perhaps some chivalrous male will move a motion and give me my freedom.

In 1998 Rick J Burbidge QC asked for the painting to be lent to his State Chambers and offered to pay the insurance costs. The painting was then valued at $15,000 and by 2000 this had risen to $30,000. (This would not be the first work of art to appreciate during controversy, although I shall sit on the fence as regards any causal link.) Three years later another set of chambers borrowed the lady for a time with the approval of the Bar Council.

The ABC prepared a television program, *The Naked Lady Vanishes*. But, according to a report in the *Sydney Morning Herald*,[28] the documentary was pulled at the last moment following a threat of defamation action by Murray Tobias QC in light of comments in it by Richard Ackland. Ackland described the program as a "mockumentary" in a *Sydney Morning Herald* article[29] in which he protested mightily while republishing the portion that had apparently been of greatest concern to the ABC, and Tobias. An edited version of the documentary went to air the following week.

A later President toyed with selling the painting but wisely relented. The painting remains at State Chambers.

28 6 June 2000.

29 "Mockumental blow to freedom of expression" *Sydney Morning Herald*, 9 June 2000.

12 Law and Religion

The law's interface with religion has often been closer than judicial citation of Scripture.[1] Bitter disputes over church governance and even theology trouble the courts from time to time. Issues of control motivate plaintiffs. Defendants tend to be both reluctant to accept the court's jurisdiction and eager to embrace martyrdom.

Early encounters and sectarian rivalries

When white settlers arrived in Australia they were blind to the beliefs and sensitivities of the indigenous inhabitants. Attitudes of supremacy, ignorance and the then prevailing doctrine of *terra nullius*[2] allowed white man's law and values to be imposed as if on a clean slate.

Aborigines neither sought nor were afforded the protection of white man's law for decades. And, when settlers were belatedly prosecuted for offences against Aborigines, the testimony of indigenous witnesses was usually rejected because the common law required a witness to believe in a future state of rewards and punishments.[3] The courage and perseverance of Attorney-General Plunkett in prosecuting the perpetrators of the Myall Creek massacre in 1838 signalled an end to a formal double standard. But it would be decades before any further prosecutions were launched despite continuing outrages by white settlers. For many years legislation to permit unsworn Aboriginal evidence was consistently voted down due to the opposition of William Wentworth and other pastoralists.

> The Myall Creek prosecution, so well intentioned, had become a fatal hindrance to extending the protection of law to indigenous Australians. Western Australia and South Australia had no such baggage, and enacted Bills allowing Aboriginal evidence in 1843 and

1 As to which see pp 194-6.

2 Early cases showed some uncertainty as to whether the Supreme Court had jurisdiction to try crimes committed by Aboriginals upon Aboriginals: see *R v Dirty Dick* (1829) NSW Sel Cas 2. The doctrine of *terra nullius* was finally abrogated in *Mabo v Queensland (No 2)* (1992) 175 CLR 1.

3 For an early application, see *R v Hewitt* [1799] NSWKR 154.

> 1844 respectively. New South Wales would not bring itself to pass the measure until 1876.[4]

Sydney was ecclesiastically a part of the Anglican Diocese of Calcutta when white settlement began in 1788 and it was assumed that the Church of England was established in New South Wales as in England.[5] This conveniently ignored the feelings of Scottish settlers who were used to the (Presbyterian) Church of Scotland as the established church where they came from. The feelings of the Roman Catholics were of course ignored for decades in official dealings.[6] No one thought about the Aborigines.

Captain Phillip's oaths of office, which he swore before the assembly of bemused soldiers and convicts mustered on 13 February 1788, included the following abjuration of the Roman Catholic doctrine of transubstantiation:[7]

> I, Arthur Phillip, do declare That I do believe there is not any Transubstantiation in the Sacrament of the Lord's Supper or in the Elements of Bread and Wine at or after the Consecration thereof by any Person whatsoever.

At that time the *Test Act 1673* (Imp) required such a declaration to be made before a person could assume any public office in England and it was simply assumed that this formed part of the birthright of white settlers. Catholics such as Plunkett and Therry were ineligible for appointment to any public office until the passage of the *Roman Catholic Relief Act* in 1829 and its adoption in the colony. Even then, Governor Bourke feared to appoint two Catholics as his law officers.

From as early as the 1820s the Presbyterian firebrand John Dunmore Lang was variously agitating *against* any (Anglican) establishment, and *for* an establishment that treated Scottish Presbyterians as they were in Scotland. Lang could certainly mix his arguments. In 1824 he persuaded the Attorney-General, Saxe Bannister, that, as New South Wales was in the (Anglican) Diocese of Calcutta, he, as a Presbyterian minister, was entitled to the privileges of an Act passed by the British Parliament in 1818 for the relief of Presbyterians in India. Governor Brisbane went along with this and issued the licence that was generally required for marriages to take place in the colony, despite the common law otherwise governing such matters.

The following year Archdeacon Scott arrived in town. He viewed the licence issued to a Presbyterian minister as a gross infringement of the legal privileges of the Anglican Church. Scott persuaded Saxe Bannister to change

---

4 Tony Earls, *Plunkett's Legacy. An Irishman's Contribution to the Rule of Law in New South Wales*, Australian Scholarly Publishing, 2009, p 112.

5 See Dixon J in *Wylde v Attorney-General (NSW)* (1948) 78 CLR 224 at 284. Cf *Ex parte Rev George King* (1861) Legge 1307, discussed below.

6 See *Trustees of the Roman Catholic Church for the Archdiocese of Sydney v Ellis* (2007) 70 NSWLR 565 at 600 [175]-[181].

7 *Historical Records of Australia*, Series 4, vol 1, p 21.

his view and withhold a licence for a second Presbyterian marriage. The poor bride and groom had to seek out an Anglican parson to guarantee the legitimacy of their nuptials and any ensuing progeny. Lang then published an advertisement in the *Sydney Gazette* announcing that it was (Presbyterian) business as usual and thereafter celebrated a number of Presbyterian marriages.[8] The law about marriage in the colony was in considerable turmoil until 1855. Lang also brawled within his own Church of Scotland. He was deposed from the ministry and ordered out of his position at the Scots' Church in Sydney, but eventually exhausted his opponents at law.[9]

Until the arrival of Muslims in numbers in the late 20th century, sectarian bitterness was primarily directed at Roman Catholics. Orchestrated anti-Catholic feeling would lead Sir Henry Parkes to renege on his promise to appoint Edward Butler Chief Justice in 1873.[10] While in Italy in 1902, Edmund Barton met with the 92-year-old Pope Leo XIII and the two of them conversed in Latin. The Pope presented Barton with a medallion. Protestants back home went hysterical, and the uproar may have contributed to Barton calling politics a day. In 1917, in *Nelan v Downes*, Barton was able to unite a healthy disrespect for unsuitable English precedent and for the same sectarianism. The High Court held that a gift for masses for the repose of a deceased's soul was not a gift for a superstitious use, but charitable, Barton saying:[11]

> This is a country without any established church. Within its bounds, all religions are on an equal footing.

Despite such sentiments, sectarian attitudes would dog judicial and other public appointments until the second half of the 20th century.

There was a sensational trial involving a young nun in the Supreme Court of New South Wales in 1921. Sister Mary Liquori left the Presentation Convent in Wagga Wagga in a distraught condition and took refuge with members of the local Orange Lodge. There were peaks of intense anti-Catholic bitterness in Australia, much of it over-heated by anti-Irish feeling stemming from two failed conscription referendums during the Great War. Bishop Dwyer, the nun's superior, obtained a warrant for her arrest on the grounds of insanity. She was taken before the Supreme Court sitting "In Lunacy" and remanded for observation, but then she was certified sane and released. With the financial backing of the Loyal Orange Lodge, she sued for £5000 for wrongful arrest and mistreatment at the mother house. Every detail of convent life was exposed

8 See CH Currey, "The Law of Marriage and Divorce in New South Wales (1788-1858)" (1955) 41 *Journal of the Royal Australian Historical Society* 97 esp at 99-101.

9 See *Purves v Attorney-General, Lang* (1860) 2 Legge 1189, (1861) 15 Moo PC 116. The proceedings against Lang failed in the Privy Council on issues of standing and (13 years) delay.

10 See p 65.

11 (1917) 23 CLR 546 at 550.

in a blaze of publicity during a lengthy trial before Ferguson J and a jury. The judge remarked in his summing-up that "it is very unfortunate for the plaintiff that, at the time she left the convent she did not meet somebody [with] a little common horse-sense". The jury concluded that the over-zealous bishop had been motivated by a sense of responsibility to the girl's parents in Ireland, not malice, so the action was dismissed.

State assistance to religious schools stirred a sleeping "DOG" in the 1981 when an organisation called "Defence of Governments Schools ('DOGS')" sooled the Attorney-General in a relator action to launch what turned out to be an unsuccessful challenge in the High Court.[12]

One aspect of the common law widely thought to be part of the birthright of the white settlers was the offence of blasphemous libel which rendered an indictable misdemeanour the publishing of material calculated to outrage or insult a Christian's religious belief. But as far as is known, there have been no prosecutions for such offence, although there has been a good deal of robust vilification. The crime of blasphemous libel has been abolished by statute in several jurisdictions and its current status at common law is uncertain.[13] The issue of religious vilification has now passed into the murky waters of human rights discourse.[14]

Anglican Establishment

In the *Red Book Case*,[15] Sir Owen Dixon observed that "notwithstanding judicial statements of a contrary tendency, the better opinion appears to be that the Church of England came to New South Wales as the established Church and that it possessed that status in the colony for some decades". It depends a little on one's definition of "established", but Dixon's view was undoubtedly correct. For example, early Church dignitaries such as Archdeacon Scott (appointed in 1825)[16] and Bishop Broughton (designated "Bishop of Australia" in 1836) were appointed by Crown Grant that spelt out considerable ecclesiastical and temporal jurisdiction.[17] An Order in Council of 1825 recognised the jurisdiction of the Archdeacon's Court. The Church and School Corporation was founded by the Governor in 1826 for the support of the Anglican Church and an educational system under its control, and it was endowed with one-seventh of the surveyed land of the colony.

12 *Attorney-General; Ex rel Black v Commonwealth* (*DOGS Case*) (1981) 146 CLR 559.
13 *Pell v Council of the Trustees of the National Gallery of Victoria* [1998] 2 VR 391.
14 See *Catch the Fire Ministries Inc v Islamic Council of Victoria Inc* (2006) 15 VR 207.
15 *Wylde v Attorney-General (NSW) (at the relation of Ashelford)* (1948) 78 CLR 224 at 284.
16 Thomas Hobbes Scott had first been to Australia as secretary to Commissioner Bigge.
17 See *Trustees of the Roman Catholic Church for the Archdiocese of Sydney v Ellis* (2007) 70 NSWLR 565 at 600-1 [175]-[176].

The assumptions underpinning these actions were rudely shocked in the 1860s by rulings that the Crown had no role outside England in the establishment of religion or the appointment of bishops or clergy.[18] But, to use a Scriptural metaphor,[19] the writing was on the wall from earlier than that, according to two notable pieces of litigation involving St James' Church in Sydney.

Edward Smith Hall was the editor of the more radical of two "emancipist" or pro-convict newspapers in the colony of New South Wales, *The Monitor*. He frequently attacked Governor Darling, who regarded him as a "revolutionary scribbler" and a "fellow without principles, an apostate missionary".[20] Hall and Archdeacon Scott were at loggerheads on many fronts. Scott accused Hall of fraud, treachery, blasphemy and a love of anarchy because of his attacks on government policy, education and religion. Hall returned the compliment with an article published in 1828 satirising Scott's attachment to his annual salary of £2000. Scott, who was close to John Macarthur and other "exclusives", was also criticised for being involved in politics. Even worse, Hall alleged that Scott was not a man of peace. For his attack on Scott, Hall was prosecuted for criminal libel of a public official. He was fined, required to enter into a recognisance to be of good behaviour for 12 months and imprisoned in the meantime. Hall appears to have raised the bond, but the following April he was back in gaol for libelling Governor Darling whom he accused of stacking the jury in the earlier proceedings.

A squabble between Scott and Hall over occupation of a pew in St James' Church, King Street, erupted into two notable trials in the fledgling Supreme Court of New South Wales.[21] In the words of Professor Bruce Kercher, "St James' was the second church in Sydney and the better of the two, socially. Its parishioners included official Sydney, whereas St Phillip's, the older church, was closer to the convicts at the Rocks and to the military barracks".[22] When he was not in gaol, Hall worshipped at St James', taking with him his eight children, including six daughters. He was a widower. One can only imagine the chagrin felt by the children at their father's conduct as later related. Hall had leased a pew, but he was informed by the incumbent, the Rev Richard Hill, that he would have to move to a less desirable part of the church. Hall saw Scott's hand in this, as it probably was. When Hall refused to move, Hill (acting on the directions of the Archdeacon's Court) ordered his eviction. Hall resisted and

18 See *Ex parte Rev George King* (1861) 2 Legge 1307 (discussed below); *Long v Bishop of Cape Town* (1863) 1 Moore NS 411, 15 ER 756; *Bishop of Natal v Gladstone* (1866) LR 3 Eq 1.

19 See *Daniel* 5: 6 (KJV).

20 *Historical Records of Australia*, Series 1, vol 12, p 762; vol 15, p 53.

21 The story is told in detail in Bennett, *Sir James Dowling*, ch 4.

22 Bruce Kercher, "Establishment, Freedom of Speech and the Church of England: Pew Disputes in Early Nineteenth Century New South Wales and Newfoundland" (2000) 6 *Australian Journal of Legal History* 135.

subsequently took matters into his own hands. Four times he tried to get into the pew, over the opposition of beadles and constables. The church authorities placed a lock on the door of the pew and even had it boarded over with decking to keep Hall out. Eventually Hall forced the lock and, as an assertion of right, remained in the pew for three hours with his hapless daughters.

Two sets of proceedings ensued. The first was a claim by the Crown against Hall for damages for trespass when Hall broke into the pew and remained there. The trial took place before Forbes CJ and assessors. The Crown was represented by the Solicitor-General. Hall represented himself and argued that Scott had no power to dispossess him of his pew according to "mere capricious whim". Hall would not accept a "cold, comfortless pew" while his own pew was barred against him, forcing him and his family "to stand like paupers in the aisle: from motives which were too notoriously known to need ... farther explanation or comment". The assessors found the facts in the form of a special verdict, an outcome that left it to the Supreme Court to determine the legal consequences. Three months later the Crown obtained an order for a new trial on the ground that there was uncertainty as to whether St James' Church was to be considered parochial or government property. (The church had been built on Crown land, at government expense.)

At the new trial Dowling J summed up the issues in a manner that was quite shocking to Archdeacon Scott. His Honour described the case as no more than "a question of Contract". He ruled that English ecclesiastical law had no place in the colony because none of the known incidents of parochial church governance such as church rates, tithes or church wardens were part of the legal framework of the colony. In short, the Church of England was not established in Australia. The case then resolved itself as a technical matter of contract law with Hall losing because the pew had originally been let to himself and another person jointly. Nevertheless, the assessors made it clear where their sympathies lay by awarding the derisory damages of one shilling, instead of the £110 claimed by the Crown. Scott was most unhappy, especially when Crown law advice in England confirmed Dowling's ruling.

But Hall was not finished. In 1829 he launched his own action against Archdeacon Scott, claiming £100 damages in trespass for having been wrongly ejected from the pew. The writ was served on the morning Scott departed the colony. The trial took place before Dowling J and a jury. Counsel for Scott waxed lyrical in an attempt to blacken Hall's character:

> Gentlemen, look at the plaintiff's conduct ... Forcing his way, with a burglarious instrument [the screwdriver] ... seeking to provoke a contest, and make the Church of God the Waterloo of his fame!

The jury were again directed that the ecclesiastical law of the mother country concerning the interior arrangements of churches did not apply in New South Wales. The real issue was whether the acts were done with Scott's privity, consent or advice. The judge said that the verdict in the earlier trial was irrelevant, because in the present case Hall did not claim any title to the pew, simply a right not to be disturbed in his possession of it without lawful authority. After a short retirement the jury returned a verdict for Hall in the sum of £25. These substantial damages were later paid by the government.

In 1861 another squabble amongst Anglicans spilled into the public domain. The Rev George King was the minister at the Church of St Andrew in Sydney (nowadays St Andrew's Cathedral). King was a combative Ulsterman (sometimes a tautology) and he objected to Bishop Barker's decision to appoint the Rev William Cowper as Dean of what became the Cathedral Church. In September 1860 there was an ordination service, on a day when the then cathedral was not required for parochial purposes. King deliberately locked the door, thereby barring his Bishop from conducting the service. Bishop Barker requested the Chancellor of the Diocese, Sir William Burton (a former Supreme Court judge), to cite King to appear before the Chancellor and four licensed incumbents in order that King's behaviour might be inquired into and reported to the Bishop. King was allowed to nominate two of the four incumbents. This was all very fair, and strictly according to Hoyle as things were done in the established mother Church in England.

But the ungrateful Mr King went off to the Supreme Court and obtained a writ of prohibition, based on findings that Bishop Barker had no power to proceed in the manner proposed. The Supreme Court reiterated that the ecclesiastical law of England did not apply in the Colony. Bishop Barker had attempted to establish a "jurisdiction by usurpation" by "the holding of a pretended Court".[23] Dickinson ACJ pointed out[24] that the Queen's letters patent did not validly confer the powers of a bishop in England on Bishop Barker. Rather, he was "a bishop ... here only over those who voluntarily submit to his jurisdiction". Wise J delivered a lecture about equality when he remarked:[25]

> [H]ow could a colony, open alike to Englishmen and Scotchmen be governed by a law which should be applicable only to a portion of its inhabitants? Just as a Scotchman, on his arrival in the colony, ceased to enjoy any rights peculiarly Scotch – so an Englishman, being a member of the Church of England, loses all legal rights which are incapable of being shared by his fellow colonists.

Poor Bishop Barker. He had bent over backwards to be fair, only stumbling because he resorted to English procedures instead of simply revoking Mr King's licence. The Supreme Court said that he had power to do so, subject to the dictates of natural justice. King later appeared before Barker under protest and his licence was revoked. Barker subsequently restored the licence and appointed King to the parish of St Peter's, Cook's River.

23 Wise J in *Ex parte Rev George King* (1861) 2 Legge 1307 at 1330.
24 *Ibid* at 1311.
25 *Ibid* at 1324.

The separation of church and state

Leaving aside the special privileges of Anglicans, there were many areas in which church and state were closer in the 18th and 19th centuries than today. For example, there were the forms of indictment used in early criminal cases. Thus, it was pleaded against a woman charged with arson in 1795 that "she, not having the fear of God before her eyes, but being moved and seduced by the instigation of the Devil" did set fire to a house.[26] A man accused of sodomy was indicted on a charge that he:[27]

> with force of arms ... in and upon one Joseph Pearce, yeoman, in the face of God, and our Lord the King, then and there being, did make an assault, and him the said Joseph Pearce, then and there did beat, wound and illtreat, so that his life was greatly despaired of, with an intent that most horrid, detestable and sodomitical crime (among Christians not to be named) called buggery ...

Depending on one's beliefs, God may well have seen what happened. But it can confidently be asserted that King George III did not. This was one of many legal fictions, some of which endure to this day. It was a stilted way of saying that a public crime was involved in very private behaviour.

The Rev Dr Frackleton resisted the efforts of the Presbyterian General Assembly to expel him for "insubordination". He was victorious at trial, in the Queensland Full Court and in the High Court.[28] The trial judge, Cooper CJ, found that a group of churchmen had acted "in concert, with the vilest motives and a common object and intent to injure". Seeing that they were all members of "a church professing the doctrines of Christianity, [the judge] could only assume that their sense of justice was obliterated by their uncommon simplicity and an innocent, although mistaken zeal, which, unfortunately gave to their judgment and their feelings an unconscious bias against the plaintiff".[29] Dr Frackleton crowned his success by suing the Church Assembly's solicitors on their undertaking to pay his costs, and by obtaining damages for defamation against a member of his own flock.[30]

An unintentional attempt to assert the superiority of the church above the Supreme Court saw a bell-ringer convicted of contempt by no less than Stephen CJ who was at the time a leading Anglican layman. In 1865 proceedings in the Banco Court were interrupted by the persistent tolling of a bell from the adjoining St James' Church. Stephen sent his tipstaff to require that the "dreadful" noise cease forthwith.

---

26 *R v Pawson* [1795] NSWKR 2.

27 *R v Wilkinson* [1796] NSWKR 2.

28 *Frackleton v Macqueen* (1909) 8 CLR 673.

29 *Frackleton v Macqueen* [1909] St R Q 89 at 108-9.

30 McPherson, *Supreme Court of Queensland*, pp 237-8.

> The sacristan, taking his own view of the matter, rather peremptorily declined to leave off, and on the officer reporting that fact to the Judge his Honor at once ordered the contumacious ringer into custody.

Dr Bennett records that:

> [T]he unrepentant offender, who pleaded that he had higher orders to obey from the churchwardens, was disabused of that notion on being found guilty of contempt of court, imprisoned until the rising of the court, and mulcted in a fine. At the court's rising, a juror and one of the churchwardens interceded on the malefactor's behalf and, after administering a severe censure and warning, Stephen discharged the sacristan, without pecuniary penalty.[31]

Despite repeated knockbacks in the 19th century, Anglicans in the Diocese of Sydney found it very hard to accept that their Church was only a voluntary association, that all denominations were equal in the eyes of the law, and that courts would bend over backwards to avoid becoming entangled in doctrinal or liturgical disputes. In the 1940s they supported litigation over doctrinal issues that went to the High Court[32] and in the 1990s they promoted and funded litigation in the New South Wales Court of Appeal.[33] Each case involved matters happening outside the diocese, in Bathurst and Canberra-Goulburn respectively. Included in the arguments pressed on each occasion were submissions that effectively ignored the 19th century cases already mentioned.

The earlier of the two proceedings is known as the *Red Book Case*, after the colour of the prayer book approved by the Bishop of Bathurst that was said to endorse a Roman Catholic doctrine of the Real Presence at the Service of Holy Communion. Following protracted interlocutory proceedings, with an appellate excursion over the technicality of a relator suit commenced in the name of the Solicitor-General being amended to show the Attorney-General as informant,[34] the trial resulted in injunctions restraining any departure from the Service of Holy Communion according to the Book of Common Prayer. There were also declarations that the making of the sign of the cross and the use of a sanctus bell constituted breaches of trusts of (Anglican) church lands.

An appeal directly to the High Court was heard by a bench of four that split evenly.[35] Dixon and Rich JJ would have upheld the appeal and dismissed the proceedings on the ground that courts of Equity should not get involved in purely liturgical disputes. Rich J would have declined on discretionary grounds

31 Bennett, *Sir Alfred Stephen*, p 419. The earlier passage is quoted from the *Sydney Morning Herald* 18 May 1865, 4.

32 This was the "Red Book case" discussed below.

33 *Scandrett v Dowling* (1992) 27 NSWLR 483.

34 See *Solicitor-General v Wylde* (1945) 46 SR (NSW) 83 where Jordan CJ (at 90) was reminded of James LJ's observation that "questions [in Chancery] are in the following order, with respect to the importance attached to them and the zeal with which they are argued, namely, practice first, costs second, and merits third and last".

35 *Wylde v Attorney-General (NSW) (at the relation of Ashelford)* (1948) 78 CLR 224.

to deal with what he described as "abstract questions involving religious dogma".[36] His opening remarks set the tone:[37]

> The subject of this unhappy controversy is only fit for a domestic forum and not for a civil court. Unfortunately it is not an example of 'charity' in the New Testament sense or of the command to love one another. The dispute illustrates a saying of Dean Swift that 'we have just enough religion to make us hate, but not enough to make us love one another'.

Latham CJ and Williams J were of a different view, although they reshaped the injunction so as to confine it to "church trust" properties. The matter was resolved in this way because the Chief Justice had a casting vote where the Court was evenly divided in such appeals.

This outcome produced two ironies. First, it bound the Church of England in Australia to greater uniformity in matters liturgical than in England, having regard to late 19th century English enactments there that were not introduced in Australia because it was by then accepted here that Parliament had no business intruding into Church doctrinal or liturgical affairs. The second irony was that the Chief Justice whose two votes in favour of strict prayer Book orthodoxy had been decisive was a committed atheist who for some years had been the President of the Rationalist Society of Victoria.

The Archbishop of Canterbury intervened more than once during the Red Book litigation to urge settlement, fearing that an appeal from Australia to the Privy Council would expose the English Church to unpleasant judicial interpretations of the Book of Common Prayer, thereby reopening the wounds of the Gorham controversy of the 1850s.[38] A threatened appeal to the Privy Council was abandoned in return for the defendants being released from the crippling costs orders pronounced by Roper J and upheld by the High Court. Bishop Wylde's leading counsel was FW Kitto KC, later a High Court justice. He endorsed the compromise in a letter from London where he was appearing before the Privy Council in the *Bank Nationalisation Case*.[39] Kitto observed that the litigation left the Church right where it was when the litigation started because the two-all split in the High Court meant that legal uncertainty prevailed except for the certainty that any fresh litigation would be cripplingly costly.[40]

Scandrett v Dowling[41] was another instance of Sydney Anglicans promoting litigation over issues of doctrine and church order that arose outside Sydney. This time there was a firm rebuttal by the New South Wales Court of Appeal,

---

36 *Ibid* at 282.

37 *Ibid* at 273.

38 Following *Gorham v Bishop of Exeter* (1850) 7 Not Cas 413.

39 *Commonwealth v Bank of New South Wales* (1949) 79 CLR 497.

40 Dr David Galbraith, *Just Enough Religion to Make Us Hate. An Historical Legal Study of the Red Book Case* (unpublished Ph D thesis), p 269.

41 (1992) 27 NSWLR 483.

resulting in the dismissal of the proceedings with costs and the triggering of an inquiry as to damages stemming from the dissolution of an interlocutory injunction that had halted an ordination service in Goulburn at the last minute. Two of the Judges of Appeal were named "Priestley" and "Hope", so the writing was on the wall for the plaintiffs from the outset.

The frequent warnings of the Old and New Testaments about the evils of believers going to law and airing their dirty washing in public[42] have as frequently been ignored, usually by believers who profess strict adherence to Biblical fundamentalism. Religious disputes over "matters of principle" have provided rich pickings for lawyers. Sadly, no one seems to learn that a secular court ruling on such matters is not going to resolve them and that martyrdom is often anxiously sought by religious zealots. Many church disputes have drawn judicial condemnation, sometimes in the form of non-believer judges citing Scripture at the believers.

Our national Constitution is janus-like with an invocation of God's blessing in its Preamble and a narrowly framed preclusion of laws for establishing any religion in s 116. That provision has had minimal impact because it speaks only of restrictions on federal legislative power and because the High Court has interpreted it narrowly. A referendum to extend the provision to the States was soundly rejected. God has blessed Australia in sparing us the horrors of church-state constitutional litigation experienced in the United States.

At other times, judges have ventured contestable views about the extent to which the Christian religion forms part of or informs the law of this country.[43] More often, they have invoked Biblical concepts to inform legal reasoning. Judges, like Satan, have been known to cite Scripture for a variety of views that are not necessarily legally orthodox.[44] The writer once incurred the wrath of Holland J when he suggested that the account of King Solomon offering to divide a baby between two women claiming custody might be relevant to a lottery case about a motor car. When Kirby P referred to the notions of redemption and forgiveness as important attributes of the shared morality of our society he was in dissent.[45]

In *Grace Bible Church v Reedman*[46] a church attempted without success to assert the authority of Scripture over the authority of Parliament in temporal matters. The Church was challenging its conviction for having conducted an

42 See *Exodus* 18: 24-26; *Deuteronomy* 16: 18-20; *Matthew* 18: 15-17; 19: 28; *Luke* 22: 30; 1 *Corinthians* 6: 1-7; 2 *Timothy* 2: 12; *Revelation* 3: 21; 20: 4.

43 See eg *R v Darling* (1884) 5 NSWR 405. On the topic generally, see Keith Mason, *Constancy and Change. Moral and Religious Values in the Australian Legal System*, Federation Press and the Australian Society of Legal Philosophy, 1990.

44 See pp 194-7.

45 *Kotowicz v Law Society of New South Wales* (unrep, NSW Court of Appeal, 7 August 1987).

46 (1984) 36 SASR 376.

unregistered school, an offence under the *Education Act 1972* (SA). The argument was put on the basis of a most unorthodox interpretation of *Romans* 13: 1-7, a passage which Zelling J pointed out[47] had been closely examined in the recent past given that Hitler's supporters had invoked it to require all German Christians to submit to the dictates of the Third Reich.

The New South Wales Court of Appeal was hearing a case involving an alleged omission by the Registrar General to register a right of way when land was bought under the *Real Property Act*.[48] Mr TEF Hughes QC was appearing for the appellants when the following exchange occurred:

> Kirby P: Where is the notice which the Registrar General gave to interested property owners?
>
> Mr Hughes: It is the one given to the Church of England Property Trust shown in the appeal book. It was common ground that this was a pro forma.
>
> Kirby P: The Church of England Property Trust must own large tracts of land in this region?
>
> Mr Hughes: The Church owns a lot of land near Goulburn.
>
> Handley JA: No unregistered right of way, I trust.
>
> Mr Hughes: Except, one hopes, to heaven!

Personal beliefs and practices

Many lawyers have become involved in religious controversies in their roles as members of church synods or church tribunals or as Advocates and Chancellors. Among Chief Justices who have been Chancellors of Anglican Dioceses throughout their term of judicial office were Stephen CJ (Diocese of Sydney), Herring CJ (Diocese of Melbourne) and De Jersey CJ (Diocese of Brisbane). Several judges of note, including High Court justices Griffith, Higgins, Piddington and Rich, were the sons of clergy. Others had been clergy before turning to law, including Cary DCJ, Geraghty DCJ, Phelan DCJ and Rutledge DCJ.

Other jurists have drawn fire from airing their own theological views. Richard Hanson who was Chief Justice of South Australia between 1861 and 1876 flirted openly with Darwin's theory of evolution, which was highly controversial at the time. He also wrote "historical" biographies of Jesus and the Apostle Paul purged of miracles and what he termed "a slavish submission to the dogmas of a self-styled infallible Church". When he addressed the Adelaide Philosophical Society in 1860, members of the Bible Society who were there demanded that he resign as president of the Philosophical Society in the light of his remarks. When he refused, they elected another in his place.

47 *Ibid* at 377-8.

48 *Dobbie v Davidson* (1991) 23 NSWLR 625. Extract from transcript of hearing on 11 April 1991.

The American legal iconoclast, Grant Gilmore, once observed that:[49]

> In Heaven there will be no law, and the lion will lie down with the lamb ... In Hell there will be nothing but law, and due process will be meticulously observed.

If the latter proposition were a matter of concern to a believer, then he or she ought perhaps to try invoking Alfred Foster who was a judge of the Victorian County Court during the Depression years. He provoked a public outcry when he told a boy witness who was being questioned about his ability to take an oath, "There is no hell, sonny".[50] Whether or not accepts this statement from this source, it does suggest that resolving some issues lies outside the competence of the law and lawyers.

49 *The Ages of American Law*, Yale, 1977, p 111.
50 Hewitt, *Judges Through the Years*, p 56.

13 Law and Sports

Courts and sports

For many Australians, devotion to a particular sport (or team) represents their true religion. As with religion itself, many disputes about access and control have spilled into the courts. Unlike the religious brawls, the sporting ones have usually been about money because rights to broadcast and advertise for sporting events mean big bucks especially if they can be made exclusive. Gambling is sometimes not too far in the background.

Sport is essentially tribal, particularly in Melbourne, and judges have been known to show their tribal colours on occasions. The following sounds more like a pitch for the Olympic Games from the Premier of Victoria than what one would expect from a Judge of the *Federal* Court of Australia. This biased Sydney-sider therefore takes objection to the following from Marshall J:[1]

> Melbourne is Australia's sporting capital. It boasts of its Spring Racing Carnival as being without peer in the country. It hosts the Australian Football League Grand Final, the Australian Open Tennis Tournament, numerous high ranking golf tournaments and many other major sporting events, including the Australian Formula One Grand Prix. In 1998 a group of friends and acquaintances were invited to a meeting to discuss a proposal ... intended to add to Melbourne's world class sporting attractions. For reasons which will become apparent, that dream was not realised.

Another Victorian judge would rule that it was contempt of court for counsel to suggest to the jury that a judge appeared to show bias, like an umpire "coming out in a Collingwood jumper ... giving decisions one way".[2]

There are now legal conferences, textbooks and undergraduate courses on "sports law", not to mention the many serious (ie tax-deductible or employment-related) meetings that happen to coincide with major events in the sporting

1 *Adrenalin International Powersports Pty Ltd v John Caines Management Pty Ltd* [2004] FCA 206 at [1]. Justice Shayne Marshall is, of course, a Victorian.

2 The conviction was set aside on the basis that the words were extremely discourteous but not insulting, according to the criminal standard: see *Lewis v Ogden* (1984) 153 CLR 682. Only one of the five justices who sat was a Victorian and presumably none of them considered that to suggest someone was a Collingwood supporter was a contemptuous insult in any context.

calendar. It is hard to think of any sport that has not had serious brushes with the law or any branch of the law that has not had sports-related cases.

As with constitutional law, many of the cases concern attempts to *exclude* a player or team from membership of a sporting body or participation in a competition; or to *monopolise* an activity such as broadcasting a sporting event.[3] Two Rugby League teams have litigated their exclusion from competition as far as the High Court.[4] Of course, some sporting participants can only blame themselves for exclusion through personal encounters with laws prohibiting race-fixing, sexual assault or drug abuse.

A wise judge observed that "in general courts should be the last resort for the determination of club and association disputes".[5] Accordingly, courts generally decline frantic pleas to overturn the results of matches or decisions as to who is selected in a team, even an Olympic team.[6] They may, however, get involved where livelihood or reputation is directly affected when sporting associations expel members without fair procedure or besmirch their reputation. Thus, a netball coach who was banned for five years for "excessively enthusiastic coaching" was reinstated when she proved that a lot of shouting had been characterised as "child abuse" in terms suggestive of sexual abuse.[7]

Since risk-taking is of the essence of many sports, it is unsurprising that the risks often come home. But this has not stopped participants or spectators from seeking to hold someone else responsible. Damages in negligence have been claimed by those injured while playing rugby, surfing, observing car racing events and by numerous golfers hit by errant golf balls.[8] Even ostensibly gentle pastimes like dolphin-watching[9] and touch-football[10] have engaged the courts. The events that cause injuries are not always those inherent in the sport. Accordingly, claims have been successfully pressed by persons injured

---

3 For example, *Victoria Park Racing and Recreation Grounds Ltd v Taylor* (1937) 58 CLR 479; *Australian Broadcasting Commission v Parish* (1980) 29 ALR 228; *Singtel Optus Pty Ltd v National Rugby League Investments Pty Ltd (No 2)* [2012] FCA 34.

4 *Wayde v New South Wales Rugby League Ltd* (1985) 150 CLR 459; *News Ltd v South Sydney Rugby League Football Club Ltd* (2003) 215 CLR 563.

5 Thomas J in *Cox v Caloundra Golf Club Inc* (unrep, Qld Supreme Court, 1995). See also *Calvin v Carr* [1979] 1 NSWLR 1 at 12 (PC).

6 *Raguz v Sullivan* (2000) 50 NSWLR 236.

7 *Carter v New South Wales Netball Association* [2004] NSWSC 737.

8 Lord Reid once observed that the lawyer who invented the maxim that a person is presumed to have intended the natural consequences of his actions had never hit a golf ball into a bunker. The plaintiff's unsuccessful submissions in *Pollard v Trude* [2008] Aust Torts Reps ¶81-989 would rank high in any list of desperate arguments. An errant golf shot that flew in his direction as he stood "well out of the way of the expected trajectory" caused the defendant to shout "Watch out, Errol!, "Look out, Errol!" or "Watch it, Errol!" The Queensland Court of Appeal was unimpressed with the suggestion that the defendant was inviting the plaintiff to observe the errant shot and that only the traditional "Fore!" could substitute for a warning.

9 *Lormine v Xuereb* [2006] NSWCA 200.

10 *Falvo v Australian Oztag Sports Association* [2006] Aust Torts Reps ¶81-831.

by kangaroos on a golf course,[11] by spectators at a car-racing event[12] and by a cyclist who collided with a man playing touch-rugby in the central area at a velodrome.[13]

Recently, Parliaments have raised the bar for establishing liability and lowered the damages recoverable where personal injuries are suffered in any "dangerous recreational activity". This term is blandly defined as a recreational activity "that involves a significant risk of physical harm". Readers may be surprised to learn that the concept did not bar the claim of one of an alcohol-affected group of men "spotlighting" and kangaroo-shooting who was accidentally shot after a companion got into the cabin of their truck with a loaded rifle that he proceeded to "clock" back and forth in an effort to unjam it.[14] Obviously some sports carry little inherent risk, but the devil lies in the "inherent" detail. What about playing chess with a homicidal maniac?

Where liability is established, the task of assessing damages is fairly straightforward although (with a professional sportsman or woman) the court has to calculate the relatively short period within which the plaintiff would have been earning big money as well as the prospect that some non-tortious curtailment of earning power might have befallen in any event. It would certainly be wrong to assume that professional players' skills are confined to the sporting field. Jarrod McCracken was an outstanding Rugby League player with Wests Tigers whose playing career was ended by an unlawful spear-tackle. He recovered damages[15] but there was no component for economic loss because his expertise as a property developer always eclipsed that as a footballer:[16]

> The plaintiff bought his first property at age 18 ... He carried on activity in this area during his football career. He said that while it took some time he could fit it in with playing football. He gave as an example that when sitting on a team bus going to Canberra he would not read the form guides as 90% of the people did but read the real estate section of the Sydney Morning Herald. He would also look at records of comparable sales.

There were no damages for economic loss because the injury allowed McCracken to employ his land-dealing competence "far more than he did beforehand".

Lawyers often get involved in sports administration and some have sat on arbitral and disciplinary tribunals. Sir Anthony Mason purchased a newspaper

11 *Shorten v Grafton District Gold Club Ltd* [2000] NSWCA 58.

12 *Australian Racing Drivers Club Ltd v Metcalf* (1961) 106 CLR 117.

13 *Canterbury MC v Taylor* [2002] NSWCA 24 (findings of negligence were made against both the touch-footballer who was playing in the central area and who was killed as he stepped onto the track; and against the cyclist who struck him).

14 *Fallas v Mourlas* [2006] Aust Torts Reps ¶81-835.

15 The claim was framed as one of assault, thereby falling within the *Civil Liability Act*'s exemption for "an intentional act that is done with intention to cause injury or death".

16 *McCracken v Melbourne Storm Rugby League Football Club Ltd* [2007] Aust Torts Reps ¶81-925 at [35].

thinking that its advertised feature story about an "Historic Court Decision" would be discussing a constitutional decision of which he was justly proud. He was surprised to find that the article was about a tribunal decision that eye-gouging contravened the rules of Rugby League.

Sportsmen and women can nowadays earn vast sums of money for endorsing products which explains, in part, why they fight so hard to get into teams and are so grievously offended by defamatory slights. The West Indian cricketer Clive Lloyd recovered $100,000 damages from *The Age* in 1984 because of a column under the headline "C'mon Dollar C'mon" suggesting World Series Cricket games were fixed.[17] In *Ettingshausen v Australian Consolidated Press*[18] an article on "hunks" contained a "grainy" photograph of a well-known Rugby League player showing "a shape between the plaintiff's legs which (despite the defendant's submission to the contrary) is certainly capable of being interpreted as his penis" (Hunt J). This exceeded any publicity that the plaintiff may have courted voluntarily.

Sporting metaphors in the law

Many sporting metaphors have passed into common language, some also acquiring legal connotations. An ancient bloodsport is alluded to when a judge is found to have descended into the arena and, by taking too active a part in the examination of a witness, been blinded by the dust thrown up by the adversarial contest. Australian lawyers seldom refer to Americanisms such as "slam dunk propositions" and "hail mary arguments". But local sports are invoked when advocates respond to questions with a straight bat, others kick an own goal or are hit for six by their opponent or by the judge. "Stumps are drawn" frequently when the afternoon adjournment is announced by the court. Mason CJ delighted once to have a Solicitor-General "on the ropes". A Solicitor-General-to-be floored another Chief Justice "point, game and set", according to one account of a verbal exchange between them.[19]

Keely J drew on a cricketing analogy when invalidating the delegation of a power under the *Migration Act 1958* (Cth) because it permitted refusal of resident status but required the officer to refer the matter to higher authority if inclined to grant it. "A test umpire who is given the power to decide whether a batsman is out or not is given one power not two."[20] Kay J preferred the metaphor of "coach" to that of umpire when describing the Deputy Child

17 The Privy Council decision upholding the verdict is *Lloyd v David Syme & Co Ltd* (1985) 3 NSWLR 728.

18 (1991) 23 NSWLR 443.

19 See Burton, *From Moree to Mabo*, p 90.

20 *Singh v Minister for Immigration, Local Government and Ethnic Affairs* (1989) 90 ALR 397 at 402.

Support Registrar as "a league footballer". The Registrar's job was "to play in the position the coach tells him to. The Magistrates Courts or any court exercising jurisdiction under the *Family Law Act* is the coach. The Deputy Child Support registrar is simply there to go and play out in the field where he is told".[21]

To say that conduct is "not cricket" is generally derogatory[22] although Meagher JA once observed that "to this submission Mr Conti QC could only reply that it was not cricket, a consideration which enhances its attractiveness".[23] "It's not cricket!" was frequently trumpeted after the notorious incident in 1981 when the Australian captain Greg Chappell directed the bowler, his brother Trevor, to deliver a mulleygrubber to prevent the New Zealand team from snatching a draw by hitting six on the final ball of a limited over match. David Fraser in his *Cricket and the Law "The man in white is always right"*[24] tells us that the phrase first surfaced in the 19th century when it was illegal to bowl *overarm*. Round-arm bowling originated around 1807 when a woman practised it with her brother because a full skirt made it difficult for her to bowl underarm. Her brother later took to this novel method at a time when it was definitely "not cricket" and found himself to be the first to be no-balled for employing it in a major match. The rules were changed six years later, in 1828.

In this fascinating book, Fraser discusses the "neglected areas of intersection of cricket and the law" and much else besides. He reminds us that:[25]

> Cricket does not have 'rules', it has laws; umpires are vested with jurisdiction only upon 'appeal', the list is long. More than the obvious, however, comes from cricket, for it is a game full of blatant and co-existing contradictions: the public and the private, the individual and the team, the spirit of the game and a strict application of the laws.

Cricketing umpires, we learn, can commit errors of fact and law. Their approaches to decision-making can, like the rulings of judges, at times strike the loser as formalistic. Like traditional Chancellors, they have to manage disputes about the spirit of rules as much as their hard edges. Causation hypotheticals present themselves with every LBW appeal.

Fraser's critical legal scholarship is revealed when he explains that:[26]

> Cricket (like all other social texts) is a contradictory and ambiguous narrative into which we insert our own extra-textual readings which

---

21 *In Marriage of Field* [1991] FLC ¶92-227 at 78,565.

22 See eg K Burns, "It's Just Not Cricket: The High Court, Sport and Legislative Facts" (2002) 10 *Torts Law Journal* 1.

23 *General Credits Ltd v Wenham* (1989) 18 NSWLR 570 at 576.

24 The Institute of Criminology Monograph Series, No 4, Sydney 1993. See generally chapter 11, "It's Not Cricket – Underarm Bowling, Legality and the Meaning of Life".

25 *Ibid*, pp 2-3.

26 *Ibid*, 243.

> become part of the new text of cricket. The story of the ball sent crashing to the boundary is not just a text about cricket or advertising, it is part of a story about race, class, gender, religion, law, ethics, etc, etc. The only end to the story is the end we impose on it. The only meaning of the story is the one we impose on it ...

Wow! Going to the Sydney Cricket Ground will never be the same again.

Justice is not a game

Despite the prevalence of sporting metaphors, the law draws the line at suggestions that justice, or even litigation, is some type of game. In *Jackamarra v Krakouer*, Gummow and Hayne JJ said that:[27]

> [T]he rules of court ... are not prescribed for the purpose of implementing what Roscoe Pound referred to more than 90 years ago as the "sporting theory of justice". They are prescribed as aids to the attainment of justice.

Or as Kirby J later put it:[28]

> [T]he ultimate duty of the decision-maker in an Australian court [is] to decide a case according to law and the substantial justice of the matter proved in the evidence, not as some kind of sport or contest wholly reliant on the way the case was presented by a party.

These admonitions have been applied in matters of evidence and procedure. Thus, Selway J pointed out that "issues of evidence are not to be treated as if they were directed to giving all parties a 'sporting chance' of success".[29] And in *Sydney South West Area Health Service v MD*, Allsop P observed that "the ambush theory of litigation is dead in this State ... Litigation is not a game. It is a costly and stressful, though necessary, evil ... Counsel and solicitors should understand their duty to co-operate to bring the real issues forward and not approach litigation as a game".[30]

A judge once explained to a jury that the standard they were to apply was that of an umpire at a cricket match. Discussing the standard of "beyond a reasonable doubt", he said that it worked in practice in the same way as when a batsman was given the benefit of the doubt following an LBW appeal. The jury "would have seen [endless appeals] in the course of World Cup Cricket [and] it is exactly that which applies in the criminal court". A new trial was ordered when the accused took his appeal to a higher court. Ipp J observed that the comparison between the task of the jury and that of the cricket umpire

27 (1998) 195 CLR 516 at 526 [30], citing Roscoe Pound, "The Causes of Popular Dissatisfaction with the Administration of Justice".

28 *Whisprun Pty Ltd v Dixon* (2003) 200 ALR 447 at [120]. See also *Blight v Warman and McCallum* [1964] SASR 163 at 171.

29 *Gumana v Northern Territory* (2005) 141 FCR 457 at 502 [164].

30 [2009] NSWCA 343 at [53], [55].

was unfortunate because it trivialised the task of the jury, which was concerned with the liberty of the accused person appearing before it. "The jury are not umpires in some game."[31]

Other judges have rejected sporting metaphors simply because of their aversion to sport.

In a speech by the President of the Bar at the farewell to Meagher JA, Ian Harrison[32] reminded his audience that the judge had "brought colour to the Court of Appeal but not, if I may say with the greatest of respect, much movement". He cited Meagher's remarks in *Trevali Pty Limited (Trading as Campbelltown Roller Rink) v Haddad* in which he had said:[33]

> Whilst all reasonable people know that any form of physical activity is both unpleasant and dangerous, and probably unhealthy as well; and whilst sport, which is communal physical activity, suffers the added feature of exposing its participants to the perils of tribal barbarism; nonetheless the law has never regarded the playing of sport as contrary to public policy or even unreasonable, and therefore the mere participation in sport cannot of itself constitute contributory negligence.

According to Harrison, it was believed that Meagher was once invited to address a conference in Stockholm on sporting injuries, which only went to show that the Swedes do have a sense of humour.

Gambling

Statute law is comfortable using chance for the selection of jurors and supernumerary jurors, determining who gets the donkey vote on a ballot paper, and for breaking deadlocks in choosing the mayor of a local council. Mediators have been known to propose tossing a coin to bridge the final gap in settlement negotiations. According to no less an authority than Sir Laurence Street CJ:[34]

> One finds frequent uncritical reference in both the Old and New Testaments to the casting of lots as a means of determining the acquisition of property.

But it is difficult to think that an appellate court would countenance jurors flipping a coin as a means of resolving some issue of fact or that its judges would draw names out of a wig when determining who should be assigned responsibility for which of several unpleasant litigants in person.

---

31 *Condo v The Queen* (1992) 62 A Crim R 11 at 13. Ipp J also noted that the laws of cricket made no reference to "reasonable doubt".

32 Then the President of the New South Wales Bar Association, later Harrison J.

33 [1989] Aust Torts Reps ¶80-286 at 60,036. See also Meagher's reflections on "it's not cricket" at p 230 above.

34 *Tahapi Pty Ltd v Avery* (1986) 6 NSWLR 138 at 141. See further pp 195-6.

The High Court has frowned upon the expression "on the cards" to explain which remote losses flow from a breach of contract;[35] although the same term was recently used by one justice (admittedly a betting man) in a tortious context.[36] Litigants are nowadays urged to place their cards on the table.[37] And the "mutually interdependent rights and obligations of vendor and purchaser upon settlement of a conveyancing transaction are no longer to be regulated by the tactics of the poker table".[38]

Negligence law often speaks of plaintiffs assuming responsibility for the risks they consciously take. Meagher JA once observed:[39]

> [A] foreign currency loan is largely a gamble; consequently it would be unattractive to the timid and the prudent. Nonetheless, there are perfectly rational people who are prepared to gamble; and it is notorious that many borrowers did enter into such transactions at the time without suffering any damage, some of whom actually made a profit.

The Gleeson High Court has been criticised for adopting a "male model" attitude to sport that skewed the duty of care owed by sporting administrators to participants. The justices viewed "sport as combative, competitive and risk orientated".[40] Cases such as *Woods v Multi-Sport Holdings Pty Ltd*[41] were said to reflect an assessment of risk orientation that is "based on a masculine rather than a feminine paradigm".[42]

Attitudes to gambling itself have changed over the years. At common law, a wager was unlawful and thus could not be enforced by the winner. This did not, however, prevent an action in fraud if there were cheating[43] nor did a person who paid a gambling debt have a right to recover the money (unless of course the payment responded to a threatened knee-capping). Legislation passed in all jurisdictions rendered gaming or wagering contracts "null and void". Gradually such laws have been watered down, often where the state wished to control and manage gambling and milk its revenue by taxes. Unsurprisingly, there was a frosty response from the Court of Appeal when New South Wales State Lotteries claimed that there was an unlawful gaming contract when an unanticipated claim was lodged, despite lotto being permitted under the *Lotto Act 1979* as a revenue-raising activity. Samuels JA wryly observed that:[44]

---

35 *Wenham v Ella* (1972) 127 CLR 454 at 471.

36 *Roman Catholic Church v Hadba* (2005) 221 CLR 161 at 174 (McHugh J dissenting).

37 See *Boyes v Collins* (2000) 23 WAR 123 at 143; *Nowlan v Marson Transport Pty Ltd* (2001) 53 NSWLR 116 at 127-8.

38 Kearney J in *Warringah Contractors Pty Ltd v Pike* (1982) ANZ Conv R 304 at 310.

39 *Commonwealth Bank v Mehta* (1991) 23 NSWLR 84 at 92.

40 Burns, *op cit*, p 10.

41 (2002) 208 CLR 460.

42 Burns, *op cit*, p 13.

43 *R v Nicholson* (1868) 7 SCR (NSW) 155 at 161 (Stephen CJ).

44 *Petranker v Brown* [1984] 2 NSWLR 177 at 179.

> It would be curious, to say the least, if it turned out that the game of lotto, established by elaborate statutory provisions and commended to the public by a most substantial advertising campaign, turned out to be unlawful; with the consequence that the holder of a winning coupon had no legal right to recover the prize. Of course, legal shrewdness and parliamentary obtuseness might join to produce such a result inadvertently. But the element in all this which is most strange is that those responsible for the conduct of lotto themselves deliberately embrace the legal propositions which are designed to attach to the newly minted empires an essentially equivocal character.

While some gaming contracts remain unenforceable, the law will intervene where disputes arise over ownership of winning lottery tickets.[45] And gambling winnings may have to be brought to account in assessing damages. Thus, the owner of a racehorse wrongfully deprived of it by the defendant was entitled to recover his losses from being unable to place winning bets and to provide what was euphemistically described as "information as to his prospects of success to others who were in the habit of betting on racehorses".[46]

Sporting participants have, at times, been tempted to throw or fix the result of a contest or to bet when aware that others have done so. In the "Fine Cotton" ring-in affair, a good horse called Bold Personality was amateurishly disguised and substituted for the much less favoured Fine Cotton in a handicap race for novices at Eagle Farm in 1984. Stewards, noticing a dramatic plunge in the betting odds minutes before the race began, checked the horse's markings and confirmed the "sting" shortly after "Fine Cotton" won by a nose. Two men were convicted and imprisoned and others, including some prominent bookmakers, were "warned off" Australian racecourses for having had "prior knowledge" of the affair.

The advent of "spot-betting" in cricket and football and the now constitutionally protected ability to bet on losing rather than just winning propositions[47] have dramatically increased the temptations for nobbling insiders of the two-legged variety.

45 See eg *Van Rassel v Kroon* (1953) 87 CLR 298; *Voulis v Kozary* (1975) 180 CLR 177.

46 *Howe v Teefy* (1927) 27 SR (NSW) 301 at 303.

47 See *Betfair Pty Ltd v Western Australia* (2008) 234 CLR 418 at 479.

Part 4

Epilogue

14 Fallible All

This book has travelled back and forth over the spread of Australian legal history. As suggested by the title, *Then and Now*, I have pointed to both the constancies and the changes in legal rules, customs and attitudes. One constancy is that folly marches forth in every generation. Every generation is also privileged with wonderment at the ignorance of forebears, sometimes with justification.

Bloopers or worse

The life of courts is detection and correction of legal error. Criminal law punishes it, tort law awards damages for the harm it causes, effective advocacy exposes it, appellate judges reveal it in others (sometimes themselves as well). Everyone makes mistakes, some of them as glaring as they are amusing. Some have greater impact than others. As Jordan CJ observed, there are mistakes and mistakes.[1]

Attempts at humour from the Bench may backfire spectacularly. "Who was the bloody idiot who granted him bail?" asked Mildren J when about to sentence a man who had committed numerous dishonesty offences while on bail. It turned out that it was Mildren himself, a feat that saw him awarded the "Judge of the Year" prize for 2004 by David Pannick QC writing for *The Times*.[2]

A recently retired judge in the Land and Environment Court of New South Wales was considering the development of a wilderness area. One proposal involved the erection of a road sign: "*Wombats Cross Here*". "What is the point of that?" asked His Honour, "Wombats can't read". Gerber DP referred once to a tiger changing his spots.[3]

A District Court judge, who until recently had been a Crown Prosecutor, was summing up to the jury in a criminal matter. Having put the defence case, he began: "But what *we* say is ...".[4] Clifford Einstein QC announced

1 *Ex parte Hebburn; Re Kearsley Shire Council* (1947) 47 SR (NSW) 416 at 420.

2 Dean Mildren tells the story against himself, with mitigating circumstances, in his *Big Boss Fella All Same Judge*, p 272.

3 *Case V65* (1988) 88 ATC 498 at 501.

4 Rick Burbidge QC recounted this story to Leslie Katz.

his appearance, explaining to Young J that a particular matter might take some little time. Einstein as counsel had a reputation for thoroughness: Peter Young J as a trial judge had a reputation for despatch, being of the mould of Judge Learned Hand who always had "an open mind but not an empty one". "Take all the time you need, Mr Einstein", was the generous reply. "You are probably going to lose". On another occasion, having learned that there was no appearance for the defendant, Young J informed counsel: "Then it's just you against me!"

In 1928 Henry Bournes Higgins, late into his stint on the High Court, wrote to the most famous old boy of the Wesleyan Connexional School, George Bernard Shaw. The judge had been chuffed to discover that the hero of *Pygmalion* was called Henry Higgins. Unfortunately he got the play's title wrong, and Shaw's evident irritation over this slip produced a more than malicious reply:[5]

> Dear Mr Higgins,
> I remember Kingsbury[6] quite well; but I don't remember you. In 1865 when you left, I was only 9 years old. If we were really at the old Wesleyan Connexional School (now Wesley College and co-educational!) together, it can have been for a short overlap only. I certainly did not call the hero of Pygmalion (not Pygmalion and Galatea, which is a play by the late WS Gilbert) after you. ...
>
> There was a boy who came and went in my time whose name may have been Higgins, though I am not quite sure of it. But he was weakminded, or rather infantile, and used to stand up and sing during roll call when the fellows next him told him that Dr Crook expected him to do it. He stayed only a very short time, and should never have been sent there. A most goodnatured creature, who may have turned out well after all. Your dates exclude the possibility of identifying you with him.

The Director of Public Prosecutions challenged the leniency of a six-month sentence imposed on a forger who had cost a bank almost half a million dollars. In the Court of Criminal Appeal matters went from bad to worse for counsel for the respondent when he suggested that the objective criminality of the offences was reduced because the victim was the Commonwealth Bank:[7]

> Scragg (Counsel for the respondent): "In this case your Honours, the crimes were not directed against members of the public or against the respondent's employer but against the Commonwealth Bank which is a large and wealthy institution. The objective criminality

5 Quoted in John Rickard, *H B Higgins. The Rebel as Judge*, George Allen & Unwin, 1984, p 305.

6 A fellow old boy of the school, resident in Brisbane.

7 *Commonwealth Director of Public Prosecutions v Machtas* (NSW Court of Criminal Appeal, Gleeson CJ, Handley JA, Badgery-Parker J, 7 August 1992) (*Bar News*, Spring-Summer 1992).

of these offences is therefore somewhat less than otherwise might have been the case."

Handley JA: "That is the principle recognised in the case of The Crown v Hood, is it not?"

Scragg: "I am not aware of that case your Honours, but we would rely upon it."

Gleeson CJ: "The case in question is The Crown v R Hood, Mr Scragg."

Scragg: "Yes, your Honour. But we submit that it is a mitigating factor in this case that these crimes were committed against the Commonwealth Bank."

Gleeson CJ: "The case that Mr Justice Handley was referring to concerned a Mr Robin Hood, Mr Scragg."

Homophones have triggered amusing mistakes.[8] An Italian contractor was suing for the cost of his services clearing land in Western Australia. Dwyer CJ, a fairly cantankerous judge at the best of times, was getting angry because the man seemed not to be understanding what he was being asked. When the judge inquired "How did you clear the land?", the question went straight over the witness's head. His Honour repeated the question: "How did you clear the land, ... did you use tree fellers?" The witness' face lit up and he said: "No, Your Honour, four fellas".[9]

Towards lunch on the second day of a trial Stephen J began to question the way in which the Crown Prosecutor was spending the time of the Court:[10]

JUDGE: Doesn't this case lie in a very small compass, Mr Magruder? Isn't it all a question of ownership?

MAGRUDER: Yes, Your Honour.

JUDGE: Isn't it simply a question whether the horses are brumbies or belong to Mr Doyle?

MAGRUDER: Yes, Your Honour.

JUDGE: Well surely the case can be shortened. You've called Mr Doyle, why don't you call Mr Brumby?

Then there are the witnesses who give themselves away by utterly ingenuous responses, like the policeman who, when asked whether he had been taught how to conduct an interview, inquired "How do you mean – physically or verbally?" Another police sergeant who was being cross-examined on the voir dire to show that a confession had been beaten out of the accused adamantly denied the suggestion. He asked counsel to remind him when the assault had occurred and then stated confidently: "It could not have happened at that time because the biff had gone out when the verbal came in".

Many cross-examiners have pressed one question too far, like the barrister who challenged a psychiatrist with the proposition that the accused "had

---

8 See also p 162.

9 Bolton and Byrne, *May it Please Your Honour*, p 191.

10 Piddington, *Worshipful Masters*, pp 227-8.

successfully attempted suicide on two previous occasions";[11] or the one who asked the accused's mother how long she had known him. A witness who had undergone a searching cross-examination about a bundle of documents was relieved to hear that all of the papers should be returned. The observant barrister noticed one document still in front of the witness – unreturned. Sensing another chance of drawing blood, he asked:[12]

> What have you there in front of you? What does THAT document say?

To which the witness replied, to the delight of the jury:

> Please lean forward to the microphone when giving your evidence.

At an inquest at Wilcannia, counsel cross-examining a witness with less than perfect recall was suggesting that she would remember significant events. When she seemed confused he continued:[13]

> BUCHANAN: Well ... if you had never been a sky diver and you fell out of a plane once, isn't it likely that you'd recall that for the rest of your life?
> (Aside, MATER): But not for long.

George Palmer recounts this blooper against himself. During a long trial before Kearney J one of his key witnesses had been discredited by having to admit he had used company money for an interstate jaunt with a secretary with whom he was having an illicit affair. In re-examination, Palmer tried to put the incident into perspective by showing that this was an exceptional departure from propriety with employees. Unfortunately, his opening question in re-examination was:

> Mr X, approximately how many female staff did you have under you at the time?

Lawyers' mistakes can prove terribly costly to themselves or their insurers, not to mention the client directly affected. Fortunately, some are rescued from the consequences of their folly because the client fails to take the advice or because a glaring risk does not come home. The author was undeservedly lucky on one occasion. For a hundred years it had been a task of the Solicitor-General for New South Wales to certify that Bills passed by Parliament were in order for assent. The role originated when Bills occasionally needed to be reserved for the monarch's assent in areas where the British government did not trust the wild colonials. Every so often a pile of Bills would arrive with standard certificates awaiting urgent signature. One afternoon the author was telephoned by the Governor's private secretary: "Keith we have a bit of a stuff-up with a Bill that received assent yesterday although it should have first gone to the people at a referendum. Don't worry, it has been torn up and a second copy will be delivered to you for a fresh certificate in the morning".

---

11 *Order in the Court*, p 15.

12 *R v Moroney & Bennell*, District Court of New South Wales.

13 *Bar News*, Autumn 1988.

An overly bold miscalculation had more serious consequences for the client of a young Irish barrister named Callaghan in 19th century New South Wales. The following account was given by Judge Dowling:[14]

> Shortly after his arrival in the Colony, [Callaghan] appeared one day at the Court of Quarter Sessions at Darlinghurst with a brief, perhaps his first. Mr Cheeke was the Crown Prosecutor and Mr Raymond the Chairman. Mr Cheeke looking at Callaghan said "I see you have a defence. What is the name of the prisoner?" Callaghan gave the name. "Oh", said Cheeke, "I do not intent to find a Bill against him, there is no case." Callaghan speaking with a rich Irish brogue replied, "Ah, my dear fellow, do prosecute, my client will get off, and then I shall have all the honour and glory of it." "Well"' said Cheeke, "to please you, I will." A Bill was found, the case was tried, and despite the able advocacy of Callaghan, the man was found guilty. The Chairman, who was not in on the secret, passed a heavy sentence. Callaghan was most indefatigable in trying to get his client released from prison. He had to make to the powers invoked the humiliating confession of how it was that the man was tried. After some delay the man obtained his freedom.

Dowling's concluding remark was that "the young barrister may learn a lesson from this incident".

Some errors of law recur with monotonous regularity. Others hopefully are things of the past, like the two-day trial in 1850 before a bench of two magistrates in which three or four different magistrates sat in, for short periods in turn, for one of the members who left shortly after the trial began.[15] Nowadays judges know that they have to stay for the duration, although some have been unable to stay awake and some appellate judges have bolted early for various reasons.[16] Starke J was once left behind on the bench by mistake and he never forgave Gavan Duffy CJ.[17]

We would certainly not do it like this today

Then there are the things done without question in one era that are universally condemned in another. In some matters, moderns can but marvel at our forebears' capacity for self-delusion. The motes in our own eyes await later detection.

The idea that those involved in the administration of justice might have a financial stake in the outcome of proceedings is now anathema.[18] Yet in the early days fines imposed by magistrates for breaches of police regulations went into

---

14 It is set out in Holt, *A Court Rises*, pp 22-3.
15 *R v Marrington* (1850) 1 Legge 643.
16 See p 92.
17 See p 53.
18 See *Ebner v Official Trustee* (2000) 205 CLR 337.

a fund for the expenses of local police administration and to the remuneration of the magistrates' clerks.[19] Field J's salary of £800 was supplemented by filing fees approximating £1200.[20] Ellis Bent arrived in Australia intent on making money. He introduced high fees for writs filed in the Supreme Court because he wanted to live on them and save his judicial salary. Governor Macquarie regulated the level of those fees, but Bent charged over seven times as much and quietly shared the excess with court officials.[21] Until 1825 the clerks to the Bench of Magistrates in New South Wales were paid fees on the issue of bail bonds (which usage required them to share with the gaoler). Pursuant to Commissioner Bigge's recommendation the clerks' interest in court fees was abolished and a regular salary introduced.

When funds were paid into court, they were invested by the Prothonotary in a special bank account attracting a small return by way of interest. It required a solemn ruling of the Victorian Supreme Court in 1856[22] to establish that the interest did not belong to the Prothonotary but was accountable to the government as public revenue. Other court officials have helped themselves to the capital of funds in court and gone to prison for it.

Until 1924 associates of High Court justices were permitted to sell copies of the court's judgments to supplement their incomes. Judges' associates in South Australia used to charge one shilling six pence for each sworn affidavit filed in the court records and their fees for copies of judgments allowed for a profit after subtracting the typist's costs. These perquisites came to an end in 1932 when the Court's financial arrangements were restructured after a Master embezzled money.[23] As a young barrister I customarily paid a small fee directly to the judge's associate for preparing a minute of interlocutory orders made outside regular court hours.

It used to be commonplace for judges to engage members of their close family as associates or secretaries. This practice came to be questioned in the late 20th century and I doubt if it continues today. For example, the District Court of Queensland adopted a protocol in 2000 requiring a transparent and accountable process that espoused the principles of merit and equal opportunity.

One Victorian judge used to read out his reasons from his notes and then hand the manuscript to reporters.[24] This would not happen today. Nowadays,

---

19 Bigge, *Report on the Commission of Inquiry, on the judicial establishments of New South Wales, and Van Diemen's Land*, p 72.

20 Castles, *An Australian Legal History*, p 109. See also *Eager v Field* [1820] NSWKR 3. Commissioner Bigge was not impressed and contended that the fees were excessive.

21 Kercher, *Debt, Seduction and Other Disasters*, p 45.

22 *Russell v Burns* (1856) VLT 479.

23 John Emmerson, "Why are you wearing a wig?" *Law Society Bulletin of South Australia*, November 2004.

24 Forde, *The Story of the Bar of Victoria*, p 290.

lengthy reasons in a reserved judgment may be dictated in Court but are more usually prepared in chambers and handed out as soon as the Court announces the result of the proceedings. A few years back, one very conscientious judge running an enormous list was anxious to finalise an urgent case before Court vacation. There was simply no time for someone to type up the lengthy reasons he had dictated and checked by replaying over the weekend. So, rather than hold up the next case, Einstein J entered Court, announced the result, published his reasons by switching on the tape, and left. During the next couple of hours, the litigants learnt their fate while the judge was able to work on another pressing case.

Some of the judgments of Sir Owen Dixon appear timeless exemplars of the judicial art. But Dixon was in many ways a man of his time (not a criticism in itself). His diaries show that he shared then commonly held racist attitudes whose expression today would get even talk-back radio folk into serious bother. Modern judges have also got into trouble for sexist comments that were widely tolerated only a generation ago, including attitudes about the testimony of sexual complainants that used to be embodied in legal rules. Judges, like the common law itself, always need to keep up with the times.

As French CJ and Kiefel J observed recently, there were striking examples of judges performing executive functions requiring their full-time absence from judicial duties during the Second World War.[25] These included the ambassadorial appointments of Sir John Latham and Sir Owen Dixon. Dixon also acted as Chairman of the Central Wool Committee, the Australian Shipping Control Board and the Maritime Risks Insurance Board. Dixon even drafted Bills for the federal Attorney-General[26] as well as judgments for other judges, sometimes in cases in which he had not sat.[27]

Several Chief Justices of old tendered advice on sensitive vice-regal matters while they held judicial office.[28] Authoritative statements in the *Boilermakers Case*[29] about the otherness of the federal judicial function and the need for it to be kept isolated lay yet in the future or were quietly ignored. In 2009, French CJ recorded many instances where vice-regal advice on legal matters had been given in the past, making it plain that it should never happen again.[30]

25 *Wainohu v New South Wales* [2011] HCA 24 at [24]. Other instances of judges conducting commissions of inquiry, some of which would be vulnerable to attack under modern constitutional principles, are collected by Kirby J in *Wilson v Minister for Aboriginal and Torres Strait Islander Affairs* (1996) 189 CLR 1 at 33-4.

26 See GKF Santow, "Transition to the Bench" (1997) 71 *Australian Law Journal* 294 at 301.

27 See pp 103-4.

28 See p 98.

29 *R v Kirby; Ex parte Boilermakers' Society of Australia* (1956) 94 CLR 254.

30 Chief Justice Robert French, "The Chief Justice and the Governor-General", Melbourne University Law Review Annual Dinner, 29 October 2009.

Switches, palinodes and regrets

According to one version of the quotation, John Maynard Keynes told a person who accused him of inconsistency: "When I find I am wrong, I change my mind. What do you do?"[31] Good judges certainly change their minds from time to time, sometimes off their own bat, sometimes in response to the arguments of counsel. They may even have been confronted with their own prior handiwork, coupled with a submission "with the greatest respect" that it requires revision.

In 1673, Vaughan CJ observed that if a judge considers the judgment of another court to be erroneous, then:[32]

> [H]e ... in his own conscience ought not to give the like judgment, for that were to wrong every man having a like cause, because another was wronged before.

Things are different now with stricter rules of *stare decisis* which generally oblige courts to follow prior decisions of courts of similar rank unless convinced that they are plainly wrong. There are limits to any judge's freedom to ignore precedent, even if it is his or her own product. Things are a little freer in the High Court of Australia, where, in Isaac Isaacs' memorable Siren-song, "it is not better that the Court should be persistently wrong than that it should be ultimately right".[33]

Stingel v The Queen[34] was a unanimous judgment of seven justices on provocation as a defence to murder. The High Court promulgated an "objective" standard whereby the reaction of the accused had to be that of an "ordinary person" with the accused's age but no other ethnic, physical or personal attributes. Only five years later, five of those same judges (Brennan, Deane, Dawson, Gaudron and McHugh JJ) would revisit the same issue in *Masciantonio v The Queen*.[35] There, the majority "explained" the Court's reasoning in the earlier case, while effecting a major retreat. McHugh J dissented, attributing his sharper defection substantially to his reading academic criticism of the *Stingel* judgment.[36]

Unlike the position adopted by the House of Lords in England in times past, the Australian High Court has never abjured the right to recognise past error and the obligation (in a proper case) to change both its collective mind

31 Quoted by Murray Gleeson, "The Constitutional Decisions of the Founding Fathers" (2007) 81 *Australian Law Journal* 791 at 797, citing an internet reference to the quotes of Keynes.

32 *Bole v Horton* (1673) Vaugh 360 at 383; 124 ER 1113 at 1124.

33 *Australian Agricultural Co v Federated Engine-Drivers and Firemen's Association of Australasia* (1913) 17 CLR 261 at 278.

34 (1990) 171 CLR 312 (Mason CJ, Brennan, Deane, Dawson, Toohey, Gaudron, McHugh JJ).

35 (1995) 183 CLR 58 esp at 67.

36 See (1995) 183 CLR 58 at 74, referring to Stanley Yeo, "Powers of Self-Control in Provocation and Automatism" (1992) 14 *Sydney Law Review* 3.

and the law. It is surely judicial best practice to be up-front about switching.[37]

The certainties of one generation can quickly disappear. For almost a decade, Murphy J was in "isolated dissent" in asserting that the Constitution established an implied freedom of political communication. With Murphy's passing, most observers expected to hear no more of such liberalities. On the day of Murphy's death, Mason J dismissed such a proposition with the curt observation that:[38]

> It is sufficient to say that I cannot find any basis for implying a new s 92A into the Constitution.

Only six years would elapse before Sir Anthony (joined by Deane, Toohey and Gaudron JJ) announced in the *Political Advertising Case* that the implied freedom had been located, as an "indispensable element" of representative government under the Constitution.[39] Their Honours declared it to be a personal freedom that might trump the common law as well as inconsistent Commonwealth and State legislation. Brennan and Dawson JJ protested against such broad conceptualisation of the freedom and McHugh J opted to sit on the fence, deciding the case on a narrower basis (albeit not quite as firmly as he would later adopt).[40] Two years later, there was a similar 4:3 split, with McHugh this time moving strongly away from the Mason bloc whose reasoning he branded as "incorrect", using the traditional minatory terms of "great respect to those who have so decided".[41] The issue returned to the Court three years later, in *Lange's Case*.[42] By this time, Mason CJ and Deane J had retired and McHugh J was able to persuade a unanimous Court to reject so much of *Political Advertising* as had derived the implication from a general principle of representative government. More importantly, the Court now rejected the human right concept in favour of the narrower limitation on legislative power stemming from particular provisions about federal politicians being "directly chosen by the people".

---

37 See eg Kirby J in *Zickar v MGH Plastic Industries Pty Ltd* (1996) 187 CLR 310 at 351. For a fine example, see Dawson J in *Street v Queensland Bar Association* (1989) 168 CLR 461 at 537-8.

38 *Miller v TCN Channel Nine Pty Ltd* (1986) 161 CLR 556 at 579. According to Gibbs CJ (at 569) and Mason J (at 579) the argument stemmed from the judgment of Murphy J in *Buck v Bavone* (1976) 135 CLR 110 at 137. Heydon J, the author of the "isolated dissent" description and himself an expert in isolated dissenting, said in *Wootton v Queensland* [2012] HCA 2 at [39] that three different decisions of Murphy J supported the attributed proposition, but that Gibbs CJ and Mason J were wrong to include *Buck v Bavone*.

39 *Australian Capital Television Pty Ltd v Commonwealth* (1992) 177 CLR 106 at 138, 168, 210-11.

40 See *ibid* at 232.

41 See *Theophanous v Herald & Weekly Times Ltd* (1994) 182 CLR 104 esp at 195, 206.

42 *Lange v Australian Broadcasting Corporation* (1997) 189 CLR 520.

One may infer that Michael McHugh was mightily pleased with this achievement. It is unknown and irrelevant whether, now in retirement, he is pleased with a successor's recent criticism of *Lange* coupled with a call for support to revisit the issue.[43] Every judge must realise that, in Lord Hoffmann's words:[44]

> Once a judgment has been published, its interpretation belongs to posterity and its author and those who agreed with him at the time have no better claim to declare its meaning than anyone else.

In a court of ultimate appeal a judge's change of mind may involve switching sides in an ongoing debate; and, if enough judges do so, the law itself will change with retroactive effect.[45] According to Professor Andrew Lynch,[46] "one of the most poignant examples of abandonment of dissent is Dixon's judgment in *Hughes & Vale v New South Wales (No 1)*.[47] With the Court poised 3:3, he cast his lot, on the basis of precedent, for the view which he personally disagreed – only to be overturned by the Privy Council,[48] which preferred his reasoning and restored his original view".

Reinforced by the views of the Privy Council, the High Court promptly swung itself unanimously behind the now authoritative Dixonian dispensation.[49] McTiernan J joined Dixon CJ and Webb J in a joint judgment obviously penned by Dixon, permitting himself the luxury of an Addendum under his name alone in which he concluded:[50]

> In the joint judgment to which I am a party there is stated, as I believe adequately, with respect to the particular problems these cases raise, what appears to be the true operation of the views which in the past I found myself unable to share. But perhaps I may be permitted to say that I remain personally far from convinced that the result is one which the framers of s 92 either intended or foresaw.

The poignancy of this Parthian shot is underscored by two matters: (1) it was almost certainly ghost-written by Dixon himself; and (2) McTiernan's doubts

43 See *Wootton v Queensland* [2012] HCA 2 at [40]-[41], [49]-[55] (Heydon J).

44 *Deutsche Morgan Grenfell Group plc v Inland Revenue* [2007] 1 AC 558 at [14].

45 See *Ha v New South Wales* (1997) 189 CLR 465. Before 1992, money paid under mistake of law was generally irrecoverable. The High Court openly changed this rule of the common law in *David Securities Pty Ltd v Commonwealth Bank of Australia* (1992) 175 CLR 353. Later cases would hold that mistaken payments made *before* 1992 were also recoverable, subject to the statute of limitations: see *Commissioner of State Revenue (Vic) v Royal Insurance Australia Ltd* (1994) 182 CLR 51; *Torrens Aloha Pty Ltd v Citibank NA* (1997) 72 FCR 581.

46 Blackshield et al, *Oxford Companion to the High Court of Australia*, "Dissenting judgments".

47 (1953) 87 CLR 49.

48 *Hughes & Vale Pty Ltd v New South Wales* [1955] AC 241, 93 CLR 1.

49 See *Hughes & Vale Pty Ltd v New South Wales (No 2)* (1955) 93 CLR 127.

50 *Ibid* at 183.

would be vindicated (not quite in the form he envisaged) 23 years later, when the High Court *unanimously* overturned all variants of the *Hughes & Vale* reasoning.[51]

When judges depart from their own published views they may or may not add a formal recantation or palinode. Some simply invoke Bramwell B's statement that "the matter does not appear to me now as it appears to have appeared to me then".[52] There is a delightful collection of similar retractions by Jackson J of the United States Supreme Court.[53]

Judges do not invariably take full responsibility for their earlier "mistakes". In *Duncan v Queensland*,[54] Griffith CJ acknowledged that he was being inconsistent with his earlier, but relatively recent, decision in *Foggitt Jones & Co Ltd v New South Wales*.[55] That case, he said, had been badly argued by counsel on the last day of a sitting and the arguments which he later found conclusive "did not then find entrance to my mind".[56]

Sir Owen Dixon told a law conference in 1955 that "I do not wish it to be thought that, looking in retrospect, I altogether approve of what I myself did".[57] Every sane human has similar regrets. Since most of the law is practised in public, many causes of regret to lawyers remain "on the record". The inevitability of this happening sooner or later is almost a comfort. It should certainly spur humility whenever we are tempted to asperity when declaring error in others.

---

51 *Cole v Whitfield* (1988) 165 CLR 360.

52 *Andrews v Styrap* (1872) 26 LT(NS) 704 at 706, invoked by the author in *Woolworths Ltd v Pallas Newco Pty Ltd* (2004) 61 NSWLR 707 at 734.

53 See *McGrath v Kristensen* [1950] USSC 97; 340 US 162 at 177-8 (1950).

54 (1916) 22 CLR 556.

55 (1916) 21 CLR 357.

56 (1916) 22 CLR 556 at 582.

57 See (1955) 29 *Australian Law Journal* 272. He was referring to his decision to perform executive roles during the Second World War at a time when he was "very depressed in relation to the war and ... feeling very restless indeed". He did not mention the judicial ghost-writing (as to which see pp 103-4).

Bibliography

Ayres, Philip, *Owen Dixon, A Biography*, Miegunyah Press, 2003

Barker QC, Ian, *Sorely Tried Democracy and trial by jury in New South Wales*, Dremweaver Pub, 2003

Beanland, Denver, *A Court Apart. The District Court of Queensland*, Supreme Court of Queensland Library, 2009

Bennett, J M, *A History of the Supreme Court of New South Wales*, Law Book Co, 1974

Bennett, J M, *Sir James Dowling: Second Chief Justice of New South Wales*, Federation Press, Sydney, 2001

Bennett, J M, *Sir Alfred Stephen: Third Chief Justice of New South Wales*, Federation Press, Sydney, 2009

Blacket KC, Wilfred, *May It Please Your Honour. Lawyers and Law Courts of the Olden Times in New South Wales*, Cornstalk Publishing Company, 1927

Blackshield, Tony, Coper, Michael and Williams, George, *The Oxford Companion to the High Court of Australia*, Oxford University Press, 2001

Bolton, Geoffrey and Byrne, Geraldine, *May it Please Your Honour. A History of the Supreme Court of Western Australia 1861-2005*, Supreme Court of Western Australia, 2005

Burns, Creighton, *The Tait Case*, Melbourne University Press, 1962

Burton, Pamela, *From Moree to Mabo. The Mary Gaudron Story*, UWA Publishing, 2010

Castle, T D and Kercher, Bruce, *Dowling's Select Cases*, Francis Forbes Society for Australian Legal History, 2005

Castles, Alex C, *An Australian Legal History*, Law Book Co, 1982

Castles, Alex C, *Lawless Harvests or God Save the Judges*, Australian Scholarly Publishing, 2003

Castles, Alex C and Harris, Michael C, *Lawmakers and Wayward Whigs. Government and Law in South Australia 1836-1986*, Wakefield Press, 1987

Cowen, Zelman, *Isaac Isaacs*, Oxford University Press, 2nd ed, 1993

Dash, Mike, *Batavia's Graveyard*, Weidenfeld & Nicolson, 2002

Dean, Arthur, *A Multitude of Counsellors: A History of the Bar of Victoria*, FW Cheshire, 1968

Drake-Brockman, Henrietta, *Voyage to Disaster. The Life of Francisco Pelsaert*, Angus & Robertson Publishers, 1963

Elvery, L et al, *In My Opinion: The History of the Crown Law Queensland 1859-2009*, Crown Law Queensland, 2009

Emerson, John, *History of the Independent Bar of South Australia*, Barr Smith Press, 2006

Forbes, John, *The Divided Legal Profession in Australia: History, Rationalisation and Rationale*, Law Book Co, 1979

Forde, J L, *The Story of the Bar of Victoria*, Whitcombe and Tombs Ltd, 1913

Fricke, Graham, *Judges of the High Court*, Hutchinson of Australia, 1986

Gregory, Helen, *The Queensland Law Society Inc 1928-1988*, Queensland Law Society Inc, 1991

Hague R M, *Sir John Jeffcott, Portrait of a Colonial Judge*, Melbourne University Press, 1963

Hannan CMG, QC, A J, *The Life of Chief Justice Way*, Angus and Robertson, 1960

Eric Edgar Hewitt, *Judges Through the Years*, Hyland House Melbourne, 1984

Holt, H T E, *A Court Rises: The lives and times of the judges of the District Court of New South Wales (1859-1959)*, Law Foundation of New South Wales, 1976

Jacobs, P A, *A Lawyer Tells*, F W Cheshire, Melbourne, 1949

Jacobs, Philip A, *Judges of Yesterday*, Robertson & Mullens Ltd, 1924

Kercher, Bruce, *Debt, Seduction and Other Disasters*, Federation Press, 1996

Leys, Simon, *Wreck of the Batavia*, Atlantic Books, 2007

McLaren, John, *Dewigged, Bothered and Bewildered. British Colonial Judges on Trial 1800-1900*, Osgoode Society for Canadian Legal History, 2011

McLaughlin, John Kennedy, *The Magistracy in New South Wales, 1788-1850*, unpublished LLM thesis, 1973 (NSW Bar Association Library)

McPherson CBE, The Honourable Mr Justice B H, *The Supreme Court of Queensland 1859-1960 History Jurisdiction Procedure*, Butterworths, 1989

Order in the Court, The Lighter Side of the Law from the Verbatim Columns of Bar News, Lothian Publishing Company, 1988

Marr, David, *Barwick*, George Allen and Unwin, 1980

Mildren, Dean, *Big Boss Fella All Same Judge. A History of the Supreme Court of the Northern Territory*, Federation Press, 2011

Piddington, A B, *Worshipful Masters*, Angus & Robertson, 1929

Russell, Enid, *A History of the Law in Western Australia*, UWA Press, 1980

Selway QC, Bradley, *The Constitution of South Australia*, Federation Press, 1997

Smith, Simon, *Maverick Litigants. A History of Vexatious Litigants in Australia 1930-2008*, Maverick Publications, 2009

Stoljar, Jeremy, *The Australian Book of Great Trials. The Cases that Shaped a Nation*, Pier 9, 2011

Woinarski (ed), Judge, *Jesting Pilate and Other Papers and Addresses by the Right Honourable Sir Owen Dixon*, Law Book Co, 1965

Table of Cases

Table of Names

General Index